Unmasking
A Woman's Journey

A MEMOIR OF COURAGE, HOPE, FORGIVENESS, AND HEALING

GLORIA EWING LOCKHART

For God, I am deeply grateful for His guiding light on this journey, always showing me favor, and never giving up on me when I wanted to give up on myself.

To my daughter, I will always cherish our unconditional love; it sustained us through all kinds of weather...I love you.

To my family, who laughed, cried, rejoiced with me, and provided the necessary tools for me to complete my journey, thank you.

To all the adolescent girls in detention and lock-up facilities throughout Los Angeles, I am indebted to you for encouraging me to write my story and instilling in me the belief that it will spark a journey of forgiveness and healing for other high-risk girls.

And, to the readers of Unmasking: A Woman's Journey, thank you for believing in my journey. I hope it becomes a blueprint to encourage you in transforming your life and becoming the champion of your own story.

PRAISE FOR *UNMASKING: A WOMAN'S JOURNEY*

A memoir of courage, hope, forgiveness, and healing

"Gloria Lockhart expresses superlative writing skills as she reveals and explores many of the major issues of our times through the prism of her life story. Her passion and determination drove her to overcome many personal and societal obstacles in her journey toward becoming a role model and counselor for others."

Coach Jim Bibbs, former coach, Detroit Track Club
Michigan State University associate professor and head track coach emeritus
Hall of Fame: Michigan State University, Greater Lansing Area and Eastern Michigan University

"Gloria broke through gender barriers as a pioneer of women's track and field. She pursued her running dreams before there was a women's track team or Title IX in college athletics. Today our female athletes stand tall because of women like Gloria who paved the way. Gloria is to be praised for her courage, resilience, and unstoppable determination. *Unmasking: A Woman's Journey* is a heartfelt testament of this."

Sue Parks
Women's track and cross country head coach
Eastern Michigan University
Olympic trials qualifier, 1972

"I highly endorse *Unmasking: A Woman's Journey*. It is an insightful account of Gloria growing up in an age of racial discrimination and misunderstanding. I applaud her ability to persevere during some of the most tumultuous times in this country's history. Her passion for track allowed her to rise above these difficult times. She was able to take her passion and pioneer track and field for women, opening the door for women to compete equitably to men."

Bob Parks
Men's track and field/cross country head coach
Eastern Michigan University, 1967–2000

TABLE OF CONTENTS

Unmasking: A Woman's Journey

By

Gloria Ewing Lockhart

PROLOGUE

It's not a church, but this room is as much a sanctuary as any room I've ever set foot in. This classroom, with its beat-up wooden table, carved with years of names and messages, its folding, metal chairs, its stained and dulled gray carpet...this classroom has heard confessions, lies, anger, and hurt. This is the classroom where I run my group-counseling sessions for high-risk, teenage girls.

Looking at the empty chairs, I can see the faces of the girls I've tried to help here; I can hear their voices. I can feel a hint of joy at a girl's small progress and also the gnawing ache of knowing a young woman right before my eyes was losing ground.

Every group is the same.

Every group is different.

I draw a deep breath and glance at my watch. Today's group will be coming in soon. Looking around the room, I can picture where each of the five young women will sit, how they'll sit; I can see their dark, guarded expressions. I wonder what they'll be able to share today and if anything I say or do will reach them. And, for a fleeting moment, as I think about how I see them, I wonder how they see me or if they even see me, really see me, at all. Can I blame them if they don't? There's so much more I could share with these young women.

As each of the girls eventually enters and takes her seat, I pay particularly close attention to Anna. Anna has been part of this group for nearly three weeks. She's tall, powerfully built, with a narrowed, angry expression. To someone with unknowing eyes, Anna gives off a sense of menace. But I only see her hurt and vulnerability. Until today, she's been watchful, careful. She's shared as little as possible.

"Anna," I say softly after we are all seated. "Would you like to share anything today?"

She scowls at me. Then she blinks. I can see her measuring in her mind—measuring me, measuring the risk. She looks at me, and then she looks down at the gray, stained carpet. I worry that even in my invitation I've pushed too hard. There's silence. But then she begins to speak in a soft, girlish whisper.

"When I was twelve, my mama told me I was a mistake," she says, her voice emotionless. "Said she hated me and shoulda got me aborted." She looks up, and her eyes are narrowed and angry, but moist with emotion, betraying her flat tone. "I hate her for hating me. She ain't never said she loved me, not once, not ever. I'm sixteen years old, and I ain't never heard my mama tell me she loves me. All I hear are her angry words in my head. I can't get 'em out..."

My breath is knocked out of me. I'm stunned at what I've heard. Not because I'm surprised by the content, but by the courage and strength Anna has shown in saying it out loud. I want to put my arms around her. I know she knows the other girls in the room understand, but how can I help her know how well I understand? How can I help her know that, just like her, I've traveled a difficult and painful path?

My mother loved me, but she gave me up, sending me on a journey that took me from the depths of my own despair to the heights of Mt. Kilimanjaro.

I know how Anna and these other girls feel. If I can find a way to tell them my own story, perhaps they'll see that there is hope—that no matter how difficult, there *is* a path forward. I have to try; it's part of my own path.

"Thank you, Anna. You're an amazing young woman," I tell her. "And you're stronger than you know. You may think those are just words some textbook told me to say. They're not." I pause. The room is silent. I lower my voice. "I know what you're capable of overcoming because of what I overcame."

A couple members of the group raise their eyebrows. Anna's expression is unchanged.

"I didn't expect that you'd just take my word for it," I continue. "That wouldn't be fair, given how much all of you have shared. So today I'm going to share, too. I want to answer your courage with my own, so you can see that no matter how dark the tunnel you're crawling through is, you can find the light."

I take a deep breath and a big drink of water. I can hear myself swallow. I'm suddenly acutely aware of my body. There's no position that doesn't seem awkward. I wonder how I look to these teenagers—like a mother or a grandmother? I know they'll relate to my experiences, but can they relate to me, and the world I grew up in? They didn't bargain for a history lesson when they came here today.

It's my turn to stare down at the stained carpet, to grapple with doubt. I can feel the girls shuffling in their chairs, crossing their legs to the opposite side, shifting their weight. My hesitation has had the unintended effect of building their anticipation.

I need to move forward. There's nothing I can say to prepare these young women for what they're about to hear, and there's nothing I can do at this point to prepare myself to tell it. I feel that in a way my whole journey has been preparation for this moment. I've brought myself to the edge of the cliff. I need to jump.

I lift my head and make sure I meet each young woman's eyes with my own, and I begin.

CHAPTER ONE

"**E**ven in the womb, you were a feisty, little thing—a ball of energy, kicking and nudging and poking me whenever you got the chance. I remember how the room smelled so sweet, like cocoa butter," Mama said, recounting the event of my birth in meticulous detail until I felt I could remember being there.

"To take my mind off the pains, I just concentrated on looking at the tiny daisies that ran along the edges of the wallpaper," she told me, and I wondered if that beige wallpaper her light brown eyes fixed on was the first thing my own eyes saw. Chances are, though, that the first image I took in on December 5, 1946, was the white man who delivered me.

Dr. H. H. Parr held progressive views for a Southern doctor in Eudora, Arkansas, at a time when segregation was in full force and it was practically unheard of for a white doctor to visit a black neighborhood. Dr. Parr even invited his black patients to take vegetables from his garden so they could stay healthy eating the greens he grew with his own hands. I was delivered into those caring hands and into a house of love, but the world outside was full of hate. My mother had no choice but to have her babies at home, even when she suffered through the difficult delivery of my older sister, Bobbie, who was born prematurely.

"In segregation, black folks couldn't have gone to a white hospital, where they would wheel a pregnant Negro woman into a back room and forget about her," my mother told me. "No, honey. For black women, home

1

births were always better." Fortunately, my birth at our home on Front Street was free from complications.

"Well, Mr. Twiggs, you should be proud of your wife and your new baby girl. She's a healthy one," Dr. Parr announced to my relieved father, who, in keeping with the times, hadn't been in the room when I was born.

"Yes, I am proud," Daddy had replied, grinning from ear to ear and displaying a vulnerability that betrayed his more than six-foot frame.

The way Mama told it, not just my father but the whole family was outright dancing for joy at the arrival of its newest member, a freckle-faced, seven-pound baby girl with a tan complexion and a mere "twig" of hair sprouting from her scalp. Given the jubilance surrounding my birth, it seems fitting that my parents named me Gloria.

Although the memory of how I entered this world seems like my own, my earliest genuine memory is from when I was three years old; it's of my grandmother, whom we called Mother Dear. What I remember most distinctly about her was her smooth skin, brown like coffee. I remember how she was strong, yet graceful like an African gazelle, despite a slight limp that I never got the courage to ask her about.

Her smile shone as bright as the sun. As if to prove the point, her front teeth were capped in gold. She swayed her hips from side to side when she walked in a sassy way that let everyone know she was the center of the universe. And in a way she was, at least of Eudora's universe, and mine, too, for a time.

Everyone in town knew my grandmother. All sorts of people would shout hello or wave at us when we were riding in her red pickup truck, and we'd shout and wave right back. On Saturdays, we'd go to Mother Dear's favorite beauty shop where she would get her "press and curl." It was located in a place in the neighborhood known to some as The One-Mile Square, where black folks did their marketing or just got together and shot the breeze.

Folks could find just about anything they needed or wanted in The One-Mile Square. There was a taxi stand for people who had money to get around but no car of their own to get around in. There was a barbershop, a market, two funeral homes, a soul-food restaurant called Miss Hammit's Place, and a nightclub called Big Sister's Place. Mother Dear owned a nightclub just outside of Eudora called State Eight. My grandmother never went to college, but that didn't mean she wasn't a smart businesswoman.

She managed her own money and hired good people to work for her. And she married a good man.

My granddaddy, Robert Twiggs, was the best electrician in town and his own boss, which was a big deal. Aside from the fact that he allowed folks to call him Bob, he was a formal man in most respects who, like Mother Dear, took great pride in everything he did. I remember how he would religiously clean the contents of his gray metal toolbox. Granddaddy always looked neat in dark-blue pants, a short-sleeved shirt, and black ox- ford leather shoes, while Mother Dear looked so fancy in dresses made of silk decorated with tiny flowers. She accessorized each dress with a thin belt that accentuated her petite waist, and took great care to match her open- toed heels and colorful hats to the flowers on the fabric.

Mother Dear was known as "the best-dressed woman in Eudora." Because of her, the women at Bethel African Methodist Episcopal church fell prey to one of the seven deadly sins, as they sat in the hard pews every Sunday worshipping the Lord and envying my grandmother's wardrobe. Most of Mother Dear's coveted fashions were homemade, courtesy of her black Singer sewing machine. She also created church hats out of straw, which women of all sizes, from the rail-thin to the big-boned, could wear with pride. I wore the pretty dresses Mother Dear made for me from the scraps of fabric she had left over from her own dresses. I looked like a patchwork quilt sometimes, but I enjoyed showing off my grandmother's designs.

In addition to what she could do with a Singer sewing machine, Mother Dear was famous for what she could do in the kitchen. Buffalo and grin- ner fish were mealtime staples in Eudora, so much so that grinner fish are now extinct there. Mother Dear cooked a mean buffalo fish, but she was known for whipping up the best potato salad, collard greens, black-eyed peas, cabbage, fried chicken, and corn bread. Perhaps it was the lard my grandmother cooked with that helped give her food such wonderful flavor. The surgeon general warns about cooking with that much fat nowadays, but my mouth waters just thinking about how good that food tasted.

Even though Mother Dear had a presence that made her seem larger than life to me, that doesn't mean my granddaddy Bob wasn't a force of nature in his own right. He was one of the best Negro baseball players in the South, but segregation kept him out of the all-white major leagues. He was so proud when he got to see Jackie Robinson break the color barrier.

Granddaddy Bob's business did well enough that he never had to work a second job at one of the cotton mills in the city, which was rare for a Southern black man in those days. Plus he owned his two-story house. It sat on an acre of land on the "black" side of Eudora, the section literally on the other side of the railroad tracks.

My sister, Bobbie, older by one year, would regularly compete with me for Granddaddy Bob's attention. We'd tug on his long legs, squatting with him as he explained the purpose of each of his tools.

"Let's see," he would begin. "We have these here linesman pliers to twist wires, a screwdriver to attach switches and plugs to the wall, a meter to read electrical currents, a hammer for attaching things. This black tape is for twistin' wires." Bobbie and I never took our eyes off whatever Granddaddy was showing us, even when we didn't have a clue what he was talking about.

And I'll never forget that 1945 Chrysler Granddaddy owned—his pride and joy, for which he paid about two thousand of his very hard-earned dollars. That was a great deal of money back then. It was common to see Chevys, Pontiacs, and Studebakers in Eudora, but most black folks drove Fords because they were the least expensive.

Granddaddy's Chrysler was a black, four-door model, and on the weekends I'd go out in the yard and help him keep it shining like new, carefully washing the thick white-wall tires, silver door handles, and wide-front windows until they were squeaky clean. Granddaddy took a lot of pride in that car. The fact was he was a proud man, and he deserved to be. His wasn't the sinning kind of pride; it was the self-respecting kind.

"Your granddad didn't go to college, but he didn't allow anyone to run over him," my father explained to me. "In his business, his prices were fair, but most black folks were too poor to afford them. Because we lived in a segregated neighborhood, that meant we were supposed to be at the mercy of white folks. But not your granddaddy.

"There was this one lady named Mrs. Greenfield who hired your granddaddy to wire her house. Mrs. Greenfield was a rude, bossy, white lady, but your granddad put her in her place. The story goes that when your granddad arrived at Mrs. Greenfield's door, she said, 'Come in, Mr. Twiggs. But I don't want you tracking dirt into my house, so take off your shoes.' Your granddad gave it right back to her. 'I'm not takin' my shoes off for you or nobody else!' Now you see, Gloria, Mrs. Greenfield got nervous when she saw your granddad turning to leave because she knew he was the best electrician on either side of the tracks. So she called for him to come back. 'Mr. Twiggs! I'm very, very sorry,' she told him, changing her tune. 'I didn't mean to offend you.' And from then on, white folks in the city wanted to hire your granddad."

It was obvious when Daddy was telling these stories how much he admired my grandfather. Granddaddy was the one who pushed him to go to college so that he wouldn't have to work as a laborer. He wanted more for his son than he had for himself. But to me it seemed like we always had enough when we lived on Front Street. It might've been the "wrong" side of the tracks, but all I knew was that I always had a solid roof over my head and plenty to eat.

Granddad was such a talented hunter that he belonged to a prestigious hunting club for black men. We never had to worry about our bellies being empty as long as Granddad was around; when he went out with his rifle, we knew he would come back with deer and rabbit. Whatever he brought home, Mother Dear cooked up.

Despite how much I loved Mother Dear's cooking and my granddaddy Bob, I was okay with having an empty belly sometimes. I just couldn't bring myself to swallow the tough meat of a deer. I was always afraid that the deer head mounted in the kitchen, one of my grandfather's trophies, would spring to life and chase me around the house, angry only with me that it had been killed, even though it really should've been mad at Granddaddy.

That large house we shared with Mother Dear and Granddaddy Bob was white with brown trim. It sat far from the gravel road where most of the other houses were built; for a long time, it didn't even have a street number. There was no need for house numbers in those days because you went and picked up your mail at the post office yourself. No mail carrier ever came to the house, but Santa Claus did. I'll never forget the red, brick chimney that brought him to us on Christmas Eve. I always wondered how he could fit through that tiny space, with his fat stomach and big sack of toys for my sister and me.

Every room in the house had stained hardwood floors with matching doorframes. The only room I didn't like was the spooky attic. I was convinced that strange creatures lived up there; I heard the noises they made when no one was around. All dark, damp places frightened me, and that attic was a bit of both. It was crammed with dusty trunks full of old clothes, boxes stuffed with yellowed newspapers, and broken furniture my grand-daddy never got around to fixing. There were also those scary monsters. I stayed away from the attic. I was brave, but I wasn't brave enough to battle monsters. Not then, anyway.

The biggest room in the house was the living room. There were cozy, red velvet pillows on the couch and clay flowerpots filled with green plants lining the windowsills. My favorite room was the dining room, where my family gathered around the pretty mahogany table to eat twice a day. I felt like a princess, sitting beneath the beautiful crystal chandelier that hung so elegantly from the ceiling—until Mother Dear would serve her all-time favorite dish of golden brown, crispy, Southern fried chicken, cooked in lard and seasoned with salt, pepper, and Mother Dear's "secret" spices. That chicken was so lip-smacking, greasy good. I ate it the way it was meant to be eaten, although not necessarily the way a princess would.

"Honey, remember your manners," Mama would reprimand me. "We taught you to use your napkin."

"It's so-o-o-o good," I'd say with my mouth full of chicken, grease all over my face.

"Let her be," Mother Dear would tell Mama. "She's just a child." I loved Mother Dear even more for defending me.

What I remember most about my granddaddy Bob's house was what a wonderful make-believe friend I had in the Chinaberry tree that presided over the backyard. I talked and giggled to her, and when it was time to play she was the first thing I visited. Sometimes, she'd drop one of her yellow berries on my head or bounce one off my shoulder, just to say hello and let me know that she'd missed me.

My friend Big Berry was old. I could see her cracked and brittle roots coming out of the ground; she was so tall it seemed she reached the heavens. She would graciously let me rest my blue tricycle gently against her while I had tea parties with my sister and my white porcelain doll. Sometimes when Bobbie and I played hide and seek, Big Berry would let me hide under her.

The only location that could rival being under the Chinaberry tree was the large front porch, where we would play games of jacks and soar on the big, gray, wooden swing that hung from the ceiling by metal chains. Sometimes I'd go so high that I thought I had wings. On sunny days, Mother Dear would sit on the porch snapping fresh green beans into a bowl. When it was time for a break, we'd fly together on the swing.

I wonder if I'm able to recall these details so distinctly because for the first years of my life, the house on Front Street and the people in it were my entire world. It wasn't until around 1950 that I took my first trip outside Eudora, when Daddy was admitted to the graduate program in theater at the University of Iowa. He'd been one of the best actors at Tennessee State and Howard University, and even though he was happy to be taking this next step toward becoming a professional actor, he knew the University of Iowa was going to be different. It was a white university, and Daddy was one of the few black students enrolled there.

Our home in Iowa was different, too. It was called a "Quonset Hut." Quonset Huts were prefabricated homes originally designed by the U.S. Navy during WWII. The University decided they were perfect for on-campus married housing. Our hut was so much smaller than our home in Eudora—only one story. There was no Chinaberry tree in the backyard or swing on the front porch. The hut's two bedrooms were really just two square boxes. There was no nice woodworking, or welcoming plants in the windows. It was all just so...plain. Instead of the privacy we enjoyed on our acre lot on Front Street, our hut was connected to other student housing.

I missed Mother Dear and Granddaddy Bob, but I adjusted to our new life. Daddy studied plays all the time, and Mama stayed home to take care of us kids. Sometimes Daddy would study at a friend's house. One of the men Daddy studied with lived down the street from us and had a daughter named Carol. Carol and I were the same age and the same height, but her hair was straight and blond, and mine was fuzzy and dark brown. Her light blue eyes matched the sky. My brown eyes matched the earth. Carol and I played together all the time. She was my first white friend.

One chilly morning, in a month when the leaves on the elm tree in front of our house had begun to turn yellow and brittle, Carol and I got into a tussle over who would ride my tricycle next. It was like any argument between any two small children, like arguments I'd had with my own sister. Until Carol yelled, "Nigger, give it to me! It's my turn!"

I wasn't sure how I knew that word was bad. Maybe I'd heard it on the news or from Daddy talking about segregation. Or maybe it was just a feeling. But I knew. I reached for Carol's arm and I bit her.

"I'm gonna tell!" she wailed, raising her neatly ironed and starched dress to cover the damage my teeth had inflicted before running off down the street to her house.

"Don't call me that bad name!" I called after her. Nothing could cover the wound her words had inflicted.

I was inside explaining to Daddy what had happened when Carol's father, Ted, appeared at our screen door, knocking frantically. He was breathing hard from his jog to our house. Sweat was beading down his flushed face.

"Robert, may I have a word with you?" Ted demanded, his face turning the same color red as his checkered shirt. He was tapping his leg nervously.

"Why, of course," Daddy said politely and let him in. Surely the man was there to apologize.

But then Ted said, "I don't appreciate what Gloria did to Carol. I want your permission to spank her."

"What?" Daddy said. I could hear the rage in Daddy's voice. "I've never heard of such a thing! Your child called my child a nigger, Ted. That's the worst name you can call a Negro!"

All of the blood drained from Ted's face. He opened his mouth to speak, but no sound came out, which was fine because Daddy wasn't finished.

"And let me tell you something. If you ever lay a hand on my daughter, Ted, I'll beat the hell out of you! Do you understand?"

Ted, realizing silence was no longer an option, began stammering. "Oh, Robert, I'm, I'm so sorry...I, I didn't know it happened like that." It was all he could manage to get out.

Ted was what my father called a liberal, and as far as Daddy had seen he treated everyone with respect. The man appeared to be truly shocked by what his daughter had said. Daddy didn't know much about Ted's wife—maybe it was her influence that had rubbed off on Carol. Like the gentleman he was, Daddy chose to give Ted the benefit of the doubt and accept his apology. I accepted Carol's later that same day. From then until my family left Iowa, Carol and I were inseparable, and she never used that word in front of me again.

We knew there was prejudice in Iowa before the incident with Carol. Daddy experienced it from his white professors when they asked him to play roles that made black people look stupid.

"My dignity is more important than my career. I love my people too much to put them down," he'd tell them.

Daddy had guts, and he also had Granddaddy Bob's footsteps to walk in. Many times Dad didn't get leading roles because they were assigned to white men, but he just kept auditioning. "Black folks got to work harder than white folks, practice longer than white folks, and stay one step ahead of them to be acknowledged as their equal," he would say. And that's what he did. Because of his perseverance, he eventually landed major roles in Shakespearean plays without sacrificing his integrity.

As for Mama, she was busy having babies. She'd given birth to another girl, Ethel, almost as soon as we got to Iowa. Ethel could have been my twin. We had the same freckles and caramel skin, and the same strong lungs. It seemed like Ethel was always crying to get her way. Shortly after Ethel, the family's pride and joy and my father's namesake, baby Robert, arrived. Daddy and baby Robert could have been twins, too, with their medium-brown skin, slanted brown eyes, long feet, and short, nappy hair.

I was still a rather sheltered child, and from my perspective the six of us were a big, happy family. I was so excited when Daddy graduated with his master's in communication and theater shortly after baby Robert was born, and we were on our way back to Mother Dear and Granddaddy Bob's house. I couldn't wait to see my Chinaberry tree again! Everything would be the same as it used to be, as if we'd never moved away.

The relationship between Mama and Daddy had been changing, though, and when we got back to Eudora, things were far from how they used to be. Mama and Daddy had fallen out of love. I didn't learn the details until later in life, details that included Mama's infidelity. But even as a child, it was plain something was wrong.

It got to where Mama and Daddy hardly spoke to each other. He was quiet all of the time. She hardly smiled. When Mama did smile, it made me so happy. I loved her dimples, and how her face took the shape of a cat's. Most of the time Mama seemed more like a mouse than a cat, silent like Daddy, and jumpy whenever he was around. Her eyes revealed her sadness.

I was five when my parents got divorced and we left Daddy. I remember Mama went to the Western Union office to pick up a money order from her brother, L. D., who lived in Los Angeles. I remember watching as she packed the little we owned into shopping bags and suitcases made of hard cardboard. Everything bulged with clothes. It's amazing how a little can seem like a lot when you don't have anywhere to put it.

Mama was reserved when she talked about our moving away. She used her words with great economy, making it even harder for me to understand what was happening.

"Honey, we're going to my hometown," she told me. "We're going to stay there for a bit."

I was too young to think of all the questions that, when I got older, I'd wish I'd asked. Looking back, it seems so strange that no one appeared to be very upset. It was like we were going on some kind of vacation. I knew that wasn't the case, but I could only believe that one day we'd all be back together again because that was how we always were. I couldn't imagine the world any other way.

One night, I pulled my cardboard cigar box, where I hid my secret treasures and keepsakes, from under my bed.

Let's see, I thought. *One, two, three wishbones from Mother Dear's yummy fried chicken. I'll make a wish for Mama and Daddy. There's my favorite small rock covered with Arkansas red clay. Yes! I'll take this new 1951 penny—it's mint. I'll hold on to these berries from Big Berry. I'm gonna miss her. I'd better say good-bye. Or maybe she'll come with us this time.*

Of course, Big Berry didn't come with us. Neither did Ethel, who was only a toddler. I was stunned that Mama would leave her. When the time came for us to take our trip, Mama brought me, Bobbie, and Robert to the front porch to say goodbye to Mother Dear, Granddaddy Bob, and my baby sister. We'd say goodbye to Daddy at the station. I couldn't understand why Ethel was staying with Daddy. Why wasn't Robert staying? He was Daddy's only son. Why couldn't I stay? I didn't ask any of these questions. I was a child. I did what I was told.

Moving as slowly as I could away from the safety of Front Street, I counted each step I took as I walked down the stairs of the front porch in my black-and-white, freshly polished saddle shoes, my Sunday best. It was as if I knew, without really knowing, what was to come. Like how I knew Carol had called me a bad name. Mama's wide velveteen skirt brushed against my face with each step.

"One—two—three—four," I counted. How can it take such a short time to leave a place and such a long time to get back?

Daddy took us to the Greyhound bus station uptown. He hugged me close without saying a word, but the tears in his eyes spoke for him. There wasn't time for a drawn-out goodbye. Maybe it was because my dramatically slow exit from the house had made us late, but we'd barely arrived at the station before we were quickly jettisoned to the back of an old, blue Greyhound bus. That's where black folks had to sit in those days, in the back.

"We're going to be fine, children," my mother said reassuringly. "Mama just has to get a new start in life."

"Where are we going, Mama?" I asked. "Where are we going?" I didn't know where her hometown was, but I sensed it was far away from Eudora.

"Just ride, baby. Just ride," she said softly.

Bobbie tended to baby Robert while Mama engrossed herself in *Glamour* magazine, turning the pages as if each contained something magical, although she couldn't have seen herself represented in the glossy photographs. Although *Ebony* magazine for blacks came out in 1945, it wasn't available in this area of the South.

"Look, Gloria, you see? I can do all of this," she said, pointing to several pale, white models wearing wide skirts with can-can slips, cardigan sweaters, and shiny, pointy-toed high heels.

"That's my dream, baby...making it as a model in New York. It'll be hard. I'll be up against white women. If you got any Negro blood, white folks won't hire you. I'll have to do the runway first, just like college. It was good experience, and I'll have a better chance that way. Watch me, honey. First I'm gonna get my life together, then I'll give New York a try."

She pulled me close to her side, smiling her wide, cat smile.

I don't know exactly how long the trip on that Greyhound bus was only that it seemed like another eternity. When Mama stopped talking about New York, I stared out the window and watched the cows and horses grazing in the rolling hills and green pastures. My eyes eventually grew tired from all the looking they were doing and the figures in the fields became a blur, their hazy shapes hypnotizing me into a sleep that was interrupted only by the sound of my mother's voice. She was telling me we'd arrived at our new home. I still had no idea where that was.

"Children, children, we're here."

"Is this New York, Mama? Are we in New York, huh?" I asked.

Mama didn't answer. She just kept looking out the window, smiling and talking to us.

"Look, we're on Main Street," she said. "Well, I'll be. Nothing has changed. The stores are still the same—Frank's Dry Goods, Sims and Hughes Clothing Store, Hamilton Drug Store, Mt. Pleasant Hardware, Ben Franklin Five and Ten Cent Store, Western Auto, Couch's Laundromat. It's like time stood still."

That wasn't necessarily a good thing. It was the red letters stenciled on the windows of the Laundromat that caught my eye and made an indelible imprint on my mind: "White Only–Colored Only." Mama noticed my confused stare.

"What's wrong, baby?"

"Why do you have to wash your white clothes on one side and your colored clothes on the other?" I asked with an innocence only a child can possess.

"That's not what it means, baby." She lowered her voice to a whisper, like she was telling me a secret, and not the good kind. "It means white people and Negroes can't use the same washing machine."

"Is this New York, Mama? Huh?" I asked again.

"No, sweetie pie," Mama answered, her voice resuming its usual self-assured tone. If the reality of our situation hit her when she saw that sign in the Laundromat, she wasn't in the least bit deterred. Mama was home.

"This is where I grew up," she said. "This is Mt. Pleasant, Tennessee."

CHAPTER TWO

I knew that things would be different for us in Mt. Pleasant the instant the white, chubby, baldheaded bus driver announced our arrival. The bus lurched and its brakes screeched as it came to rest at its designated stop, next to a Standard Oil station where gas was all of fifteen cents a gallon. Mama, continuing her role as tour guide, informed us that the Standard Oil was one of only two gas stations in town.

"Mt. Pleasant has always been more of a farming town," Mama explained. "Around the turn of the century, the land around here was rich in something called phosphate, a mineral that fertilizes the ground and helps things to grow. It was very important to the people of Mt. Pleasant, to their agriculture—like gold. I bet you children didn't know that if it wasn't for phosphate, you never would've even been born."

"How's that?" I asked, scrunching my face. I couldn't guess how something I'd never heard of could have played such an important part in my existence.

"It was in the phosphate mines just outside Mt. Pleasant that my parents, your grandparents, first met. If they both hadn't been working there all those years ago...in 1908, I think it was...they might never have found each other and we wouldn't be here today," Mama said matter-of-factly.

I wasn't so sure I wanted to be "here" in terms of my arrival in Mt. Pleasant, but it was out of my hands. Just then the driver bellowed in the slowest Southern drawl I'd ever heard, "All righty, y'all, this here is Mt.

Pleasant. Final stop befo' Nashville. Mt. Pleasant, folks!" I could barely understand him.

"Does he have bubble gum in his mouth?" I asked Mama.

"No, sweetie pie. He's chewing tobacco. You can't see it, but it's tucked under his bottom lip," she said, pointing to her own lip.

"What's tobacco?" Bobbie asked.

"Growing tobacco is how a lot of people in the South pay their bills. This kind of heat is perfect for it. When the big, brown tobacco leaves are ready, they pick them and dry them in the hot sun. Then they chop them into little pieces to sell to folks to chew or smoke. Remember, though, tobacco's no good for you. Now come, children."

As I took my final step off the bus, all I could see were dozens of pairs of shoes shifting from side to side. At less than four feet tall, I was too short to see all the anxious, waiting faces. But they could see me, and before I knew it, I was face to face with Mama's parents. Violet and Earl Young were standing proudly out in front of everyone else, waving and smiling. Mama told Bobbie and me all about them during the long bus ride; they looked just like Mama had said.

"Your granddaddy Earl takes after his father, James Erwin 'Big Red' Goodrum. He was Jewish," Mama told us. "Your granddaddy's mother, Mary Young, was fair-skinned. She was black, but also a Cherokee Indian. James and Mary were your great-grandparents, but they were never married."

"Why not?" I asked. "Didn't they love each other?"

"Yes, baby, they loved each other very much. But back in Maury County in the 1870s, the law said that whites couldn't marry Negroes, and that's what the law said Mary was," Mama told us. "So James built Mary a house in the valley with fat white columns like the ones you see on old plantations. She lived in that big white house with all eleven of their children, and James lived in a small house on a hill nearby. It's been reported by our relatives that, by the time Mary died, she'd accumulated eighty-five acres from James Goodrum."

"Eleven children?" Bobbie questioned, completely unimpressed by how much land our family had come to own. "That's a lot!"

"Your great-grandmother actually had fourteen children, but three went to live up in heaven."

As my granddaddy Earl approached me for the first time, I took notice of his features, which were decidedly "white." His silky, blond hair was straight, but did wave slightly at the ends. His eyes were hazel—the exact same color light green as Big Berry's leaves. He wasn't very tall, maybe five-foot-eight but, like big granddaddy Bob, he was a proud man and stood with his shoulders back and his head high.

Granddaddy Earl was handsomely dressed in a dark suit with a narrow lapel and a skinny, light-blue tie that sat perfectly straight under the stiff collar of his white shirt. The laces of his black, pointed-toe shoes were thin and round and reminded me of spaghetti. Mama admired Granddaddy as she hugged and kissed him.

"Daddy, you look good. You still like your Florsheim shoes...they're nice. Are they new? You always told us to never wear run-over shoes," she remarked.

Granddaddy Earl laughed. "Yes, Daughter."

Mama went over to Grandmamma Violet and greeted her with a kiss. Grandmamma was a bit shorter than Granddaddy, and beautiful with high, round cheekbones. Her skin was pretty and smooth, like Mother Dear's, and the same rich, medium-brown color as milk chocolate.

The outfit Grandmamma was wearing was one I'd see her in again on Sundays. The navy-blue rayon dress with its delicate, white lace collar bare-ly skimmed her calves, allowing me a peek at her muscular legs. I would soon learn that they got so strong from all the housework she did. The thin, black netting attached to Grandmamma's navy-blue straw hat protected the sanctity of her pressed "bubble" curls. The black, suede heels she wore, which opened only enough to reveal a small glimpse of her toes, added just about two inches to her height. She smelled sweet when she kissed me, like talcum powder—like Mama.

We pulled away from the bus stop in Granddaddy's black, four-door, 1939 Chevy, which, at six hundred dollars , was a bargain compared to Granddaddy Bob's car. I liked the outside of it very much; it was adorned with long, silver handles. But I liked being inside, sitting on Grandmamma's lap, even more. "My, my, you chil'ren are beautiful, just like your mama," she gushed. "Robert, you're gonna be tall like your daddy. You got those long feet," she said playfully to the baby.

Bobbie and I made sure to mind our thank yous as we lapped up the compliments from our "new" grandmother. The attention was enough to at least momentarily take my mind off the grandparents I'd left behind.

I could see from the window of the Chevy, just as I could out the window of the bus, that Mt. Pleasant was a lot different from Eudora. The sights of small-town life in this particularly small country town would grow familiar to me during my short stay. There was a cleaners, a shoe store, a hardware store, a family clothing store, and, of course, the Laundromat. There was a Church of God for Negroes and a Baptist church for whites. The streets and yards were generously populated with majestic elms and the overburdened boughs of weeping willows, but there wasn't a Chinaberry tree in sight. Unlike the trees in Eudora, the trees in Mt. Pleasant provided little protection from the hot, glaring light of day.

In Mt. Pleasant, my fellow citizens were white children with straggly hair, who ran barefoot and played in the streets. I would see their fathers in dark-blue overalls and black work shoes. Their mothers and elderly family matrons wore light cotton dresses and wide straw hats as shields against the oppressive sun. Everyone tried as hard as they could to be still, sitting on long, wooden benches taking in the day. A slow turn of the head and a slow-motion wave to passersby was the extent of their exertion, as they called out in that distinctly lazy, Southern drawl, "Hi do, how y'all doin' today?"

Mama explained, "You have to move slow and talk slow. Otherwise, you'll drop dead from a heat stroke."

Everyone seemed friendly—whites waiting out the heat on their benches, black folks sitting on adjacent benches designated just for them, like the pews of their separate churches. The streets were also segregated. White folks walked on the sidewalk, while blacks were supposed to walk in the street, close to the curb. Mama said she never did, though.

Mama said, "My daddy always believed he was equal and refused to walk on a separate sidewalk. He said God made us all, and He made us just the same. White folks thought Daddy was white, so they never bothered him. And we children followed his example."

"We did plenty of walking, too," Mama said. "When we were your age, my brothers and sisters and me, we had to walk miles to school in all sorts of weather. It's hard to believe, given this scorching heat, but it does snow here. The two churches Daddy's pastor of are miles apart. We never would've made it to services on time if we had to walk, so then we drove."

"Not a lot of people in Mt. Pleasant own cars," Mama went on, clearly proud that her family, our family, was one of the ones who did. "Like I explained, this is a farming town. Gas is used mostly for tractors and kerosene lamps. No, not much has changed in this small town since my childhood," she said with a sigh. "I can't imagine much ever will, being that when kids grow up and leave, they don't come back."

So why had she?

The house I would inhabit during my stay in Mt. Pleasant was only about one mile from the bus station, and just like a bus driver giving a tour of celebrity homes, when we arrived, Granddaddy Earl announced, "Children, this is 304 Cross Avenue. It's where your mother and her nine brothers and sisters were born and grew up."

The house was white, with trim the color of a healthy, green lawn. It was smaller than my home on Front Street; how Mama and all her siblings could squeeze into it confounds me to this day. Yet, the house gave me a feeling of happiness and familiarity. Maybe this is what Mama came home for; what Eudora was to me, Mt. Pleasant was to her.

The front yard of the house was close to the gravel road, and pretty yellow daisies and rose bushes haphazardly lined its edges. There were all kinds of tall green plants on the porch—mother-in-law tongues, ferns, scheffleras, and spider plants, just like at Mother Dear's. What reminded me of Front Street the most was the gray swing that hung from the porch ceiling. I'd still be able to swing to the sky!

I could tell that Mama was happy to be there. "Come on inside," she said, smiling and walking fast. "Let me show you children the house."

It must have been about ninety degrees outside, which was normal for mid-July, and inside didn't feel much different. There were fans in the corners of each room, but they certainly didn't seem to cool things off any. I suppose circulating the hot air was better than letting it sit, and that a warm breeze was better than no breeze at all.

There was a fireplace in the living room, just like at Mother Dear and Granddaddy Bob's. All the rooms had wood floors stained dark brown except the kitchen, which was covered in beige linoleum. Here I encountered for the first time a funny-looking round heater called a potbelly stove. There was one in the front bedroom and one in the back. Wooden logs were used to heat the stoves, and the stoves heated the house when it got cold. Despite what Mama had said about the snow, I found it hard to imagine that being cold was ever an issue in Mt. Pleasant.

After showing us the inside of the house, Mama took us on a tour of its vast backyard. Bobbie and I walked while Mama, carrying Robert, led us toward an old weather-beaten shack made of wood that, even from a distance, I could tell stunk to high heaven.

"Yuck!" I said, trying not to breathe in. "It smells bad!"

17

Mama slowly opened the rickety door, releasing more of the stench. She seemed to be immune to it. "There's no bathroom inside, so you'll use this," she said with authority. "Come, children. You have to learn."

I crept in and looked down a deep, dark pit into a pool of poop that had been there for a long, long time. After assessing the situation for a moment, I said with a conviction that matched my mother's, "Mama, if I sit on it, I'll fall in. Are there snakes down there? Are there bugs?"

Mama, in her singular comforting way, said, "No, honey. You won't fall in and there are no snakes or anything else living down there. Don't worry. I'll come with you at night. Or you can use the bedpan I'll give you."

She handed the baby to Bobbie and carefully picked up the empty white porcelain pan sitting next to our new toilet to demonstrate. "Just like this," she explained. "See how it's round and fits right under the bed? When you have to use it, you just squat. The next mornin,' you'll be responsible for emptying it into the outhouse here. Okay?"

I nodded. I'd already decided I'd just hold my pee until morning. I trusted Mama, but there was no way she could see all the way down to the bottom of that big hole, and I didn't want to get bit by something.

I was so relieved to leave that outhouse and breathe in the fresh air, hot as it was, as we walked up a hill to meet the prettiest animal I'd ever seen, Granddaddy's tan cow, Betsy. I knew instantly that we'd be the best of friends.

As we made our way back to the yard, I took note of how many chickens there were—big ones, little ones, brown ones, white ones. Some were sleeping under the back porch, which was on bricks. Some were flapping their wings trying to fly, but they kept landing back on their feet. Some were bobbing their heads up and down and pecking their beaks into the ground. None of them could hold a candle to Betsy.

"Mama, are they eating dirt?" I asked.

"No, honey," Mama corrected. "They're picking up small pieces of corn and wheat. That's what's called their meal. Do you like the chickens? You and Bobbie will have to feed them every morning," she said. "Let me show you."

Mama took us inside the place where the chickens lived. It was called a coop and seemed a lot like the outhouse. As I opened the wobbly, gray wooden door, I saw poop everywhere. It was on the dirt floor, the walls, the ceiling. I tried to avoid stepping in it because I was still wearing my new Buster Brown shoes, but it was an impossible task. The chickens seemed happy, though. They were snuggled into their nests high on shelves. Some slept and some stared at us. Mama said they had to be up there to protect them from wandering cats at night.

Our last stop was Grandmamma's pride and joy, her tremendous vegetable garden. She grew everything that we'd eat for dinner, from mustard greens, green beans, lettuce, tomatoes, broccoli, and carrots to okra, potatoes, and tiny peas. I liked walking between the rows and rows of beanstalks and corn. I thought it would make a good place to play hide and seek. That was before I knew we were there to work, not to play.

At dusk, our tour ended. It was time for bed. "Your baby brother's getting too heavy to carry," Mama said. "Let's go to your new room and I'll read you a story."

The three of us children were going to room together in the large attic. This attic, with its two big, shiny brass beds, reminded me more of a fairytale than a ghost story. Our pillows were stuffed with chicken feathers, although I hadn't yet made the connection, and the white pillowcases, made from flour bags, had been starched and ironed. The pillows were hard as rocks, but they still felt good under our sleepy heads. We managed to stay awake just long enough to hear Mama finish reading *Goldilocks and the Three Bears*. It had been a long journey and a big day for such little people.

Even so, we were up by 7:00 a.m., being introduced to what would become our daily ritual of breakfast, Bible devotions, and chores. Grandmamma made sure we understood that she was the boss in the kitchen and of us. She liked to say, "No chil'ren of mine gonna grow up to be lazy adults. Housework never killed nobody."

Grandmamma believed in working all the time. We'd start in the kitchen, the largest room in the house, by setting the table, and washing and drying the dishes. Sometimes in the early morning, even before breakfast, I'd go with Granddaddy to milk Old Betsy. But that was more fun than work. "Now, take the nipple and squeeze it like this," Granddaddy would demonstrate, gripping the sagging skin of the cow's udder with his own firm hand, squeezing it then moving it up and down.

"Well, well, Betsy's on her last leg...can hardly get any milk," he remarked one day.

"But Granddaddy," I said, counting. "She has one, two, three, four legs..."

"Oh, no," Granddaddy said. "That means she's been around a long time, since your mother's days. Old Betsy's 'bout ready to kick the bucket."

"What does that mean?" Bobbie asked.

"Means she's about ready to die," he said.

I couldn't bear the thought of losing my new friend so soon. My cigar box still contained the berries from my tree. What part of Old Betsy could I save in that little box?

I remember the first time I saw Granddaddy make buttermilk from the milk Old Betsy gave. He filled a big Mason jar and left it on the kitchen counter to sour for days, until it curdled like cottage cheese, leaving a silky smooth butter floating on top. Then he crumbled corn bread into a tall glass and poured the buttermilk into it. The sounds he made while he was drinking made it seem so delicious. "Ah-hum, good...mighty tasty, ah-hum," he'd say to himself between taking big, messy slurps. It was because of Granddaddy Earl and Old Betsy that I acquired a taste for buttermilk. Since most of the time Granddaddy and I were the only ones drinking it, I got the impression that not too many folks loved buttermilk the way we did. It was something special, between us.

My chores weren't done when breakfast was. Afterward, I'd usually go to the garden with my sister and gather corn, greens, green beans—anything that Grandmamma would need for dinner. After that, we'd move on to sweeping the floors and dusting each piece of furniture, even if we'd just dusted it the day before.

We had to be extra careful in the living room, where my grandmother's breakfront china cabinet was, and a mahogany floor lamp that had belonged to my great-grandmother. My favorite piece of furniture was the mahogany upright piano. It was so shiny from being polished all the time. The top was always pulled down to keep dust off the keys. The piano belonged to Mama's brother, my uncle Frederick Young. He was a child prodigy, who learned to play at three years old for Granddaddy's church. When Uncle Frederick grew up, he went to college and earned a doctorate in music then became a famous composer in Chicago. Grandmamma was so proud of what that piano represented. Every child who stepped foot in the house was given orders not to touch the piano unless we were going to be like Uncle Frederick. None of us ever touched the piano.

My grandparents put a value on everything—the piano, furniture, and especially work—and they wanted to instill the same values in us. They doled out discipline generously, especially Grandmamma. She would always talk first, softly, never raising her voice. Then she would cut us a warning with her eyes, and if we didn't listen, she'd send us to the front yard for weeping-willow switches. She'd braid those switches and whip our legs real fast, all the while never raising her voice. Mama told us that's how it was when she was growing up, too. I guess Mama didn't like it very much because, although she could give a good scolding, Mama never spanked us.

Granddaddy didn't talk much, but when he gave an order we kids better have acted on it immediately. If we didn't, and we heard him raise his voice and saw his face turn beet red, we knew we were in trouble. Turning red didn't always mean Granddaddy was angry, though. It was also something that happened every Sunday when he preached.

He would start with a familiar scripture, like Psalm 23, "The Lord is my shepherd..." Then he'd get emotional, gesticulating with his hands and moving his head from side to side. Soon, he'd be walking down the aisles, preaching and wiping sweat from his forehead. Everybody loved the passion of Granddaddy's preaching.

"Preach, Reverend Earl, preach," church folks would say, cheering him on.

When he'd finish, he'd give the altar call to accept Jesus. "Come to Jesus. He'll wash away your sins. Let Him come into your heart today, so you'll have eternal life in heaven. It's either heaven or hell. If you're sick, God can heal you."

I looked up to my granddaddy because I saw how everybody else looked up to him, especially church people. He was the first man of color to build and pastor a Church of God for blacks in the South. He had one church in Sandy Hook and another in Lawrenceburg. Because of segregation, blacks weren't allowed to worship at white churches, so they went to Granddaddy's church.

I did grow genuinely fond of Granddaddy, mostly because he didn't make us work as hard as Grandmamma did. And when he did, he gave us treats. Every Saturday, Bobbie and I would go to the mill with him to help with chores. We'd have to walk about a mile up a dusty, dirty, red clay road and, while we walked, Granddaddy told us all about our roots.

"I come into this world October ninth, 1891," Granddaddy said. "And I've been working pretty much since the day I first drew air."

Granddaddy explained that he only stopped working at the phosphate mine the year he met Grandmamma in order to start working at the mill his father co-owned, shortly after it was officially incorporated by James Erwin Goodrum and his four partners as the Maury Milling Company. It would be forever known in my family simply as "the mill."

"I was seventeen years old when I started at the mill, Gloria. When my father died, they made me lifetime manager."

"What's that mean, Granddaddy?" I asked.

"It means the mill will always be there to feed my family," he answered. "'Course, my first love is preachin'.'"

By the time we got to the mill, my white cotton socks had slipped into my Buster Browns, and my legs were covered with red dirt. Granddaddy spat on a rag to clean me up. He understood I had to keep these shoes until I grew out of them because Mama wasn't working. The man really did seem to care a lot about shoes.

The mill was big and painted bright red like a barn. A small wooden sign hung over the door: *Maury Milling Company.* When I stepped inside, I felt dwarfed by the piles of corn kernels and dry shucks of corn ears that were everywhere.

"Children, see that big machine upstairs? Well, that's where the kernels go. You grind 'em up, and it comes out feed," explained Granddaddy. "Farmers from all over Tennessee buy bags of this feed for their cattle. That machine up there runs back and forth from the first floor to the second floor, like an elevator without a door. I built it, wanted to get a patent for it, but didn't have the money. It could have made us rich by now. Let's get busy, girls. Sweep the cornhusks into piles, and when you're done, we'll go to White's grocery for popsicles. How's that sound?"

"Oh, goody, Granddaddy!" we'd squeal, jumping up and down. Apparently we could be bought, and cheaply at that, since those popsicles only cost ten cents.

We hadn't been with my grandparents too long when my aunt Mildred, one of Mama's sisters, visited us from Lansing, Michigan, with her sons, Jerome and Teddy. Aunt Mildred was pretty with a nice figure. She had fair, smooth skin and brown eyes. She and Mama may have looked alike, but Aunt Mildred and I had the same brown freckles running across our faces, the same high cheekbones and fine sandy-brown hair. I looked more like her than I did like Mama.

The one thing different about Aunt Mildred were her hands, which were large like a man's, with protruding knuckles. I later found out that she worked hard on the assembly line at Fisher Body factory. It was common for women to hold factory jobs after World War II. So was the harassment women had to put up with while doing them. Aunt Mildred did the same work as men, but instead of getting their respect was subjected to their put-downs, inappropriate comments about her body, and sexist remarks. My aunt Mildred had spunk, though. She would argue with the men until they shut up.

My cousin Jerome was just a toddler, but Teddy was five years old, like me. Teddy was a big kid, though, a head taller than I was and chubby like a bear. He loved to tease me, always searching for new ways to make fun of my last name. Teddy also liked to entertain himself by pulling the neatly ironed white ribbons from my hair. Mama painstakingly starched those ribbons every day, but Teddy didn't care. He would even hit me when no one was looking, then he'd run into the next room laughing like a crazy person. Grandmamma didn't approve.

"Children, I'm not going to have that fightin' in this house. Wherever you hit, you kiss. You hear?" she said.

"Yes, Grandmother," we'd respond in unison.

If I hit Teddy in self-defense, he would run and tell Grandmamma, and I'd end up having to kiss him on the seat of his brown corduroy pants because that was the only part of his body I could take a swipe at, given my height disadvantage. He was only made to kiss me when I pleaded my case by crying and yelling. Teddy was often told to kiss me on the lips, which were usually dry and brittle from the heat, prompting him to refer to them as "alligator lips."

One day, I finally got my revenge in what went down in family lore as "The Chicken Chase." It all started with a request from Grandmamma. "Bobbie, Gloria, Teddy—get me a chicken for dinner tonight. And don't play."

Grandmamma had shown Bobbie how to wrangle a chicken, but Cousin Teddy wanted his chance at it. He exploded like a ball of fire into the chicken coop, flinging the door open and startling the chickens, causing them to raise a ruckus of their own.

"Teddy, don't! Don't do it like that. Shhh, be quiet. Here, watch me," Bobbie told him.

She grabbed the closest chicken by the neck and ran out the door, with Teddy trailing close behind. I lingered where I was, feeling deep sorrow for the imminently dead chicken, which Bobbie was holding by its neck as tightly as she could, twirling it around and around in a circle.

"I wanna do it, let me try!" Teddy called out.

Bobbie, not wanting Grandmamma's wrath to be aroused by Teddy's yelling, handed the chicken to him. He laughed and spun around, wringing its neck until it snapped off. The limp chicken fell to the ground, and Teddy stood holding the head. After resting for a few seconds, the chicken's body began flapping its wings and running all over the yard, headless. I was frozen. I couldn't figure out if the chicken had any sense without a head, but rather than wasting time trying to figure it out, I ran to the corner of the house, where I squatted at a safe distance.

"See, Grandmamma! Grandmamma Violet, I did it, I did it!" exclaimed Teddy proudly.

"Okay, son," she said. "You, Bobbie, and Gloria, follow me now. Let's clean this bird up. Stand here right next to this tub of boiling water and we'll pluck the feathers. Now where's Gloria?"

"Over there," Teddy said, still laughing, but this time at me.

"Come on, Gloria, you have to help, too," Grandmamma said.

I walked slowly toward the tub. The smell of the feathers and blood mixed with the hot water made me sick, but I knew I had no right to speak my mind. We soaked the dead chicken in the hot water, and then plucked its lifeless body clean. When we were finished, we were surrounded by millions of wet feathers. The chicken's head was sitting on top of a newspaper.

"Now I'll take this heart, liver, and gizzard, cut it up, and make us some good gravy tonight." Grandmamma, barely finished with one task, had already moved on to the next.

All of a sudden Cousin Teddy grabbed the chicken head and began chasing me through the backyard, out the gate, and down the street. "Ha, ha, ha, I'm gonna get you now!" he yelled.

"No, you can't. I can run faster than you!" I yelled back.

When I looked back and saw those chicken eyes popping out and blood dripping everywhere, run is just what I did. I outran Teddy. I might have been smaller, but I could run faster. I felt so vindicated; I could actually do something better than my cousin. I didn't know it then, but it would turn out this wasn't a fluke; I had a gift. I could run faster than a lot of people.

Teddy and I created such a commotion that the neighbors came out to see what was happening. They all started laughing. For the first time in the short time that I'd known her, I saw Grandmamma laugh. She tried covering her mouth with her apron so we couldn't see her, but her whole body was shaking. The adults around me so rarely showed their humorous side, especially Grandmamma, who seemed to take everything so seriously. I was surprised she didn't make us kiss that chicken head.

Instead, all she did was give us a slight admonishment. "Now, children, that's enough," she said. "Come in and help me with dinner."

That night, I refused to eat the chicken whose murder I had been an accomplice to. Mama gave me a litany of reasons as to why I should. At the top of her list were the children starving in Africa.

"Honey, those children would love to have your food," she told me. "Be thankful, and eat your chicken."

I didn't know anything about those children in Africa, but I knew Gloria Twiggs in Mt. Pleasant, Tennessee, had no choice but to eat. I took a bite, chewed it, and pretended to swallow it. When no one was looking, I spit it into my paper napkin. The napkin stayed on my lap until I got up to clear the table. Nobody knew my secret, not until now…not even Teddy.

At the end of that summer, another of Mama's sisters, Frances, and her husband, Reverend Harry Ewing, came to visit for a week. They lived in Lansing, too. My aunt Frances, like my aunt Mildred and Mama, was also pretty and petite, but she had bigger hips that stuck out when she walked. She was light-skinned with a few tiny moles on her face. Black folks said moles were beauty marks that God made so that special people would stand out.

Aunt Frances wore her shoulder-length, dark brown hair in curls like Shirley Temple. When she was younger, she'd been a singer with four of her sisters. They would sing for their father, my granddaddy Earl, when he preached. Auntie Frances had the most talent, and she kept singing after she left Mt. Pleasant. She had a clear, soprano voice, which made her famous in black churches throughout the South. Some even called her the second Mahalia Jackson, one of the best gospel singers who ever lived.

At this point, Aunt Frances's life was with her husband. She sang wherever he preached in black churches in the South. You could just tell she could sing by the melodious sound of her laughter, and she had such a presence. I was so amused by her gestures, especially when she'd laugh, clap her hands, and roll her head backward all at the same time.

My uncle Harry was tall with bulging muscles. He reminded me of Popeye, except much better dressed. He was a handsome man who, like my father, stood more than six feet tall. He often sported a turquoise-blue hat that had been made by Dobbs Fifth Avenue of New York. He matched everything to his blue suit and smooth, dark, blue-black skin. His nose was broad, and the moustache beneath it was carefully groomed. He had beautiful, light-gray eyes, like the sky just before a rainstorm. Since he was a preacher and evangelist, and sometimes a pastor when a church needed him, you might think he talked a lot, but it was Aunt Frances who was the talker. The only time she'd stop was when she was sleeping.

With Aunt Frances, Uncle Harry, Aunt Mildred, Teddy, Jerome, Mama, my grandparents, and us three children, we were one big, happy tribe squeezed into my grandparents' small house. I must have been a more impressive child than I'd given myself credit for because Auntie Frances and Uncle Harry seemed to like me the best out of everyone. One day, they called me into the living room for a talk. The entire family was there. My uncle sat me on his knee.

"My, my, you're such a cute one, Gloria. Your aunt Frances and I like your spunk. How would you like to come home to Lansing with us?" he asked.

I looked at Mama for direction, to see what I should say. She nodded and smiled. "Yes," I answered shyly.

Only then did Mama speak up. "Honey, I've talked this over with your aunt Frances and uncle Harry. Mama needs time to get a job and find a house, so we can be together as a family again. I'll come for you in December, at Christmas. Does that sound okay, baby?" she asked.

I nodded. If it was what Mama thought was best, it must be okay, but I had questions. "Where will Bobbie and Robert be?"

"Bobbie will stay here with your grandparents. I'm going to Chicago with Robert. Everybody says Negroes get good jobs there. I can start modeling in Chicago, and then maybe in New York," Mama said.

"You'll make new friends. We'll go to the zoo at the Lake Lansing amusement park and of course to church," Aunt Frances chimed it. It was surprising that she'd managed to stay silent that long.

"Frances, don't forget to tell Gloria about my favorite place, where we go every Sunday after church...the Dairy Queen. Do you like the Dairy

Queen, Gloria? And don't worry about missing your brother and sister too much. Cousin Teddy stays with us while your aunt Mildred is at work. Besides, December is just around the corner," Uncle Harry said.

Whatever it took for Mama to get her life together and for us to be a family again, that's what I wanted. It all did sound pretty fun to me. This would be my fourth move in the five short years I'd been breathing air. It was becoming a game, moving from city to city, meeting new people and family members. Maybe it was like a vacation after all.

Mama squatted down and pulled me close. She whispered something that was special, something that was only between the two of us. "I love you. I'll be back for you soon. Don't worry, baby, I'll be back. Harry and Frances love you, too. They'll take good care of you."

Mama put her soft, red lips to my cheek and gently kissed it. I looked into her moist eyes. "Okay, Mama. I love you, too," I said softly, as a tear fell down my cheek. To this day I'm still not a hundred percent certain whether it was Mama's or mine.

Soon after that talk in the living room, I was climbing into the back seat of Uncle and Auntie's new Oldsmobile. It had that distinct new-car smell and large doors with shiny handles, and a big wheel for steering. You could see the whole world out of the wide windows, just like Granddaddy Bob's Chrysler.

I kneeled in a corner of the back seat so I could see Mama. Everybody around her was waving frantically, but they all seemed to blend into the background. I only saw Mama. She stood smiling and waving her hand back and forth, back and forth, like a beauty queen. Her pretty, red, sleeveless dress stood out from the many petticoats she wore. Her long ponytail, held together by a small red ribbon, bobbed from side to side. Everything Mama had on was red—her high heels, her clip-on flower earrings, her lipstick and rouge. Red was her favorite color. She looked just like the models in the fashion magazine she was flipping through when we were traveling on the bus to Mt. Pleasant. My mama was the most beautiful woman in the whole wide world. I'd miss her but, like Uncle Harry said, it wouldn't be for long.

CHAPTER THREE

Lansing was a long way from Mt. Pleasant, and we couldn't, or Uncle Harry wouldn't, drive over the fifty-five miles per hour speed limit. Yet there was never a boring moment. How could there be, with Aunt Frances in the front seat? She talked about church and how God had healed her as a baby when she was stricken with scarlet fever and deafness. She was so animated when she spoke. She'd clap her hands and let loose with a "hallelujah" for emphasis. When she got really excited, she'd speak in a language that made no sense to me. She told me it's what's called speaking in tongues. And then she and Uncle would burst into their favorite song, "At the Cross."

At the cross...where I first saw the light and the burdens of my heart rolled away. Auntie's high soprano vocals, better suited for a church than an Oldsmobile, rang in my ears. She wanted me to join in.

"Come on, baby, now you sing. You're a little soft, but we'll get you out of that."

I didn't have the confidence or the interest. Compared to my aunt, I sounded like a mouse caught in a trap. What did interest me was knowing what my new home was going to be like and who my new friends would be.

Eventually, we pulled up to 914 Olds Avenue, named appropriately for the Oldsmobile factory directly across the street. It was the largest factory in the city, stretching several blocks. Uncle Harry worked on the assembly line there, making Oldsmobile cars.

"Well, baby, we're here," he said. "You'll like it with us."

"Wow, this is big." I stared wide-eyed at the street. It had four lanes. "The road's got black stuff on it," I said.

"That's tar, honey," Uncle Harry said.

My new house was like all the others on the block, except it was the biggest. It was made of wood and painted white, and it proudly sat away from the street on about half an acre of land dotted with elm trees and lilac shrubs, and plenty of rose bushes. The front porch had two long, white columns. In the back, next to the back porch, were stairs that led to a sun deck.

The first thing Uncle and Auntie did was show me my room, which was a small den off the living room. It had been freshly painted the color of eggshells, like the rest of the inside. A twin-size bed and a dresser had been squeezed into it, along with an antique mahogany table filled with Uncle's favorite plants, mother-in-law tongues and spider plants. Every room in the house except the kitchen and bathroom had slick, sandy-colored hardwood floors.

"No running in the house, no playing. Before Christmas, we'll clean and wax all these floors. Got to take good care of the things you own," Aunt Frances said. She sounded just like Grandmamma Violet.

Uh-huh, I thought. *Sure would love to skate on these floors in my socks, just me and Teddy. It'll have to be when no one is around...sure would be fun.*

I felt positively swallowed up by the living room, with its wide walls, bay windows, and high ceiling. Even the furniture was humongous: the sky-blue sofa that folded out into a bed for guests, the golden high-back chair, and Uncle's tall, mahogany, Victorian desk. My favorite thing in the room was the RCA phonograph, on which Uncle played records of Mahalia Jackson and Tennessee Ernie Ford; sometimes he'd make records of Auntie singing.

The upstairs was a whole other house, with a kitchen, two bedrooms, a bathroom, and a dining room. Uncle was going to rent it to his cousins. "A little extra income will help pay off the mortgage in about ten years," he said, explaining that he'd paid ten thousand dollars for the house, a sum a little girl who thought ten-cent popsicles were a treat couldn't even begin to comprehend.

The basement was our last stop. The gray brick walls were cold like ice, with spider webs hanging from the ceiling.

"Uncle Harry, what's a basement?" I asked.

He smiled. "All houses in the North have basements, Gloria. They protect us from storms and tornados."

"We never had a basement where I was before," I told him.

"We've been blessed not to be in a tornado here yet, but we've come mighty close. You have to prepare. It rains...thunders. I've seen trees torn into pieces, houses blown away. But if you go down to this here basement, you'll be pretty safe."

One wall was lined with cabinets, which Auntie stocked with canned food each fall. On another wall stood a General Electric freezer, which held bulk quantities of frozen chicken, fish, beef, and vegetables.

"We got to be prepared for the nuclear war that we're gonna have with the Russians," Auntie told me. This impending war was news to me. The basement's supposed safety didn't make it any less creepy.

We quickly moved to the next room, which was Uncle's dark room. It could only hold two people. He showed me how he developed wedding pictures to earn extra money. Next to the dark room was a corner devoted to Uncle's television repair shop.

"I'm the first and only Negro in the city to repair TVs and take wedding pictures," he said. "You can't let people stop you from your dreams."

The very next day, I had to go to the basement alone. It was the last place in that big house that I wanted to be all by myself, but Auntie said, "Gloria, honey, run and get me a handful of potatoes for dinner. Your legs are younger than mine." I didn't know how to tell her that I was afraid of that cold, gray room, so I went down, my heart pounding with each step. Behind the last one, I found something mysterious.

"Auntie, Auntie, there's a hole down here!" I shouted. Aunt Frances appeared at the top of the stairs.

"That's nothing to be afraid of. When this house was built in the twenties, people used coal to heat their houses. That's what the hole is for."

"What's coal?" I asked.

"It's a small, shiny black rock that burns really hot. A big truck would dump coal through a side window off the driveway into that hole. But we don't need it now. We have electricity. Are you okay now?"

"Yes," I lied.

I wished Uncle was with me. He had a way of reassuring me, same as Mama. I ran to the bottom shelf of the cabinet to an orange wooden crate where Auntie stored the potatoes. They certainly didn't look like any potatoes I'd ever eaten, or ever wanted to eat.

"Auntie, Auntie, there's little white worms comin' out the potatoes. They're movin'," I said.

I could hear Auntie snicker. "No, honey. Those are sprouts. They can't move and they won't hurt you. I'll cut them out. Hurry up now."

I grabbed a rag from the barrow nearby, wrapped a bunch of potatoes in it, and skipped up the stairs as fast as my legs could take me, hoping Auntie would never send me back again. But Auntie's dinner of pot roast and potatoes, carrots and peas, with corn bread on the side, was so delicious it almost made the descent worth it.

Within a few weeks, Teddy was spending more time with us. His mom dropped him off before going to work at the factory. Sometimes he'd even stay the night. He didn't tease me as much as he did in Mt. Pleasant, probably because Auntie was always close by. It felt like we were becoming more like brother and sister than cousins. But one night, after we'd gone to bed, Teddy did something that wasn't at all like what a brother's supposed to do.

"Do you want to play doctor?" Teddy asked.

"Yeah," I said innocently. I'd never played that game before. I didn't want Teddy to know; he might make fun of me.

"Pull down your pants," he said.

I did.

Teddy pulled his penis out of his pajamas and rubbed it against my vagina, although at the time I didn't even know what my vagina was. I felt Teddy's penis get hard, like a rock. I didn't understand the pleasant sensation I was feeling, where it was coming from, or what was making it happen. Teddy kept rubbing against me. That's just what playing doctor was, I supposed.

"What are you children doing?" Auntie's voice interrupted us. "Why are you still talking? It's after nine, past your bedtime. I'm coming in there if you don't hush," she said.

"Okay, Auntie," we said at the same time. We were giggling. I know I didn't know any better, and I don't think Teddy did either. I never told a soul.

That September, I started at Lincoln Elementary School; it was just three months before my mother was due to come for me and even sooner than that I was going to turn six. I was the oldest in the class, but the shortest and smallest. The red, brick, two-story school was a stone's throw from Uncle and Auntie's house—right around the corner, in fact. On the outside of every entrance to the school hung a yellow metal sign decorated with three triangles that said, "Fallout Shelter Site." Whenever there was an air siren drill in preparation for a nuclear attack, students evacuated with their class to the school's basement.

Teddy went to Main Street Elementary School, about two miles away, but we still played together in the yard in the afternoons every chance we got. Most days we had to meet Uncle at the factory gate a few blocks down the street when he got off work. He'd always give us the same explicit instructions the night before, repeating them over and over.

"Just walk two blocks straight down Olds Avenue and turn right at the light. You'll see a metal gate when you cross. Stand by it and wait. Other people will be waiting, too. When the whistle sounds at three o'clock sharp, don't move. That's when I'll come out. Is that understood?"

Teddy and I nodded in agreement. "No head shaking; you're no horse. Open your mouth and talk. You're smart children. I want you to be smarter than me. I had to drop out of school in the third grade to help out my mama. You children are going to college."

"Yes," we said together.

A lot of people were always waiting at the gate, mostly white children with pale skin and stringy hair like the children in Mt. Pleasant. They were nice to us, letting us squeeze in between them to jockey for a good position. We waited eagerly, making sure we didn't miss Uncle among the multitude of factory people running to the tall, wire gate splattered head to toe with paint that matched the color of the cars they'd painted that day.

Leftover inside Uncle's lunchbox was always my favorite treat, carrot sticks. He told me that they'd make my brown eyes sparkle like stars. I shared them with Teddy gladly, knowing that he would share his raisins with me. Uncle told him that raisins would make him strong. Since I was eating carrots and raisins, I knew I had to be a pretty strong little girl, even though I was still such a tiny thing.

Uncle would pick me up and carry me home, saying, "Honey, you as light as a feather. We got to put some meat on them bones." I'd smile, enjoying the walk while Teddy gripped Uncle's khaki work pants. Teddy was much too heavy to carry. Uncle was strong, but he had a slight limp in his right leg.

"Uncle, how come your leg is like that?" I asked one day while he was carrying me home.

"O-o-oh," he said, looking down at it. "That happened back in 1918. I was 'bout eighteen. I wasn't thinking about the Lord then. I was running around, smoking, gambling, and doing a lot of things just not pleasing to the Lord. This guy and me started arguing one night, and things got heated and he shot me," Uncle told us.

He rolled up his pants to show Teddy and me his wound, which had shrunken and shriveled into a round circle around his knee. "There are pieces of the bullet in my leg to this day."

"Did it hurt? Did you cry?" I asked.

"No, men don't cry much," he said, smiling.

"Why?" Teddy asked.

"We supposed to be strong," Uncle replied. "But I sure did holler, calling on the Lord to help me. When I got to the hospital in Dansville, Kentucky, no white doctor would help me. 'We don't help your kind. We'll get to you when we can,' they said. I forced myself onto a gurney, and some-one wheeled me into an empty hallway to die. I bled so much, then my leg started turning dark with what's called gangrene. I was at death's door, but the Lord, hallelujah, touched a white doctor's heart. He saw me lying there and got angry 'bout the bad shape I was in. He operated right away and took out as much of the bullet as he could without taking my leg. Later, he said I would have died if he hadn't seen me. Now, when I think about it, I get happy and thank my Jesus. Hallelujah. Praise His name. There ain't nothin' my God can't do."

Uncle Harry's eyes watered a bit at the end of the story, but he didn't cry. I was growing very close to him. I started wishing he could be my real daddy.

I didn't have an easy time fitting in at school. Fortunately, I had made a good friend in Theresa Tomes shortly after I moved in with Uncle and Auntie. The Tomes lived three doors down and were good friends of Auntie and Uncle. Their daughter, Theresa, was five like me; they also had a son, David, who was six and very skinny and tall, and another boy, Joey, who was just a toddler. Mrs. Tomes's name was Sarah. She wore her dark hair in a long braid that wrapped around her head. Her husband, John, always welcomed us into his home with a handshake. Tetti, the children's grand-mother, never greeted us; she would only peek her head out the door as we were leaving.

I was all smiles whenever I visited the Tomes. I missed my sister, Bobbie, terribly and was so happy to have a little girl to play with again. David, Theresa, and Joey were born in the United States, but the rest of the family came from Syria, which they referred to as "the old country." The Tomes all had long noses, black eyes, thick black eyelashes, and heavy eyebrows that ran together. The hair on their heads was thick and black, and they all had the smoothest, light-olive complexion.

Theresa and I often played together at my house. We made mud pies or drank tea, which was really only water, out of my miniature porcelain tea set, with our white dolls as our guests. We played at Theresa's house, too, but it was smaller than mine, or maybe it only seemed that way because there was stacks of newspapers packed neatly in every corner. The furniture was dark and crowded into small spaces on the thinly carpeted floors. The entire house smelled like onions and lamb.

One day, when I was at the Tomes', Tetti decided to make her presence known. Theresa and I heard the slam of her bedroom door before we saw her enter the living room. Tetti never smiled. She wore wire-rimmed glasses on her wrinkled face. She was probably more than seventy years old and no taller than David. Her long, gray ponytail touched her hips, and she wore a white apron over her dark-blue dress and the same black oxford shoes that all old ladies seemed to wear.

I was afraid of Tetti; I couldn't make direct eye contact with her. The reason she had come out of her room was because Theresa and I were raising a ruckus during the *Mickey Mouse Show.* Every time we watched that show together, we'd stand in the middle of the floor, marching and singing with the Mouseketeers: "M-I-C-K-E-Y M-O-U-S-E!" We knew every Mouseketeer on the show.

I told Theresa, "I'm goin' to marry Bobby when I grow up. He's my favorite."

Tommy was the object of Theresa's affection, but she related the most to Annette. "I like Annette," Theresa would say. "Her hair is fluffy and black like mine."

It was after our marching ritual, and after we'd plopped on the couch, exhausted, that Tetti appeared. She walked over to me grimacing so hard I could see the veins in her neck popping out. She lifted me from the couch by my arm and pulled me to the side door, then pushed me out onto the small cement porch, where I stumbled. I caught myself and managed to stand up straight; my legs were always the strongest part of my body. Tetti spoke in Syrian, then in broken English.

"I don't like you. You colored. Go! Get out. Don't come back."

I could hear Theresa pleading with her. "No, Grandma, please... Gloria's my friend."

I left and ran straight to Auntie, who tried her best to console me and told me not to pay Tetti any mind. "Just ignore her," she said.

"But she doesn't like me!" I cried.

"Some people are prejudiced, baby. I know for a fact Sarah and John aren't like that. I'll talk to your uncle when he gets home and we'll settle this," Auntie promised.

Uncle was upset. He went straight to Theresa's parents, who were also upset by what had happened. They said that Tetti didn't understand American culture, but they would speak to her and tell her that she'd have to accept me because I was Theresa's best friend.

The very next day after school, I was sitting at the Tomes' table eating a wonderful meal of tabbouleh, lamb, kibky, Syrian bread, grape leaves, raw tomatoes, and cucumbers dipped in vinegar. Tetti stayed in her room. It took many months for Tetti to greet me kindly when I was there playing with Theresa, but she did come around.

I also became best friends with Diane Burton. Both of our families attended St. Paul Church of God in Christ, where Uncle Harry was superintendent of the Sunday school and Diane's mother was the choir director. Diane was pretty, with smooth, caramel skin and long, thick hair that her mother pressed and curled every Sunday. Diane wore fancy clothes from Knapp's and other expensive department stores in Lansing, even though she was from a working-class family like mine. Her mother loved nice clothes and wore something new every Sunday herself.

Diane and I became inseparable. Each week we attended prayer meeting, choir rehearsal, and Sunshine Band together. We went to children's Sunday school class, then to regular church, which lasted three hours. At night we'd go back for the Young People's Willing Workers. That was the way of the sanctified church. We were what folks called "holy rollers."

The folks at our church could get emotional and often expressed themselves through music and dance. They played tambourines, the piano and organ, the drums. During the holy dance they would jump all over the place to loud, fast songs, rolling under benches and running down the aisle. They'd get so caught up in the spirit that they'd cry and raise their hands to God, testifying about how He had healed their body. Some parishioners would talk about how thankful they were to have a job at the factory. By the time the evening reached its climax, it wasn't unusual for the entire congregation to be doing the holy dance and speaking in tongues. Sometimes, when Uncle would preach, he'd end with a holy dance that looked like the jitterbug.

Diane and I, too young to be so genuinely moved, would imitate what we saw. One evening we got caught by Uncle Harry doing our version of the holy dance, throwing our hands, talking, and laughing. He warned us not to imitate God's people because something bad would happen to us. Then, when Uncle was preaching, Diane and I got called out for talking and laughing. Uncle stopped his sermon.

"Now, this is the Lord's house. Gloria, Diane…you girls aren't gonna embarrass me before the Lord. Gloria, sit by your aunt. Diane, get up and sit by your mother. You know better," Uncle said.

Diane's mother rolled her eyes at Diane from the choir stand. I knew Diane was in trouble, and that I had it coming when I got home. Uncle resumed preaching like nothing had happened while I sat stoically by Auntie, even though I felt like hiding under a church pew. I got a serious tongue-lashing from Uncle and Auntie later on, and I never talked and laughed again while Uncle was preaching.

December 5, 1952, came quickly. For my sixth birthday party, Auntie made me a two-layer vanilla cake from a recipe that she'd submitted to Betty Crocker. She served it with vanilla ice cream, my favorite. Theresa, David, Diane, and Teddy helped me blow out the candles. Mother Dear sent me a pink cotton dress with flowers. And, that day, I got a card from my real father with six dollars for turning six. It was a surprise hearing from him, since I hadn't since August. My thoughts drifted to Mama, who would be there soon for Christmas. I missed her so much and, despite how settled I'd become in my new home with my new friends, I was eager to go back to Chicago with her.

A few days before Christmas, as Auntie had promised, I was hard at work on my hands and knees scrubbing all the floors. It seemed like there was enough floor in that house to cover a football field. We cleaned so the house would look nice for the many guests who would come during the holiday, mostly from the church. But the whole time I was scrubbing I was thinking how nice I was making it look for Mama.

When she arrived Christmas Eve, she was the prettiest mother I'd ever seen, prettier than when I said goodbye to her in August. My brother, Robert, came with her. By that time he was a toddler, running around and getting into everything. Mama had a new apartment and was doing a little modeling to pay the bills. While she worked, Robert stayed with Velma... Aunt Velma, that is. Although she wasn't our blood aunt, we had to call her that out of respect. Velma came to Lansing with Mama to help with the drive and with Robert.

Christmas Day was special. Mama played in the snow with me and helped me build a snowman. We gave it real character—rocks for the eyes and mouth, and a carrot for the nose. Mama said if we stayed outside in the cold too long we'd get pneumonia. As soon as we were inside, she immediately got me out of my wet clothes and laid my soggy, gray wool leggings and coat on an opening in the floor where the heat came up from the furnace. I loved having her look after me again.

We stopped by Aunt Mildred's house for the holiday. Uncle Wayne, her husband, and Teddy and Jerome and a big group of their friends enjoyed a feast of turnip greens with ham hocks, corn bread, fried chicken, ham, sweet potatoes, tossed salad, and pineapple upside-down cake. After dinner, we went to our friends' homes to exchange Christmas gifts.

And that night, everyone went to church to hear me recite my Christmas speech. You'd have thought I was a Spiegel model, with all the compliments I received about my dress. Auntie had made it. It was pink nylon with a can-can slip underneath to give it fullness, which my small frame so badly needed. I had big pink ribbons tied to my pigtails and thick bangs covering my protruding high forehead. My pink cotton ankle socks and new black patent-leather Buster Browns set the outfit off perfectly.

I had the longest speech of anyone my age because Auntie believed that kids should be challenged to learn more than what people thought they were capable of. That was fine with me. I enjoyed reciting. And everyone in my family was so proud of me. They stood and applauded, along with a congregation of folks who numbered about two hundred. Their clapping sounded like thunder.

"You're such a good actor, honey, just like your father. You knew when to raise and lower your voice," Mama told me, beaming with pride. Out of all the compliments I got, hers meant the most. I wanted her to see what I could do, to make her proud so I could go back to Chicago with her.

Early the next morning, before she began her packing, Mama came into my room and sat on my bed. Cuddling next to her, I could still smell the lingering scent of Chanel No. 5 from the day before. She had something to tell me.

"Mother won't be able to take you back with her, honey. I'm not ready, financially."

"But you promised!"

"I don't have money coming in regular every week. I'm only working part-time doing interior design, some modeling. I still don't have anything steady," Mama explained.

I looked into her soft, brown eyes. She must've seen the sadness and hurt in mine. "When can I come then?" I asked her.

"Well, maybe after you finish school this year. Then you can start first grade in Chicago next fall. It's not that I don't want you with me, baby, it's just that Harry and Frances can do more for you right now than I can. I've talked to them about you staying on, and they're happy to have you. Maybe before you come to stay, you can come on the bus to visit me."

"Promise?" I needed Mama's reassurance. Even though I was heart-broken, I didn't cry. I couldn't let Mama know how disappointed I was. I wanted to show her that I was a big girl, big enough that if she would only send for me, I could travel to Chicago all by myself on the Greyhound bus.

We all gathered to watch Mama leave, and still I held back my tears. I really did believe she would be back for me soon. The winter quickly passed and spring came. Before I knew it, summer had also come and gone. In September of 1953, I was still waiting for Mama. Instead of coming to Lansing or sending for me, she phoned.

"I'm sorry, honey. I'm still looking for steady work. I'm a seamstress for Marshall Fields now. It's not steady like I wanted, but it's something. You have to remember, it's hard for Negroes."

"But I miss you, Mama. When can I see you?"

"Maybe I'll send for you next summer, when school's out. How does that sound?"

"Okay," I said softly, trusting in the sound of her voice and clinging to the belief that, one day, I'd be with her in Chicago. Not only did I want to be with my mother, but the idea of starting at a new school somewhere else was appealing.

I was not having an easy time at my school in Lansing. Most of the students were black, but the teachers were white. The few white children who did attend Lincoln lived in the same neighborhood that I did and, like me, had parents who worked on the Oldsmobile assembly line. Despite my small size, I was wiser than many of my peers, perhaps owing to the fact that Uncle, in his forties, and Auntie, in her twenties, were older than most parents. Still, my maturity didn't prevent me from becoming the victim of merciless bullying; the chief bully was Alvin Mask.

Alvin was always bragging about how he and his numerous brothers and sisters all loved to beat up kids just for the fun of it. He wore wrinkled T-shirts that were riddled with tiny holes and were always too snug, as if they were hand-me-downs from a younger rather than an older sibling. His faded corduroy pants, also a size too small, rose above his ankles, and the soles of his brown shoes were paper thin.

The smell of Alvin's breath and clothes reminded me of Granddaddy Earl's outhouse. His hair was matted into rolls of tiny naps, and he made a habit of wiping the snot from his nose onto his shirtsleeves. His dark, cat-like brown eyes were always filled with white mucus. Several of Alvin's fingers were just stubs, and most of his nails had been bitten to the quick. He was the only classmate of mine whom I feared. Because of him, I dreaded going to school.

Today, Alvin would be referred to as a gang leader, but back then he was simply known as a ringleader. He provoked fights with me, taunting me by saying, "Ha, ha, ha, you yellow, high yellow. Your name be different from your mama and daddy. Look at that cute hair you got. You think you so cute, huh?"

The kids who ran with him joined in. I noticed the kids who teased me the most had dark skin and sad faces; some of them managed to top Alvin in their taunts. "You think you white 'cause you got light skin and that nice hair," they'd say. When I walked past them in class, they would stick their foot out in the aisle to try to trip me. Sometimes, when we were outside, they would tear the clothes Auntie had worked so hard to make for me. I was tormented like this every day.

My teacher, Mrs. Palmer, smiled and said hello to me each morning; I could tell she really liked me. When I'd tell her the things Alvin had done, she'd send him to the principal's office. Still, I was the one who got punished—with a beating from Alvin after school. Even though Mrs. Palmer didn't succeed in stopping Alvin, I liked that she was calm and soft-spoken. And that she had brown freckles splattered across her face the same as me, and blazing red hair that barely touched her shoulders.

Sometimes Cousin Teddy's school, Main Street Elementary, let out early, and he'd come and pick me up at Lincoln. When Alvin, his brothers, and the other bullies saw my cousin, they'd run. They knew they were no match for Teddy, who was built like a linebacker, chunky and tall. When Teddy was around, no one bothered me and I felt safe. I never told Auntie or Uncle about Alvin because I knew things would end the same way they did when Mrs. Palmer intervened.

To keep the beatings to a minimum, I began to steal money from Uncle. Alvin and his crew would accept whatever I gave them—nickels, dimes, pennies. It was my only recourse. But I wasn't a clever thief or a good liar.

"Gloria, I had rolls of quarters and dimes in my desk drawer. Where are they?" Uncle asked me one day, using his most firm tone.

"I don't know," I answered, my voice and body quivering.

"Come closer...let me see those eyes. They'll tell me if you're lying. I had about twenty dollars in change here, and I know nobody walked into this house and stole it."

"Maybe they did," I prompted.

"And maybe you're lying through your teeth. Tell you what—I'll just sit here all night 'til you tell the truth. I don't care what you've done, but you got to tell the truth. God hates liars. I do, too."

"I didn't steal the money...I didn't," I swore to Uncle, with tears in my eyes.

He called Aunt Mildred to see if Teddy had taken it, but he said he hadn't, so Uncle confronted me again. He sat and waited while I stood there in the same spot for hours. At last, the tears fell; they quickly turned to loud, messy sobs.

"I did it! I did it! I took it and gave it all to Alvin Mask. I didn't want him to beat me up anymore." It's amazing my Uncle could understand a word I'd said, given how hysterical I was.

"Gloria, why didn't you tell me?" he asked, his demeanor softening. "Your aunt and I know how bad those Mask children are. We could have helped you."

"I was scared."

"Tell you what. I'm goin' up to that school and get this thing straight with the principal. If that doesn't stop it, I know Alvin's mother. I'll talk to her. You're not gonna live your life in fear."

"Don't tell, Uncle! Alvin will beat me up!" I pleaded.

"That's not gonna happen. I can't let this continue, Gloria. We'll give it a few days if you want, but if nothing changes, I'm gonna have to take action," he said.

The next time I saw him at school, Alvin asked for more money. I told him that Uncle was going to tell his mother about the teasing, beatings, and extortion. To my surprise, the threat worked. For a whole week my life was bliss. Alvin didn't speak to me, and he didn't beat me up. Unfortunately, that didn't mean things had changed between us.

I was playing in my sandbox one Saturday morning with Teddy, Theresa, and David, when suddenly I heard a loud pop, like a gunshot. Teddy was big, but quick on his feet. I heard him yelling as he ran to the back door, "Aunt Frances, Aunt Frances! Gloria's bleeding. Hurry! Gloria's got her eye shot out!"

"You're gonna get it!" Teddy screamed at Alvin and his brothers, who were running toward the playground.

As I made my way slowly to the house, I began to sway. I was dizzy, unable to see well, and growing delirious. I pressed my hand to my eye to try to stop the bleeding, but blood continued to gush from my head. I left a trail of it behind me as I entered the kitchen. Uncle got a cold towel for my wound, settled me into the car, and drove like a madman to the Sparrow Hospital emergency room while Auntie applied pressure to my head with the cold washcloth, hoping the blood would clot.

I'd been hit on the left side of my head with a sharp rock. The doctor told Uncle Harry I was fortunate to still have my eye. I had to get stitches and was donning a large, white patch over my forehead. As angry as I'd seen my uncle in the past, I'd never seen him as angry as he was at that moment. Still, he managed to politely thank the doctor for his good care. He was saving his ire for Mrs. Mask, with whom he wanted to speak immediately.

Mrs. Mask lived on the west side as we did; her house was about eight blocks from ours. It was only a short time after we left the hospital that Uncle was urgently pounding on the Masks' flimsy screen door. I was standing next to him, and Auntie was standing next to me.

It didn't take long for Mrs. Mask to appear. She was a dark-brown, full-figured woman, and her short, black hair was slicked back with grease. Her cotton dress was worn and was mostly covered by a wide white apron. She was calm and polite, two things Uncle was finding it hard to be.

"Hello, Mrs. Mask, I'm Reverend Ewing. I need to have a word with you about what your sons did to my daughter."

"Why, yes, Reverend. Of course, I know who you are. Come in, please," Mrs. Mask said, speaking slowly.

A tattered couch was pushed against one of the living room walls and in front of it was a small television set, positioned on a chair, with a wire hanger where the antenna once was. There were a few chairs for sitting scattered throughout the room. The scent of fried chicken wafted in from the kitchen. I saw no trace of the rest of the Mask tribe.

"Today I come to you not as a minister, but as a parent, and an angry one," Uncle said. He was being hard with Mrs. Mask, but he was quite gentle with me as he pointed to my injured head.

"Your sons did this. They were throwing rocks at Gloria today. The doctor said she coulda lost her eye!"

Mrs. Mask's own eyes widened as she took in what Uncle was telling her. Her mouth hung open as if she was about to say something, but it took a few moments before she could get any words out.

"I'm, I'm so sorry, Reverend," she stammered. "I didn't know this happened. I'll talk to my sons. I'll make sure nothin' like this happens again." Mrs. Mask began nervously wiping her hands on her apron.

"I can't say for sure which of your sons did this, but I believe Alvin is the instigator. He's been beatin' up Gloria every chance he gets. I won't have it," Uncle said to her firmly.

She reiterated her apology and her promise to handle the situation with her boys. Uncle didn't wait on Mrs. Mask to discipline her sons; he met with the principal that Monday, and I never saw Alvin again. I never had trouble from any of the Mask boys after that. I heard students say that Alvin was attending the Lansing Reform School, which might have been enough to teach his brothers a lesson, too.

That wasn't the end of my troubles at school, though. A boy named Gerald Richardson, who could've been Alvin's clone, chased me home one day and tried to pull off my dress. I clawed his face something fierce, so much so that I got expelled over the incident, despite Gerald being the aggressor. After I was reinstated, none of the boys at school ever messed with me.

It wasn't long after I was expelled that Uncle had a serious phone conversation with my mother about their arrangement, which after two years no longer seemed temporary. He and Auntie told me about it later.

"Thelma," he'd said to Mama, "we'd like your permission to adopt Gloria. It would be cheaper on us. She could have my medical benefits. If she had our last name, it would keep children from teasing her."

Uncle Harry made a solid argument, but my mama was still my mama, and she intended to stay that way. Uncle said she issued her reply in a soft but firm voice.

"Harry, I appreciate everything you and Frances are doin' for Gloria while I get my life together. Truly I do. But I hope you understand that I can't give up my rights as a mother."

Uncle did understand; he never talked about adopting me again. He continued to pay for my care, out of pocket. Fortunately, I was a healthy child, and Uncle Harry never complained. After the situation with the Mask boys, I began to feel even closer to him. He had stood up for me and protected me the same way a real father would have. I hadn't heard from Daddy in more than a year, since he'd sent me that birthday card with the money in it. I started to think about him less and less. And as much as I loved Mama, it was Aunt Frances who tucked me into bed at night and nursed me when I was sick.

I began to love Uncle Harry and Aunt Frances so much that I cried at night over not having their last name. I went as far as to write "Ewing" on my school papers, instead of "Twiggs." My teachers warned me not to use Ewing. They would cross that name out and write "Twiggs" above it. They told me it was against the law to use a name that wasn't legally mine. But I never listened. No matter what the law said, this was my family—in the same way that my great-grandparents James and Mary were truly husband and wife.

I began calling Uncle "Dad" and Auntie "Mom," except when my mama Thelma would phone. Then I didn't refer to them at all, for fear of hurting her feelings.

It was in 1953 that Mom Frances got pregnant with a child of her own. She and Dad said they wanted me to have a sister. I was ready for one, too. Having Teddy around got boring, and even with my best girlfriends to hang with, I still missed Bobbie.

One day, Mom started bleeding badly, and it wouldn't stop. There were puddles of blood everywhere—on the bed, on the green rug next to it, and all over her clothes. Dad rushed her to the hospital while I stayed home alone; children weren't allowed in hospitals back then, unless they were being born or receiving care. Later, I learned this was Mom's second miscarriage.

When Mom came home, she had to rest a long time. She didn't talk much about it, except to Aunt Mildred.

"My body wasn't ready for a baby. This was God's way of cleansing it. When it's time, I'll have a healthy one," I'd hear her say to her sister.

A year later, Mom gave birth to a tiny six-pound girl with a pinkish complexion who burped a lot, but she made up for it by being so angelic and calm. She had the prettiest light-brown eyes and straight, dark-brown hair. Mom and Dad named her Shenell after a niece who used to live with them before I came.

The first week after Shenell was born, Mom rested, and I helped out with the feeding. The worst chore wasn't taking care of what went into the baby, but cleaning up what came out of her! Like a dutiful big sister, I changed Shenell's stinky diapers all day long. But something went terribly wrong in Shenell's second week of life. The doctors at the hospital discovered that she'd been born with a hole in her heart. They said she was too weak to live.

"Our heavenly Father, we come to you as humbly as we know how. If it's your will, Lord, work a miracle in our baby's life. You've opened blind eyes and healed the lame. I know you can do this," Dad would pray out loud.

But the miracle never came, and Shenell died. I'd never experienced death before, and I didn't understand it but I felt sad. Mom tried to explain it in children's terms. "It just wasn't God's will or Shenell's time," she said. "She's gone to Glory and is flying around with all the other little angels she's met."

Dad held a service for Baby Shenell at Riley's Funeral Home, the only black funeral home in the city. Shenell's pretty, white velvet casket was no bigger than she was. Mom Frances was sad for a long time. Then, in 1954, when I was eight years old, she got pregnant again.

For nine months, Mom was on bed rest—doctor's orders. He gave her multivitamins because of her low blood count. Mom listened to everything he said, wanting to make sure she did everything right to have a healthy delivery and baby. It seemed like no time at all before she was yelling to Dad Harry that her water broke.

I stayed with Aunt Mildred while Mom Frances was in the hospital delivering a little baby boy. Baby Ewing weighed in at almost nine pounds. Dad said he was handsome enough to break girls' hearts. He had straight, sandy-brown hair and green eyes, and smooth skin that was nearly white. Baby Ewing didn't look like Dad Harry or too much like Mom Frances; he was the spitting image of my granddaddy Earl.

I never got a chance to hold my new brother. He died in Mom Frances's arms in the hospital a few hours after he'd been born. The umbilical cord had been wrapped around his neck. Seeing him in his tiny white casket, dressed in a pretty, white-silk lace gown made me sad. I was so confused about death and why there had been so many in my new home. Somehow, Mom Frances found the strength to handle the deaths of her babies.

"God knows best. He has a plan," she'd say.

"But why do people have to die?" I asked her.

"Honey, this is God's way. He gives, He takes. I know one day I'll have a healthy child," she told me with the conviction of her faith, but there were tears in her eyes.

A few black folks were wagging their tongues. They said Baby Ewing didn't look like Dad Harry because Dad was almost fifty. They felt he was too old to make babies, and maybe too old for his wife, a woman twenty years his junior. Of course, our family knew the truth. Mom Frances was loyal to Dad Harry, and they both had enough life in them to make a new one.

Not too long after Baby Ewing took his first and last breaths, Grandma Violet and Granddaddy Earl were in a bad car crash. Mom Frances had to go to Mt. Pleasant to nurse them. I was heading into the fourth grade and couldn't ruin my perfect attendance record, so I stayed with Dad, who knew by then how to take good care of me. He cooked oatmeal for breakfast, ironed my dresses, and even plaited my hair.

One night, while Mom was away, there was a terrible storm in Lansing. The wind, rain, and hail pounded so hard against my window I thought someone was trying to break into the house. The roar of the thunder reminded me of the lion I saw at the Lansing Zoo. I was terrified. I pulled the blankets over my head, hoping to block out the noise of the ravaging storm. But I couldn't, and it just got louder and scarier. It sounded like it was inside the house. I became convinced a monster had gotten into my room, looking for something good to eat. I had to find a safe place.

I jumped straight up out of bed and landed on my feet like a cat. I ran quick as the lightning that was flashing in the windows, through the living room, the dining room, ignoring the chill of the hardwood floors on my bare feet. "Where's your house shoes?" Mom Frances would've reprimanded. "Always wear your slippers—you're gonna catch a cold," she would've warned. But Mom wasn't there.

I jumped into the safety of Dad Harry's bed. I nestled comfortably next to him, drifting off to a world far away from the storm, thinking, *Nothing in this whole wide world can harm me now, not even the monster.*

I woke up when I felt a hand on my right leg. Then it slowly crossed over to my other leg. Then it moved downward. And then it stopped.

Mom Frances had taught me what my vagina was. That's where the hand was, on my vagina. And it happened again, and then...again. It didn't seem right. I remained perfectly still, pretending to be dead like Mom Frances's babies. I just lay there holding my breath, hoping it would stop.

I couldn't understand why this was happening. I thought it wasn't real, like a bad dream. I wished and wished that it would go away. But it didn't stop. It was real. I carefully and slowly allowed myself to breathe, letting out the air in gradual, shallow increments.

On my last breath, I prayed, *Dear Lord, please let his hand go away.* I knew it was his hand, Dad Harry's hand. It was soft, and I could smell the glycerin and water concoction he used every morning and every night to ward off calluses from his hard work on the assembly line.

Dad Harry's hands lifted me. They took care of me when I was hurt. They defended me and provided for me. Now his hands scared me. They scared me so bad, I was afraid to hold them again.

CHAPTER FOUR

I remember the relief I felt when Mom Frances finally came home. She had barely walked through the front door and I was in her arms, hugging her close. I so badly wanted to tell her what had taken place in her bed a few weeks before, and what was still going on during my baths.

Dad would lather the washcloth and begin washing my back, slowly moving to the place my breasts would've been if I'd had them, then down to my vagina. He would wash me thoroughly, pause, and wash me again, always paying careful attention to those same parts. I had strong, shapely legs, just like my natural mom. But my body was physically immature for a nine-year-old. I tried to convince myself that Dad was only examining me like Doctor Harrison did when Mom Frances wanted to find out why I wasn't growing.

"Now, Mrs. Ewing, don't worry about Gloria. She'll be fine. One day she'll shoot up like a bean pole, and you'll wonder what happened."

Dr. Harrison was Lansing's only black doctor. He was gentle and kind, and when he examined me, I didn't feel it was wrong the way I did when Dad Harry was rubbing my body in those places.

Dad never talked to me about what he did, never told me not to tell. He didn't have to. Even if I'd known whom to talk to about it, I wasn't sure I would be believed or that I wouldn't be blamed. Maybe they would say it was my fault for not having been brave enough to stay in my bed that night and face the storm and monster on my own.

After that night, there were monsters everywhere. Every time the floors cracked or the wind whistled, or I heard mice dancing between the walls and drunks cussing as they walked down the street, I got spooked. But I'd just close my eyes real tight until I fell asleep. No matter how afraid I was, I promised myself I'd never run to Dad again. I didn't want it to happen again.

I just wanted everything to go back to the way it had been. I yearned for normal things, like going to school, meeting Dad Harry at the factory gate, playing, and going to church. The molestation would always be with me, though; things would never be as they were. It was only once I began to develop breasts and pubic hair that I was able to put an end to Dad's washings.

"Honey, it's time for your wash," he'd call through the locked bathroom door.

"I can do it myself, Dad," was my quick response, as my heart throbbed against my chest, hoping I wouldn't hear his hand turning the doorknob, trying to get in.

It was too late, though. The little girl who believed that trees, and grownups, could be trusted was gone. In her place was a girl who felt helpless and lost, and not much like a child at all anymore.

I had convinced myself that, as much as I wanted to, if I ever told Mom Frances, she would say I was lying. She never listened when I tried to explain my side of anything; often her verdict was that I was to blame. Sometimes she'd wash my mouth out with a big chunk of Ivory soap until I gave in and told her what she wanted to hear, whether it was true or not. Mom would follow my forced "confession" with a litany of do's and don'ts.

"Children should be seen, not heard," Mom would say. "You don't know anything about life; you're just a child. You ain't been livin' as long as me. Discipline didn't kill me, so it ain't gonna kill you. The Bible says, 'spare the rod and spoil the child.' You not raising yourself, nor are you gonna grow up a heathen. You a preacher's child. You not gonna embarrass me."

I'd try to defend myself. "But, Mom," I'd begin.

"Hush, don't talk back," she'd cut me off. "That's why children end up in prison. They don't respect their parents, and their parents don't discipline them."

Sometimes my punishment was standing in a corner on one foot.

"Get that foot back up! Don't think I didn't see you. I got eyes in back of my head. You want me to add more time?"

"But, Mom, I'm tired. My legs hurt."

"You should've thought about that before you sassed your teacher."

It was best, I decided, that the molestation remain my dark secret, buried deep inside for as long as I could keep it there.

Dad's punishments weren't as frequent as Mom's, but just as memorable. He'd make me strip off all my clothes in the bathroom, and I'd watch as he'd wrap the end of his leather belt around his large, muscular hand. When he began whipping me, I'd scream. I'd outright yell like he was killing me. Because I was fair-skinned, it didn't take long for welts to appear over my entire body.

"Don't you ever lie to me! Do you hear me? If you lie, I'll beat the truth out of you."

"Yes, Dad. I hear."

After the first beating, I never lied, although that didn't stop me from being punished. Of all the punishments, the worst was when Mom Frances would haul off and slap me for giving my opinion, which she called "talking back." She hit hard, and blood would run from my nose like a faucet until Mom applied a small piece of brown paper bag under my top lip. Mom wasn't the least bit daunted by the bleeding, and the slaps continued.

I still felt fortunate to have Mom Frances and Dad Harry, grateful even. At that point, I hadn't heard from my real father for years. Mama stayed in touch, but I hardly ever saw her. I was beginning to doubt that she was ever going to send for me. If Mom Frances and Dad Harry hadn't been caring for me, I didn't know who would be. And I genuinely loved them. More than that, I wanted their love.

So I did what I had to do. I learned to keep my feelings to myself, swallowing hard and saying little. There was so much going on inside of me, so much to keep down. Shortly after I was first molested by Dad Harry, I was traumatized by another experience—a kidnapping.

Mrs. Thurman was a short, stocky white lady who babysat for our next-door neighbors, the Jacksons. She had long gray hair that she pulled back into a bun and covered with a matching hair net. She always wore a white apron on top of her cotton, flower-patterned dress that hugged her large breasts. She would wave to me while she was hanging sheets on the clothesline in the Jacksons' backyard. I'd wave back from my sandbox, where I played with Cousin Teddy and my friends Theresa and David.

Playing in that sandbox was my favorite thing to do in the whole world. It allowed me just for a little while to forget everything bad that had happened. Sometimes I'd play in the sand with John and Helen, the children Mrs. Thurman watched during the day. Their parents worked at the factory like Dad. Their house was plain and the dark green paint on the front was peeling. There were no pretty flowers in their yard like there were in ours. There was nothing pretty at all about their old wooden house.

One day, Mrs. Thurman peeked through the sheets waving pieces of candy at us. She smiled. I smiled back.

"Come, come inside, I'll give it to you," she said, beckoning us with the candy.

Teddy, Theresa, and David followed my lead onto the concrete side porch, then into the kitchen. Once we were all inside, Mrs. Thurman quickly slammed the door. As I heard her turn the top lock, I knew something was wrong.

Mrs. Thurman's voice was no longer kind. She began yelling and stomping from the kitchen through the other rooms in the house. She found John and Helen and yanked them by their arms.

"Stand here—John, Helen—in this line."

She lined all of us up, beginning at the locked back door in the kitchen into the dining room, near the table. We were silent with fear. Mrs. Thurman pulled the dining room shades down and walked slowly into the living room to lower the shades there as well. Then she flopped herself down on the couch, which was in the room across from where we were standing. Someone must have moved.

"Stand here. I said stand!" she yelled. "You deaf?"

Then she picked up a belt that had been lying on the couch. It was long, like Dad Harry's. She jerked it quickly; when it hit the floor, it made a loud snapping sound.

"Come here, you bad kids. Helen, you first. Lay across my lap."

Helen, who was so skinny her bones poked out of her knees, walked slowly to the couch. She was about four years old with long, brown, stringy hair that was always hanging in her face.

"No, please. I won't do it anymore!" Helen cried.

"Shut up! You talk too much. Don't make any noise," Mrs. Thurman warned.

She pulled Helen onto her lap and began whipping her. Helen began to cry.

"I said shut up." Mrs. Thurman covered Helen's mouth.. When she was through whipping her, Mrs. Thurman pushed Helen onto the floor. The little girl curled up in a fetal position at her feet, whimpering.

"John, hurry up. You're next."

John, like his sister, walked slowly toward Mrs. Thurman to receive his beating. He was about six and was dressed in brown corduroy pants that didn't go a smidge beyond his ankles and a too-tight plaid shirt pulled taut across his stomach. He lay down across Mrs. Thurman's lap, tears sliding silently down his face, which was scrunched tight in anticipation of the pain.

I was already blaming myself. Mom and Dad had taught us never to leave the yard or go with strangers. But Mrs. Thurman wasn't a stranger. We'd known her for years. That hardly seemed to matter.

"We have to get out," I whispered to Teddy, who was standing next to me.

"Gloria, another word, you'll be next. You hear me?"

I nodded. I was terrified. I had to find a way out. Once Mrs. Thurman was through with John, David was next, then Theresa, and then me. Teddy, the biggest and tallest, was standing at the end of the line, next to the kitchen door. I knew he was tall enough to reach the lock. I wanted him to turn it so badly. That's all it would take; we could run faster than fat old Mrs. Thurman.

I whispered to Teddy, "Unlock the door and run." Thank the Lord, he obeyed.

In a matter of seconds, Teddy and I were out the door and back home.

"Hey, come back! Come back…here's your Tootsie Rolls!" Mrs. Thurman bellowed after us at the top of her lungs.

We ran like we were in a race for our lives, straight into the arms of Mom Frances and Dad Harry, who were standing in front of our house waiting with our nervous neighbors. It was Dad who spoke first.

"Where have you chil'ren been? You had us scared stiff."

"Mrs. Thurman was beating all of us," I said.

It was Theresa's mother's turn to ask the questions. "What? Why were you over there? Haven't we told you children not to go anywhere without our permission?"

"She had some candy for us," Teddy tried to explain.

"You know better," Dad said, looking us over carefully. "Don't think we won't be talking more about this at dinner."

We never saw Mrs. Thurman again. And from then on we stayed close to home..

Shortly afterward, I began to withdraw. Already a quiet child, I was now a particularly fearful one. I spoke up when it was demanded of me, but for the most part, I was afraid to talk about anything at all. Mom Frances and Dad Harry often asked if I was okay.

To them I would always answer, "Yes."

Mixed with the trauma and abuse, there were moments of joy, like in 1955, when Mom gave birth to Eva Maria, a beautiful baby girl with smooth, medium-brown skin and a full head of hair. Eva Maria was pretty like Mom. Her eyes were slanted like Dad's. Everyone who knew our family called her a miracle baby. Although we were ten years apart, I was proud to have a little sister to care for.

To help pay for the cost of a new baby, Dad rented the upstairs out to his cousins. The Sanders family consisted of Gene and Estella and their daughter, Eugenia. Eugenia was my age, but a little taller with more meat on her bones. The most delicate term that could have been used to describe her father was "flirtatious." Gene was definitely related to Dad Harry.

One afternoon when Mom was running errands, I was alone in the basement ironing the culottes she had just made for me to wear to our church picnic. I didn't know Cousin Gene had come down until I felt him standing close to me. The smell of him made me think he'd been drinking.

"Gloria, what's this?" he asked.

"What's what?" I asked.

"This."

He extended his index finger and poked at the Janzen logo on my polo shirt, which happened to be covering one of my emerging breasts.

"I, I don't know what you're talking about," I stuttered.

"This," he said, touching my left breast again.

I felt like my legs were cemented into the cold, concrete floor. Despite all I had done to suppress them, the memories of Dad Harry molesting me surfaced. I couldn't understand why it was happening again, or help but wonder if this would be the outcome of every interaction I had with an adult male.

Suddenly I found myself running. My body was taking me as fast as it could away from Cousin Gene, my legs skipping every other step as they ascended the basement stairs. I didn't stop running until I realized I was outside, where I stood alone in the middle of the driveway. I was still afraid, but I knew Cousin Gene couldn't hurt me outside, out in the open where everyone could see. When he walked out of the back door, he said nothing to me. He just smirked. I watched him go back to his house upstairs. It was an hour before Mom returned—an hour that I stood in that spot in the driveway, waiting for her.

This time, I told her everything, at least about Cousin Gene. She was furious.

"That low-down, dirty, good-for-nothing dog! When your dad gets home, he'll hear about this!" Mom promised.

Dad took the news calmly. He said he'd talk to Cousin Gene. But after a week or so, when Mom asked if he had, he said no. I could only assume it was because of what Dad had done to me himself. From then on, all I could do was run every time I saw Cousin Gene. With too much to live with already, I decided I didn't want to be alone with a man ever again. As an adult, I learned from family members that Gene had molested other girls, possibly even one of his own daughters.

It's ironic, given all the bad things that happened to me, that Mom Frances and Dad Harry were overly protective to an extreme; I had no life outside of church. One Sunday, though, we strayed from our usual routine.

It was February 17, 1957. Instead of heading to another church service, we crammed into the Lansing Civic Center with hundreds of other black people to hear a speech given by the nephew of Pastor Joel King of the Union Baptist Church. I noticed the man everyone was there to see before he was even introduced because he looked a little like Dad, with a handsome, full face, thin mustache, and hair that was closely cut to his head. His skin was lighter than Dad's, though. When Reverend Toussant Hill of Detroit introduced this gentleman, everybody in the civic center rose to their feet.

"And now I present the greatest civil rights leader of our time, Dr. Martin Luther King, Jr., of Atlanta, Georgia!"

The applause echoed for minutes. When it quieted, Dr. King spoke in a broad, monotone voice, which Dad said was the Baptist in him. Dr. King's voice began to rise, and he started preaching with great emotion, punctuating the air with his fist and shaking his head from side to side. Lines of sweat trickled down his face, forming droplets that landed on his dark suit.

Dr. King spoke a long time about a lady by the name of Rosa Parks and how she was tired of segregation. Her refusal to give up her seat on a bus to a white man in 1955 led to the Montgomery Bus Boycott. Blacks wouldn't ride the buses for many months, not until things were integrated. This was the beginning of Dr. King's journey to becoming a great leader. But Dad Harry warned, "Not all Negroes care for King."

Even Mom had her opinion.

"King is gonna mess around and get a lot of black folks killed. He shouldn't be stirring up stuff between the races. It's best to leave it alone. It'll work out on its own."

"I tell you, if it hadn't been for him, black folks in the South would still be livin' in segregation, though," Dad said.

While the country was ushering in a new chapter in its history, my natural mother was beginning a new chapter of her own. In the winter of 1958, she finally came to see me again. My greatest wish was to go back with her to Chicago; it was all I thought about. But Mama's life had changed. She brought a man with her to Lansing—her new husband.

Harold Hoffenkamp was a handsome, debonair white man who stood well over six feet tall. His dark brown hair was slicked back with Brylcreem. His blue suit was tailored in a way that gave the impression of wealth; it wasn't a false impression. When he met me, he hugged me and gave me a few one-dollar bills and a teal blue winter coat from Marshall Fields. Harold seemed nice, but his presence greatly interfered with what I wanted, which was for my mother to remarry my father so that we could be a happy family again. My mother had different plans.

"Harold's family has a lot of money. They don't know we're married. If they knew Harold married a Negro, they'd disown him. So, in a few months we're going to Liberia and Monrovia, West Africa. I'm going to help Harold start a car business there."

"But, Mama, I don't understand."

"That's just the way things are with some whites, baby. They're prejudiced. Harold's parents don't have to know, and everything will be just fine. Don't worry, Gloria, I'll write you. And when we come back, in a year, you can come to Chicago to visit us."

The way she explained it, it was like she was taking a trip to the market, not another continent. I didn't know what to say except, "Okay, Mama. I love you."

Instead of Mama reassuring me, I reassured her that I'd be okay. I wanted her to know that I was a big girl who could deal with disappointments. I wanted to make her proud.

Although Mama never said that we wouldn't be together again, her actions spoke plainly enough. She was living her life, without doing much to help me live mine. I had to handle things on my own, and I had learned that the best way to do that was by being silent and pretending.

Whenever Mama and I spoke, she would say, "You're a mature child. I can always count on you to make the right decisions. And you have Frances and Harry to guide you. They give you a good home."

Mama had no idea the kind of home I had. She didn't know how much I longed to be with her, that if I could've ripped my heart out and handed it to her to prove how much I loved and needed her, I would have. I was jealous that Mama put Harold before me. But, like always, she compensated by showering me with kindness. From West Africa, she sent postcards and letters that expressed her love for me. They meant everything and nothing to me at the same time.

While I put my best face forward for Mama's sake, I continued to grapple with problems I wished she'd been there to help with. I had experienced discrimination when I was with Mama in the South, riding on the back of the bus. Shamefully, I had even dealt with it in the schools in Lansing, where black kids had taunted me, calling me "high yellow," sometimes "white," and sometimes even calling me "uppity." I simply learned to ignore my own people. But I couldn't ignore the pain white folks began to cause me when I started at West Junior High School.

I entered seventh grade in 1959. I became a real grown-up that year, at least according to Mom Frances. I was going on thirteen years old and had gotten my first period. Mom Frances explained what menstruation was, or at least what it meant to her.

"You're now a lady. You can get pregnant. So you're to keep your dress down and your panties up. Don't let boys feel on you. That leads to other things, like having a baby."

Mom Frances avoided using the word "sex" the same as if it were a curse word. Instead, she would say, "when two people get together."

Every month, when I had my period, Dad Harry would put an "X" on the calendar he kept on the wall near his desk. He said he had to keep up with me to make sure I wasn't fooling around.

Like all schools in Michigan, West Junior High School was integrated. That didn't mean there wasn't racism there. Mrs. Smith, my school counselor, was my personal tour guide on the journey that taught me to hate my color.

"Well, it seems according to your test scores that you're a slow learner, Gloria," she explained to me during one of our meetings. "You'll take remedial reading with Mrs. Johnson and we'll see how you do."

I had no say in my placement. But putting me in classes with students whom the state had labeled "retarded" caused me to receive a lot of abuse from the students who were in regular classes.

"Something is wrong with you. You're in that class for special students," they'd say.

"I'm not. I'm taking reading, that's all," I'd try to explain.

The fact was it was the only reading class at West Junior, and most of the students in it were black. My teacher, Mrs. Johnson, was a short white lady who wore a lot of pleated skirts with matching sweaters and shoes with open toes. Mrs. Johnson would walk around the classroom like a drill sergeant, overseeing the small cluster of wooden tables at which we sat. The class consisted of fifteen black students and two white students who were poor. When Mrs. Johnson bent down to help the black kids, she'd cover her mouth with a large, white hanky. But she never used the hanky when she helped the white kids. As soon as the bell rang, she'd move quickly to the door and open it, using her hanky to cover the knob. She never smiled or said goodbye.

I began to think that something really was wrong with me.

Why isn't she treating the white kids the same way? Why just us black kids? Do we smell? Is there something wrong with being black?

Although Mrs. Johnson's actions bothered me, I wanted her to accept me. I began hating my blackness.

One day on my way home from school, I stopped at the corner drug store. I knew that if I was just one minute too late, Mom would come looking for me. I made a beeline to what I had come to buy; I had the few dollars that I had saved from my weekly allowance counted out in my pocket. My earnings were going to be spent on a jar of Dr. Palmer's Bleaching

Cream. I read the directions. If I followed them carefully, my skin would turn as white as a lily:

Apply a small amount on dark areas daily. Rub into skin gently. You will have lighter, prettier skin in days.

I applied the cream every night after I said my prayers, and then hid it under my bed. A night didn't go by that I didn't apply that slippery, white cream to my face, just as the directions said. But Dr. Palmer overpromised. My skin stayed the same.

I was disappointed, but not defeated. I moved on to trying to change my broad nose. It had to be narrow, like the white girls in *Seventeen* magazine.

"I read that Chinese parents attach a clothes pin to their child's nose at birth to make it smaller," Mom Frances once told me.

"It's got to hurt, though," I'd said.

"I'm sure they clip it on just a short time," she said, laughing.

I decided to brave any potentially painful consequences and give it a try. I clipped the wooden clothespin to the wide part of my nose. It did hurt, but if suffering a few minutes a day would change my nose size, then it was worth it. Nothing changed, though; I never got my white nose.

Next I tried the Playtex girdle that Mom Frances bought me. She said every woman wore one, and she wasted no time investing in one for me after I officially became a woman.

"You can't be enticing the boys. Your hips need to be firm, not one saying, 'Here I come,' and the other saying, 'Get out the way,'" she told me.

I just wanted flat hips like white girls. But I soon discovered that the girdle did nothing for my figure. All it did was cut off the circulation around my thighs. The fact was I was petite without the girdle.

I couldn't see anything positive about myself. Instead, my self-hate campaign worsened. I became obsessed with my hair. Whenever it would frizz up, I'd press it repeatedly with a scorching hot comb so that it would be as straight as white folks' hair. The little naps in my "kitchen," that's the little curls on the back of the neck, drove me crazy. As soon as I saw a hint of those curls, I'd rush for the hot comb.

After a year in junior high, I was a confused black girl who had denounced her blackness to embrace anything associated with being white.

Mom Frances never knew about my identity crisis. She was too busy preaching to me about keeping my dress down and my legs closed. She was too concerned about me being influenced by smoking, drinking, and wearing make-up to notice the rage growing inside me. Some of this festering rage was directed toward Mom Frances. She was too strict and too holy, always prohibiting me from expressing myself. I was angry about everything and with everybody—except white folks.

I was angry with Dad Harry and Gene for molesting me.

I was resentful toward Mama for never coming back for me.

I was furious at Daddy for forgetting about me.

I hated school. I hated myself.

The consequences of being black weighed heavily on my slight shoulders. It was whites who got the breaks in life. They were embraced, not belittled by society. I couldn't stop thinking how much easier my life would be if I could just be more like them.

The year 1959 was dreadful for me, but I was still just an adolescent. I had my entire life before me, and there was a lot of sorting out I needed to do.

CHAPTER FIVE

As I progressed into the eighth grade the following year, things did begin to sort themselves out a bit. I found a less self-destructive way to cope with my feelings of anger and resentment, one that involved embracing instead of rejecting who I was. It started in gym class. All of the students in the school had been put through a battery of required physical fitness tests, and it turned out that I had attained the highest scores. I was the fastest female runner in my gym class, the fastest runner in basketball, and the quickest volleyball player at West Junior High School.

For the first time since I left Eudora, I felt equal to whites, if not better. My self-esteem soared.

Soon after I got the results of the fitness tests, an announcement was posted on the gym bulletin board: *Tryouts: Looking for energetic girls to be on the cheerleading squad.* I immediately knew that I wanted to do it, but I also knew I had to clear it with Mom Frances and that it would be a hard sell. I was nervous to ask, but my newfound self-esteem also gave me a self-confidence that I hadn't had before. I knew I was good, and I didn't want anything to get in the way of my proving it.

When I approached Mom about the tryouts, her reaction was along the lines of what I'd expected.

"You know how I feel about that worldly stuff, Gloria. If it's too much twisting and shaking, then the answer is no."

"They're just tryouts. I may not even make it, Mom."

She took another moment to think about it. "Well, I guess there's no harm in just seeing how it works out. But you come straight home afterward."

I felt like I'd already cleared a monumental hurdle by just getting Mom's permission. When I stood before the cheerleading coach and the fifty or so girls who were trying out with me, I was able to hold my head up, knowing I was the fastest girl in the school. I thought my execution of the routine we were taught was impressive enough. I jumped, kicked, and did a perfect cartwheel. But when I finished, all I heard was, "Okay, thank you. Next girl."

I'd been hoping for a more emphatic affirmation of how well I'd done. I tossed and turned all that night, thinking about how much I wanted to make the squad and how upset I'd be if I didn't. The next morning, before class, I walked slowly to the gym door, where the names of the girls who had been christened cheerleaders were posted. I took a deep breath and held it as I carefully read the alphabetized list.

"Yes, thank you, Lord!" I whooped, finally letting the air out of my lungs when I got to the E's and saw my last name.

I was sure I was the happiest girl in school. I was not only a member of the junior varsity cheerleading squad, but I had become one of the few blacks in the school's history who could claim that achievement. I'd share the spotlight with a black girl by the name of Ann Diamond. Other black kids said she was conceited because she had fair skin and a full head of thick, pressed, curly hair. But Ann was always nice to me. We practiced cheers together until we were hoarse.

It didn't take long to notice that the coach always put Ann and me on the end or in the back, never in the middle, where the white girls were positioned. It bothered me a little, but not enough to say something. I was glad white folks had recognized my talents. I saw cheering as a way to gain equality and credibility with them. I cheered at all the games until suddenly, with three months of the season remaining, Mom wanted me to quit.

"You're spending too much time after school shaking your hips, not enough time in God's house, Gloria."

"Mom, please, please!" I begged. "I like cheerleading. I'm so proud to be on the squad. I still love Jesus."

Mom had no knowledge of afterschool sports. She'd never seen me cheer and hadn't planned to.

"Well, no more practice then. That's that." Mom's tone was harsh and her verdict was final.

"If I don't practice, I can't be on the team. Please Mom."

I cried. I begged her. Because of Mom and Dad's strict beliefs, I was already scorned at school by black and white kids alike for being a religious fanatic. I'd worked so hard to gain the small amount of acceptance that I had; I didn't want to revert to being an outcast. How would I face Miss Anderson, the coach? When my begging failed, I had no choice but to go to her office first thing the next day and tell her exactly what Mom had told me.

"Gloria, you're so good. But you know if you don't practice, you can't cheer. Those are the rules. I'm sorry; I can't make exceptions."

I had to find a way to stay on the squad. Maybe I could lie to Mom and sneak into practice. But the chance was too high that she would come looking for me and embarrass me in front of my classmates.

The next day, girls on the team asked why I hadn't been at practice. I told them I had something to do after school. After missing a week of cheering, I was miserable. As a last resort, I took my troubles to Dad. I felt, since he had more experience with the world than Mom, that maybe he'd understand. Not only did he understand, but he petitioned Mom on my behalf.

"Sweetheart, it's important that Gloria be in sports. It keeps her off the streets. You know a whole lot of children end up with babies, drinking, smoking, robbin,' and killin' when they don't have anything to keep them busy. I'm talkin' 'bout church folks' children. They're the worst."

"I'm concerned that she won't stay in church. I don't want her to forget God. She shouldn't be up there shakin' her hips all over the place like she's some monkey in a zoo," was Mom's response.

"She's not goin' to do anything to bring shame on us. Show me in the Bible where it's wrong to be in sports. It's clean fun," he said.

Mom sighed. "Okay, we'll let her try it again," she said softly.

"You and I've debated this before. The church's actions aren't always biblical. We've got to make sure our actions are biblically sound," he told her.

Then Dad warned me that if I sneaked around and tried to get away with doing something that was wrong, he'd know because he had spies in the neighborhood who would tell him. I believed him and meant it when I promised to be a good kid.

When I met with Miss Anderson the next day, she was kind enough to let me back on the squad. I went on to make the varsity squad in the ninth grade. Eventually I was involved in every sport white girls were: basketball, swimming, tennis, volleyball, baseball, and field hockey. I had become the best athlete in the school. Excelling athletically was my way of expressing that being black wasn't an impediment but a form of equality.

I was making strides in all sorts of ways. I developed my first crush. It seems I had a fondness for basketball players. There was one in particular I really liked by the name of Ronnie Rainge. He was more than six feet tall and muscular with smooth, chocolate skin. Ronnie was a fine man. Whenever I cheered, he'd turn from the court, no matter where he was shooting from, and flash me that killer smile of his. For all his bravado on the court, he was so shy when he passed my locker that he'd just grin sheepishly and rush by. Since my parents prohibited dating, my admiration for him remained just that.

My giftedness at sports did make me popular with white kids and my white teachers. White kids would call me their friend, although they never came to my house because their parents wouldn't let them. They lived in neighborhoods that weren't so near to the factory and their parents had white-collar jobs. The factory had taken the place of the railroad tracks in terms of there being a right and a wrong proximity from it.

Although I wasn't wearing name-brand clothes, I was beginning to blend in more with whites. Mom cared very much about my appearance and the clothes she made for me were the latest fashions, at least the ones that measured up to her standard of decency.

I wore shift dresses, wide skirts with a can-can slip, and cardigan sweaters that buttoned down the middle. The fad of wearing thick white bobby socks rolled to the ankle gave my legs more definition. I saw bold white girls wearing fashionable pants known as peddle-pushers, but they came down only just below the knee and I couldn't wear them because it was against my religion. It was supposed to be against the rules to wear them to school anyway, although some girls still did. Teachers would often comment, "Why, you can't tell the boys from the girls. What are they going to come up with next?"

Despite my conscious attempt to assimilate into white culture, I was still loyal to my black friends. I knew I had to be true to my race. After all, I lived in the black neighborhood, went to a black church, and had black blood. Although 1961 still presented an uphill climb, it was a better year in terms of white acceptance than any that had come before.

The following year, I started at J.W. Sexton High School. I was sixteen years old and popular for being the most outstanding female athlete. During my first semester in the tenth grade, I decided to try a new sport, track, because I knew I was fast. In Lansing, track was a sport dominated by boys. I was the first girl in my high school to run. As a sign of the changing times, I was allowed to practice with the boys' track team. Many of the boys were afraid to run with me because I was faster than they were.

It wasn't easy being the only female runner. I was ridiculed by whites and blacks. Black kids would congregate in what was called "coon" alley, which was a section in the hallway next to our lockers, just before class. It was impossible to avoid the crowd, and the boys were especially relentless.

"Gloria, you keep runnin,' you gonna grow big muscles like them Russian women, big and burly. And you ain't gonna have a boyfriend lookin' like that. You ain't gonna be fit to marry. No man's gonna want a woman with big muscles."

Then they'd flex their muscles and fall to the floor laughing.

White kids dished it out, too—again, mainly the boys. "You keep running, you not gonna have kids. You'll look like a man with big hands, big feet, big legs."

Sometimes they said things behind my back instead of to my face, but I heard the rumors, the whispers in the hallway.

"I think she's queer. You think she's homosexual? You never see her with a boy."

Dad Harry helped me through this rough patch. He always said, "Sticks and stones may break my bones, but names never hurt me. Always remember, being black, you got to be one step ahead of white folks to be equal to them—get up earlier than they do, be smarter than they are, think faster, and practice longer than they do."

Dad Harry's words of wisdom reminded me of the advice my natural father had passed down to me and of his struggle to get good roles in the theater program at the University of Iowa. I knew both my fathers were right. So I listened to them.

I ran the 75-yard dash, the 220-yard dash, and the 440-yard run at different Amateur Athletic Union (AAU) meets around Detroit. My results were published in the school newspaper, the *Zodiac.* One day, a few white girls asked if I would train them to run. Although I knew little about coaching, I was flattered. I pretended to know. They did whatever I did at practice, which meant wind sprints, interval work, and repeat 440s. A gym teacher took an interest in what we were doing and began coaching us, and soon we joined girls at other high school track teams in the city.

I maintained Cs and Bs in physical education, drama, English, book-keeping, science, and general math. But Mom didn't think I was getting enough from my education. She knew I'd need more than basic classes to get into college. She decided to pay my guidance counselor a visit.

"Mrs. Lawry, I want Gloria to have college courses. What she's taking is too easy. They're for children who are slow. My daughter's not. She's going to college. The classes now are to keep Negro children out of college, you know that?"

"Well, I've never heard of anything like that, Mrs. Ewing. We have to place students at levels where they're capable of doing the work. It's all based on test scores. I don't think Gloria's capable of college."

"Well, if you're thinking she's gonna work in a factory, you can forget it. Gloria's gonna make something of her life."

"Well, Mrs. Ewing, her scores show that she's average or even a slow learner in some areas, like reading. She's just not capable. I would suggest sending her to community college."

"No. My daughter's going to take the courses white children are taking. That means biology, literature, history. Now, if you don't agree, I'll go straight to the school board."

Mrs. Lawry's tune quickly changed.

"That's not necessary, Mrs. Ewing. Why don't we try some classes and see how she does?"

The classes were extremely hard. I had to stay up late to memorize the parts of a frog and events in American history. Everything seemed to be over my head. It wasn't because I was stupid, but because I had never been exposed to any of the material before the way my white classmates had. The first semester in college prep, I ended up with Cs, Ds, and Fs. But Mom and Dad encouraged me not to quit. Every time Mrs. Lawry put me on probation and threatened to send me back to general studies, Mom would convince her to give me another chance. Track helped me focus and work harder at my academics. I eventually brought my grades up to average.

In 1964, I joined a new girls' track team in the city called the Lansing Lightningettes. The coaches, Vonda Gerow and her husband, Gerald, were the only husband-and-wife coaching duo in the United States. They had seen me at a meet and asked me to join their team. This was the first time white folks truly acknowledged my talents. Not only that, they believed in me.

We competed with other all-girl track teams in Detroit and Ohio, mainly in cross-country. We'd go to track meets nearly every Saturday in small cities like Utica, Holt, and Pontiac, but the big cities like Detroit and Toledo were where girls' competitive track flourished. The first time I ran the 880 in Lansing was the first time that Mom came to see me there.

"Go, Gloria, you can do it! Run, pick 'em up, put 'em down!"

I could hear Mom Frances yelling across the track. I had never before seen her express how proud she was of me. It was exactly the kind of emotion that I'd been seeking from Mama.

I took fifth place, which was also last place. That did nothing to lessen Mom's pride as she watched me receive my ribbon on the podium.

Mom wasn't able to come to another meet because of the demands of caring for my little sister, Eva, plus she was helping Dad pastor his new church. I was just happy that Mom at last approved of my participation in sports. There were times when she still annoyed me with her strict, conservative rules, though.

"Honey, your shorts are at your thighs, so make sure you put your sweat pants on after you run. You don't want to entice the boys. You can only trust them from the waist up."

"Okay, Mom," was my pat answer.

I knew I had pretty legs and shapely hips, taking after my natural mother. But Mom eventually gave me a complex, so I seldom exposed them. Besides, even though I had my crushes, I was only interested in running, not in dating. I knew boys would be a distraction from my goal of going to the Olympics one day. The Olympics were all I could think about, and all I wanted to think about.

Besides, I never got asked out. The boys at school knew Dad was a minister, and they didn't want to call my house for fear of hearing his voice on the other end of the phone. The one boy who was brave enough was my senior prom date.

I was eighteen years old, and Boyd Lewis was my first date ever. Boyd was a popular, second-string varsity basketball player. He was handsome, with a small Afro, fair skin like mine, and a baby face. He smiled so wide that his eyes would squint almost all the way shut, and his chipped front tooth would be exposed. It was his one dimple that charmed me into saying yes to his invitation. My girlfriends said he'd always had a crush on me, but was too shy to tell me.

When Boyd asked me to be his prom date, he was so nervous his voice shook, and sweat was pouring down his face. I was equally shy, and my acceptance just as shaky. My first choice for a prom date had been Ronnie Rainge, but he had to leave for Texas to be with his grandmother. When it came down to it, I was just so happy to be asked.

"Are you sure your father will allow you to go?" Boyd asked cautiously.

"Of course," I reassured him. "It's my last year of high school."

Mom and Dad didn't have an issue with me going to the prom, but I had a curfew of ten o'clock. My date was a big family affair. Mom made me a beautiful, floor-length satin dress. It was soft yellow and sleeveless, with a scooped neck that bordered my breast line; tiny white, silk flowers strategically covered my cleavage. I wore satin shoes that had been dyed at Bakers to match my dress and long, white gloves that went up to my elbows. Aunt Mildred pressed my hair until it shined like white girls' hair. I wore a hairpiece shaped like a beehive, which was complemented nicely by bangs cut to my eyebrows.

The entire family sent me off: Aunt Mildred and Uncle Wayne, Teddy, and my cousins from upstairs. Boyd arrived promptly at seven.

"My name is Boyd Lewis, sir," he said, extending a nervous hand to Dad.

Boyd's hands were strong, firm, and large enough to each hold a basketball. It was amusing to see hands like that so unsteady. Boyd was handsomely dressed in a tailored tuxedo with black pants, a light yellow suit jacket, and a light yellow shirt that matched the color of my dress. His bow tie and lapel flower were black. The scent of Old Spice emanated from his entire body. He handed me a beautiful yellow orchid, which I wore on my sleeve.

"It's good meeting you, Boyd. I know your parents. You have my daughter back by ten sharp, understood?" Dad said firmly, but with a smile meant to ease Boyd's nervousness.

"Yes, sir, I understand."

Other kids were staying out until after midnight or even after dawn. But I didn't make a big deal out of it. If I had, Dad would have told me to stay home. It was the white kids who got drunk and spent the night in hotels. Black kids stayed until the prom was over, and then had dinner at different restaurants. I had warned my black classmates about my curfew, and they seemed to understand. They had grandparents who were strict like my parents; it was accepted as part of our culture. My black friends were just pleased that I was able to attend the prom at all. My white classmates didn't understand, even though I'd tried to explain it to them.

The minute we walked into the school gym, I saw Tyrone Fletcher and Larry Davis, the most handsome, popular ballplayers in my school. I had a crush on both of them. I'd wanted one of them to ask me to the prom, but neither could bear the prospect of facing Dad. I was happy with Boyd; I couldn't have asked for a better date. We had fun laughing and dancing, but I was careful to heed Dad's advice. He'd warned, "Dancing is okay if it's in moderation. Don't get too close. It'll make man's nature rise." When Dad said "nature," he meant penis.

We did the mashed potato, the watusi, and the twist by Chubby Checker. We danced to Mary Wells' "Two Lovers," the Shirelles' "Soldier Boy," the Supremes' "Where Did Our Love Go?," The Righteous Brothers' "You've Lost That Loving Feeling," The Beatles' "Ticket to Ride," and Elvis Presley's "Hound Dog."

When I wasn't dancing, I was sitting with the other black kids at a small table sipping root beer, which some kids pretended was rum on ice. The girls gossiped about who was or wasn't a virgin, while the boys talked about basketball. Ten o'clock rolled around quickly and, before I knew it, I was home again.

I told Boyd not to be surprised if Dad was waiting at the front door, which sure enough he was. Dad eased the door open, and then went into the next room so Boyd and I could say goodnight privately. He sneaked me a quick kiss on the lips, my first kiss ever, and told me what a great night he had.

I felt a tingling and wanted more. Boyd was so nervous, though, that he could only bring himself to give me that one kiss. I had barely closed the door when the inquisition began.

"Tell me, how was it? What'd you do?" Dad asked.

"It was nice. We listened to music and talked."

"Tell me more," Mom prompted.

I didn't tell them about the dancing because I knew Mom would say it was a sin.

The next day at school there was considerable buzz about my pretty dress and how nice Boyd and I looked together. Everyone wanted to know if he'd kissed me. I was too shy to respond, so I deflected the questions with a coy smile.

The truth was track occupied my mind more than any boy ever could. I didn't particularly want to date, plus the young men felt dealing with my parents was too much of a hassle. Instead of dreaming about love letters and proposals, I focused my dreams on the 1968 Olympics. I wanted to compete more than I wanted to eat or sleep.

Every weekend, I competed in local track meets. My coach, Vonda, recommended that I change coaches and track clubs to acquire the speed I needed; she didn't have experience coaching sprinters. I was going to miss her very much. She had shown me through her coaching that she wasn't prejudiced. Color didn't seem to be a deciding factor in athletics. What mattered was the passion and dedication that the coach and athlete had for the sport.

Vonda had introduced me to the coach of the Detroit Track Club, Mr. James Bibbs. He was well-known among runners and coaches in the United States as one of the top coaches for high school girls in Michigan. He had female sprinters on his team who were quick as lightning. He told me that if I joined his team, he could train me to run faster. He believed in me the same way Vonda did, and under his coaching as a member of the Detroit Track Club, I increased my intensity and dedication. On weekends when I wasn't busy at church, I took a Greyhound bus either to Detroit to train or out of state to attend meets. All my new teammates were black, and they were as fast and as serious about running as I was.

Since I was graduating that year, Coach Bibbs thought I should pursue a scholarship to Tennessee A & I University in Nashville. That thrilled my dad, who had always told me that when I graduated from high school, I had two choices: to get a job or to go to college. Wasting my time as a couch potato wasn't an option.

"Dad, A and I University is where Coach Bibbs thinks I should go. It's the only college in America with a women's track team. The Tigerbelles are famous," I explained. "Their coach, Ed Temple, is tough, but good. He's coached the team to national titles. He coached the U.S. Olympic team in Rome, and he made a star of Wilma Rudolph. You know she's my role model, right?"

I had always wanted to be like Wilma. She was the only American to win a high number of medals at the Rome Olympics. I had read all about her in the encyclopedia. She was born into poverty in Tennessee, the twentieth of twenty-two children. She weighed only four pounds at birth. She suffered from pneumonia, scarlet fever, and polio. She wore a leg brace until she was eleven years old. Then one Sunday at church, she took it off and walked down the aisle. She never even ran until she was thirteen years old.

"If she could overcome those odds, I can run fast, too," I told Dad.

Dad was never a talker. He just smiled. Although he knew nothing about women's track, he listened intently to everything I was telling him.

"Well, I'll tell you what," he said. "As long as I have the means and God gives me strength, I'll send you to college. You know I only finished the third grade. Your mom, now she did two years at this same college you're talking about."

Dad said black colleges were started because blacks either weren't provided with the academic preparation needed to get into white colleges, or didn't have access to the same opportunities as whites, or because of blatant discrimination. Tennessee State accepted me even with my average grades. I was doing the holy dance all over Mom's pristine hardwood floor. I wanted to take the letter and wash Mrs. Lawry's face with it, but that wouldn't have been very Christian of me.

In June 1965, just before I was slated to graduate, my senior class of almost five hundred students voted me the best athlete at Sexton High School. I was going to be one of the few blacks in the school's history to receive this honor, and since I was involved in every sport, I had earned it. Every day after I found out about the award, I would stand in front of the mirror and rehearse how I would accept the gold-plated, four-foot-high trophy.

"Thank you! Thank you!" I would say, nodding graciously to the huge crowd of students in the auditorium, all of whom were applauding my achievement. "It's with great pride that I accept the honor of being named Sexton High School's Best Athlete of the Year."

I practiced the smile I would flash my classmates as I walked off the stage, clutching my large prize.

On the day of the assembly, every seat was filled, just as I'd imagined, mostly with white students and teachers. My eyes got big as I counted the trophies arranged in a perfect line on the floor of the stage. Even in the poorly lit auditorium, each one radiated as if it were reflecting the sun. I wondered which one of those beauties had my name on it. Students who were the smartest in the sciences and mathematics were the first to be called to collect their respective awards.

In preparation for the ramifications of my nervousness, I'd washed with 20 Mule Team Borax and put on a dab of deodorant, but it hadn't helped. Maybe the fact that my armpits weren't accustomed to deodorant was what was causing them to sweat so excessively. Mom said deodorant could cause cancer, so I seldom used it. Not only was I soaked with sweat, but my heart was racing. I turned to Karen Flowers, my best friend, and asked if she could hear it.

"Hear what?"

"My heart, it's beating out of my chest," I said.

"Girl, no!" She laughed as quietly as she could. Karen's laugh always made me laugh. She had beautiful white teeth that protruded like a beaver's.

The wait for my name to be called was killing me. Finally, the principal began making the announcement. After all my anticipation and expectations, the whole thing took only fifteen seconds.

"Now for the most outstanding female athlete in the class of 1965," Principal Christian Roosenraad began. "Pat Kelly, please come forward."

I had started to stand, but collapsed back into my chair. Karen was saying something to me, but I couldn't hear her, nor could I speak. I had been voted number one. They published it in the *Zodiac*. Besides, Pat was only the captain of the cheerleading squad, only played a sport occasionally here and there. Maybe she was on the basketball team, but that was about it. She didn't come close to having the athletic credentials that I did.

But Pat Kelly was white.

I had worked so hard for that moment. I had gone through so much to prove myself to those people. I thought they had finally accepted me. I wanted to vomit.

Instead of bile, I felt that familiar rage rising within me. I looked around and was repulsed by the sight of all the white folks in the auditorium, clapping for Pat Kelly, even though they knew the trophy she was holding was rightfully mine.

The next day was the last day of school. Absolutely nothing was said, by me or anyone else. Silence was becoming an all-too-familiar theme in my life, being forced to live with the knowledge that something wrong was going on, without any open acknowledgement of it. To keep it together, I had to turn my attention to college and not look back. College was my ticket to prove to white folks that I was equal to them, that I was somebody. And if success was the best revenge, then making it to the Olympics would be mine.

That fall, I matriculated at Tennessee State University. It was a black school. At least there I'd be sheltered from the wrongdoings of white folks.

CHAPTER SIX

In September 1965, Mom and Dad drove me to Tennessee State University in Nashville so I could pursue my dreams. I noticed the South had changed since I was a child. There were no signs that read, "Colored Only" and "White Only." Blacks and whites rode and sat together on buses. They even walked on the same side of the street. Dad had been raised in the South, but moved north as a young adult because he had a better chance of getting a good job there, of being successful. He was surprised at the drastic change in the way things appeared to be operating since the end of segregation.

"Sweetheart, look at Woolworth," he said to Mom. "Negroes can sit with white folks to eat now. If I was living in the South back when segregation was goin' on, it would have been nearly impossible for me with my third-grade education to ever learn how to read like I did, get a diploma at night school like I did. I would have had trouble passing that literacy test they gave black folks before they could vote."

"Dad, remember someone named Stokely Carmichael?"

"I can't say that rings a bell, no."

"He was the leader of the Black Power Movement. He did a lot to help restore pride in the black community by using the 'Black Is Beautiful' slogan."

"Now, hold on, Gloria. I'm not black. I'm Negro. Don't you go getting wrapped up in all that Black Power mess. You'll end up raising your fist to white folks and, before you know it, they'll be throwing you in jail. That kind of carrying on scares white folks."

"But, Dad, whites have been putting us down since we came here, 'til we didn't believe in ourselves. I love the 'Black Is Beautiful' slogan. It's a good thing to own our businesses—you do, right?"

"Yes, but integration makes us equal to whites. Black Power is just a way to separate us Negroes from each other. Some of us want it and some don't. I'm sending you to college to get an education, not to get tangled up in Black Power, hear me? Stick to your studies. Can't afford to get you out of jail."

"Okay, Dad."

If I pushed the debate, Dad would say I was talking back, so as usual I said nothing. What I really wanted was to join a student sit-in movement to fight discrimination, maybe the Student Nonviolent Coordinating Committee (SNCC) or a march like the one on Washington led by Dr. King. In my heart, I just wanted to find some way to protest the injustices of white folks toward black folks. But my family felt getting an education was more important than marching in the streets.

Dad and Mom stayed to help me settle into my dorm. Before they left, Dad gave me more instruction.

"Baby, go as far as you can. You can be whatever you want. You've always been a smart cookie. As I've always told you, there'll be lots of temptation, but if you keep your mind on the Lord, on your studies, and on track, you'll not be swayed by the world. Keep Jesus in your heart."

"Don't worry, Dad, I'll be fine. Don't you worry either, Mom. It's not good for the baby. I'll be praying that he or she arrives safe and healthy."

My new sibling was due the following month. Mom said this one had surprised her, but she was excited about it. She was just over forty and still had regular periods. It was Dad she expected to be infertile; he was sixty-five, after all. After Eva's birth nine years earlier, the doctor warned Mom that if she had another baby, she would die; her body wasn't strong enough. Mom and Dad had faith, though. Before they left, they prayed for me and reminded me to go to church with my grandparents in Mt. Pleasant, which was just fifty miles from the university.

When I saw students walking around campus, heads high, proud to be black, I knew what I had wanted from the skin bleach and the clothespins was wrong. That was in the past. All that mattered now was that I had come to Tennessee State to become a Tigerbelle.

My new roommate, Charlene Bussey, was a teammate of mine from the Detroit Track Club. Everybody on the team used to call Charlene "Lightning." When she ran the 100 and 200-yard dashes, all you could see was the blur of her track uniform whizzing past your eyes. I had the stamina to outdo her in the longer races like the 440- and 880-yard runs, though. We both were aiming to qualify for the 1968 Olympics in Mexico.

Charlene was from a poor family. She ran to make them proud. I loved her honesty, humor, and cavalier spirit. She wore heavy black eyeliner around her slanted eyes, reminding me of a gypsy. Her hair was short and coarse, requiring frequent heavy-duty pressing with Royal Crown hair oil. Her skin tone was medium-brown, and she stood about five feet, two inches. When I met Charlene, one of my first thoughts was how nice it was to finally know someone in track who I was taller than.

Charlene and I didn't date or go to movies or parties. Our lives revolved around running and schoolwork, in that order. It was our track coach, Ed Temple's, regime that dictated our daily existence. Coach Temple was serious about rules. He laid them out clearly the first day of practice on the cinder track.

Coach Temple had a reputation for being borderline necrotic. I never saw him smile, although he was frequently grimacing, with his forehead wrinkled up like a bulldog's. He always held his five-foot-five-inch frame perfectly erect, maybe to look taller than he actually was. His bald head peaked like a mountain. When he spoke, he jerked his hands around spasmodically. There were fifteen of us on the track team, and we attentively hung to his every word.

"All right, ladies. Here's how it's gonna be. If you can't live by my rules, get on the first train smokin.' Anybody who wants to be on my team shows up every day. Some of you are on scholarships, some will be later, but everybody follows my rules. Be on time at three every day. That's rain, shine, sleet, or snow. Saturdays, there's practice meets to prepare you for the national AAU meet and the Pan Am Games. No track on Sunday. That's church day. No staying out late. No drinking. No smoking. Live a clean life. Keep your grades up, you'll keep running. You should act like a dignified lady, but run like crazy. Some of you will go on to the Olympic trials, then the Olympics. You're here for one thing and one thing only, that's to run and to win. Understand?"

"Yes, sir," we said in unison, nodding.

Some of the veteran team members said that Coach Temple didn't want us dating, especially the freshmen. They said if we dated, not to let him know because if he found out, he'd question us for days. The girls advised that we save ourselves the embarrassment and just not date.

Our two-hour daily workouts began on the track with stretches. Then we'd take a long run on dirt roads, along paved streets, through the black neighborhood and cow pastures, over rolling green hills, and up steep valleys for a good cardiovascular workout. When we returned to the track for speed work, everybody was out of breath, but I could keep going. I enjoyed distance running more than sprinting. But that's not what Coach Temple wanted. He wanted quick runners—Olympians. I lagged behind during the speed drills. It was especially hard to keep up with Wyomia Tyus, an Olympic gold medal winner, and Edith McGuire, an Olympian who broke one of Wilma Rudolph's records.

I became frustrated and turned to Charlene for answers.

"How can I get the speed my teammates have? I get in the blocks, keep my head down, and come out low. Then after a few yards, I can't maintain the speed. How can I get faster like everybody else?" I asked.

"It's 'bout repetition, girl. Just keep doing the drills. I'm faster now than I was in Detroit. Just keep at it."

"You don't think speed is inherited? If you don't have it, you just don't have it?"

"Yeah, but I also think you can train hard to get faster. So we just have to keep doing it over and over."

We decided to train more than our teammates. We got up at the crack of dawn, ran the streets for cardio, and did speed workouts on the track in the afternoon.

Coach Temple told Charlene and me that we had become Tigerbelles. We considered it an honor to practice every day with the team, but Coach Temple only took the fastest runners to competitions. We two slowpokes got left at home.

In October, Mom called. She was ecstatic over the birth of another healthy baby girl, Lydia Viola Ewing, who weighed in at eight pounds and nine ounces and loved to eat. I couldn't wait to see her during winter break.

Not only did I get a new sister that semester, I got to meet Wilma Rudolph. She was standing in the doorway of the gym watching her husband shoot hoops. She was such a beautiful woman, not at all resembling the physical stereotype of a runner, which was muscular and ugly. Wilma's short, curly hair was cut in a style that flatteringly framed her flawless, caramel face. Her six-foot-tall body was beyond graceful as she stepped inside the gymnasium toward the small congregation of spectators sitting on the bleachers. I quickly rose with my hand outstretched.

"Hello, Wilma, my name is Gloria. I'm from Michigan. I'm running with the Tigerbelles. I'm so glad to meet you. You've always been my hero."

Wilma blushed and began to smile. Then Charlene walked up and introduced herself. I couldn't believe I was in the presence of a woman who was in history books and every sports magazine in the world.

Wilma, speaking softly, said, "Thank you. Coach Temple told me about the new girls from Detroit. I'm happy to meet you." When Wilma smiled, small dimples punctuated the corners of her mouth and her straight, white teeth gleamed. She just looked like a superstar.

"Do you have any running tips?" I asked.

"Just keep runnin'. Practice every day, and don't get discouraged. Stick to it."

I followed Wilma's advice. I also managed to get average grades, except in biology, which I was flunking. I had to do something to make the F up as best I could, so I paid a visit to Professor Anderson one brisk morning that fall. The classroom was cold and quiet, and the wooden floorboards squeaked as I entered. The room was lined with shelves holding microscopes, and jars of frogs and other reptiles preserved in formaldehyde. Professor Anderson was clad in his white lab coat and wearing wire-rim glasses. His short Afro had a spattering of gray. His face remained expressionless as we exchanged the customary pleasantries. His stern demeanor was intimidating as he glared at me from behind his large desk.

"Well, Gloria, what can I help you with this morning?" he asked, getting down to business.

"Professor Anderson, I want to know if there's anything I can do to bring my grades up. I can't fail your class."

"Your problem is the weekly tests. You've got Ds and Fs. Your homework is okay, but that's not what will pass you."

"What about writing a paper, doing research? Whatever it takes. I have to have a C average for track, and this is the only class I'm failing."

"Hmm," he said, resting his eyes obviously on my breasts. I was wearing my gray track sweats, although I supposed my breasts were somewhat visible beneath the thin material.

"Well, now, you could get a passing grade, if you…" He lowered his voice to what he must have considered a sexy tone and continued to fixate on my breasts. "You could, well, you could go out with me and we could, you know…talk about it."

Professor Anderson finally smiled. He propped his elbows on the desk and slowly interlocked the long, thin fingers of his hands before resting his chin on top of them. He sat in that position, his eyes probing me from behind those wire rims, waiting for a response.

I heard Dad's voice saying, "Keep Jesus in your heart."

"Professor, my father's a minister. I, I can't compromise my values like that."

Thoughts of Dad hadn't just brought Jesus to my mind. Dad started molesting me when I was eight years old and only stopped when I approached puberty. The flashbacks never stopped. When Professor Anderson made his advances, I again became that little girl in the bath, at the mercy of her father's hands touching her where they shouldn't. I covered hundreds of miles in track trying to run away from these memories.

Instinct kicked in, and my feet were moving me as fast as they could out of the building, away from Professor Anderson, before I was even aware that I was running. For the rest of the day, I couldn't think. Once again I felt like I couldn't tell a soul what had happened, not even Charlene. It seemed that no matter where I went in this world, I would never be safe.

It was excruciating to return to Professor Anderson's class, but I had no choice given what was at stake. The professor didn't acknowledge what transpired, made no apologies or restitution. At least I flunked the course with my dignity intact.

Shortly thereafter, I took a weekend break to Mt. Pleasant to see Grandmamma Violet and Grandfather Earl. I didn't have to ride in the back of the bus, but instead sat proudly in the front near the black driver. Riding down Main Street in Mt. Pleasant was different, too. The Laundromat was no longer segregated, and black and white folks sat on benches together.

My grandparents' house was the same, except there were fewer chickens running around outside acting crazy. The garden had fewer vegetables, and dear Old Betsy had finally kicked that bucket my grandfather told Bobbie and me about. My grandparents were more complimentary and respectful of me. I didn't feel like I was working on a plantation. In fact, I didn't have to lift a finger to do housework while I was there because they knew I had research to do for school.

"We're so proud of you, honey—of how you turned out. You make us proud going to college the way you are. You made something of yourself. But remember to keep God in your heart," my grandmother said.

Sunday was still a church day for them; we went together. While I was at church, I thanked God for the courage to stand up to Professor Anderson.

When it was time to head back to campus, my grandmother handed me a sack lunch she'd prepared—crispy fried chicken stacked between several pieces of white bread, carefully preserved in wax paper. I smiled gratefully. It had been a nice visit, and I was glad I'd made the trip.

Back at school, there was a reality check waiting for me in the form of a letter postmarked "Michigan." I knew it was from Dad Harry. He wrote that he was disappointed in my biology grade and knew I could do better. I wanted to explain about Professor Anderson, but I wasn't sure if Dad would understand. I decided it was a discussion better left for when I went home for Christmas break.

But when I was home, I got cold feet. I couldn't tell Dad about Professor Anderson. The incident conjured up too many emotions; any discussion would have come too close to confronting Dad about his own inappropriate behavior with me, and I wasn't prepared to do that. I spent my time at home helping Mom take care of Lydia and playing with Eva. Just before I returned to Tennessee State to complete the year, Dad sat me down and told me that when that semester was over, he wouldn't be able to fund my education anymore. He had paid several thousand dollars for tuition plus a monthly allowance. He was supporting a new baby and paying my schooling all on his retirement income and what little money he was getting from his TV-repair business. Dad's poor health was affecting his ability to work. He'd been having seizures for some time that came on without any warning, and their frequency was increasing. Doctors were mystified as to the cause, which meant they couldn't provide a cure.

81

One time, Dad was incapacitated by a seizure when we were driving home from a revival meeting in another city. I reached over from the back seat and grabbed the wheel, managing to steer the car away from pedestrians and other vehicles. We ended up on a sidewalk next to a newsstand, which was dismantled by the accident. Thank goodness that newsstand was the only casualty. After that, the doctors ordered Dad to never drive again.

I was more worried about Dad's illness and its impact on my sisters' ability to have what they needed than I was about not having next year's tuition paid. I told Dad not to worry about us and that I'd talk to the coach about a scholarship. I didn't know why, but for some reason I couldn't imagine things not working out. Maybe it was because the thought of not being able to run track was unfathomable to me.

At times, there were other things in my life besides running. When I returned to Tennessee State in January 1966, I went on my first real date. I hadn't been out with a boy since I attended the prom with Boyd. Boyd and I never went out after that because Dad made him nervous. Now I was having dinner with Eldridge Dickey, the most popular football player on campus, and Dad didn't even know about it. Eldridge was one of the fastest college quarterbacks in the United States. He was a fine black man with a clean-cut look and muscular body. He only stood about five-foot-nine and weighed less than one hundred and sixty pounds. It was his smile and dimples that made my legs go weak.

For our date, I wore a blue, wool shift dress with short, black leather boots that had chunky heels. Mini-dresses were popular, but not at this college. My bangs and ponytail were in style. Eldridge dressed with simplicity. He wore a light blue shirt with straight-leg wool pants and a navy blue pea coat, perfect for the thirty-degree temperature.

We cruised down Jefferson Avenue in Eldridge's navy blue Ford, listening to the Supremes and the Four Tops. We picked up Claude Humphrey, Eldridge's best friend, who was also a famous football player and the biggest man on the football team. He weighed more than three hundred pounds and looked like an actual giant next to his date. He was planning to play for the pros when he graduated.

We ended up at a soul food restaurant—a shack that leaned like the Eiffel Tower. The sun had bleached the wood to the bone, and the door with its torn screen only closed halfway. But they had the most mouthwatering collard greens, corn bread, and crispy fried chicken in the world (except for Mother Dear's, of course).

I picked at my food because I was too shy and nervous to eat. When we returned to my dorm, Eldridge was a perfect Southern gentleman. He opened doors and didn't try to kiss me. It wasn't until several dates later, at a drive-in movie, that we kissed for the first time. Eldridge's lips were soft, and his touch was gentle. He put his tongue in my mouth when he kissed me, giving me my first French kiss. When his muscular arms embraced my one-hundred-fifteen-pound frame and he pulled me close, I felt a tingling sensation surge through my body and penetrate my heart. When Eldridge looked into my eyes and spoke, I turned into putty. I don't think I heard one word that he said that night; I only heard my heart beating. I had become infatuated. Maybe I was even falling in love.

"Goodnight. I'll see you soon. I had a nice time," Eldridge said when he dropped me at my dorm later that night.

All I could manage to get out was, "Me, too."

For days, I felt guilty about giving my heart away so easily, through a kiss. Dad's voice kept echoing: "Now you don't want to get too close. It makes the nature in man rise. Kissing leads to other things."

Eldridge was a nice guy. I couldn't imagine he would ever do anything like what Dad said. In fact, he continued to treat me like a proper Southern lady. He told me how pretty and smart I was, and how much he liked me. But the date he invited me on after our romantic interlude at the drive-in was different.

"Glo, I got a friend who's having a party at his house. Want to come along? Everybody's gonna be there…the football team…the cheerleaders. We'll dance, have lots of fun."

I had heard through my track teammates about house parties off campus. They warned me not to attend because they were wild with drinking and sex.

"I'm sorry, I can't go. It's against my religion to party."

"We're just gonna have fun, that's all. I know you're religious. I respect you and would never do anything that goes against your beliefs," Eldridge promised.

"I'm sorry, I just can't."

I didn't, and Eldridge never asked me out again, although we remained good friends. I harbored a mad crush on him for a long time, but I knew he was living life in the fast lane off the football field. My feelings eventually dissipated, and I was able to rededicate myself to focusing solely on track for the rest of the school year.

That June, Coach Temple gathered the Tigerbelles on the bleachers for a meeting.

"Now we've had a good year. Your training program is on target for the '68 Olympic trials. We're gonna beef up our workouts. They're gonna be longer, harder, and faster. Some of you will be back on scholarship. Some won't. Some will have new scholarships with me."

I held my breath. This was the moment.

"'Detroit,' you girls have stuck it out. It's obvious that track is your life. I like that."

So far, so good, I thought.

"But next year, we got to focus on faster girls. What that means is that I can't offer you a running scholarship. Here's what I can do, though. I can offer both of you scholarships as trainers. I need trainers bad to help me coach."

He pointed to me. "Now, 'Detroit,' you got stamina. You're good at distance, but I ain't looking for distance runners, don't have time. I need sprinters. That's the best I can do. If you want to keep runnin,' you'll have to find another coach. I can't help you."

Even though I didn't want Coach to see me cry, I couldn't hold back the tears from my eyes.

"I understand," I told him, after I'd started breathing again. "But I can't give up running. Thank you for having me on your team."

Charlene felt the same way. We both had running in our blood.

I hadn't expected things to turn out the way they did, but I was determined to keep running, no matter what I had to overcome to do so.

Track was why I lived. Track was my passion. Track was all I had.

CHAPTER SEVEN

At twenty years old, I had just finished my freshman year at Tennessee State University. Although it had been a huge accomplishment just to get into college, I didn't view my first year as a success. Coach Temple wanted me on the track team as a trainer, not a runner. I had failed biology, which brought my GPA down to a D. And Dad could no longer afford to pay my tuition.

Returning to Lansing to live among a white majority wasn't something I looked forward to. I had no interest in repeating the past, of having to prove myself to whites and having to work to promote equality for female runners. Lansing wasn't always proactive when it came to women in sports. I wanted to live where I could foster my dreams and my goals in an equitable society. I didn't want the burden that came with living in Lansing.

I became withdrawn, as I'd been in my youth. I said little to my family. I'd already lost touch with most of my high-school friends. Those who were still in Lansing had started families, worked in the factory, or were in prison. Shortly before summer ended, Dad and Mom asked me to sit with them at the gray Formica kitchen table where we always had our family conversations.

"You've been quiet around here lately," Dad said.

"Yes," I said. That one word was all I could manage.

"Look, you're too young to get discouraged. Life's just startin' for you. We've always taught you, 'A winner never quits and a quitter never wins.'

Now you just got to get up and try again. We've all had disappointments in life, but the Lord will help you through."

"I tried to run faster and couldn't. I failed biology. I just can't..."

"No buts. There are no can'ts in life. You keep trying and trying until you make it," Mom chimed in.

"But I need to tell you this," Dad went on. "If you're gonna stay here, you got to go to somebody's college or get a job. You can't live here and do nothin.' Go to Lansing Community College, get your grades up, and then go to a university like MSU. I know they don't admit too many Negroes, but you could be one."

I felt better hearing them tell me I should keep trying. Dad wanted more than to rally my spirits; he wanted me to take action.

"Tomorrow morning, bright and early, we'll go to the college, a deal?" he asked.

"Yes," I said quietly.

I knew my parents meant business. At eight o'clock the following morning, we were standing in front of a female admissions counselor. It felt a little strange seeing so many white folks. Dad did the talking. He had the experience of dealing with all sorts of folks. He stood erect, head up, and looked into the eyes of the counselor.

"May we help you?" she asked.

"Yes, I'm Reverend Ewing, and my daughter, Gloria, here needs to enroll in classes to bring her grades up. She spent a year at Tennessee State and will need to transfer her credits."

"That's not a problem. She'll have to complete this standard application, after which we'll send for her grades. Once we get them, we'll determine what classes she'll need. We'll call you once everything is in place. It shouldn't take but a few weeks. She can attend our first semester mid-September," the counselor said politely, with a smile.

I started LCC that fall. I had to repeat a lot of the first-year courses that I took at TSU, like English, math, and biology. Admissions said it was because academic standards were different in the South than in the North. I was able to pay for tuition by working part-time for minimum wage, which at the time was $1.25 an hour.

I loved my job as an elevator operator at Knapp's, the most expensive department store in Lansing. The elevator was old-fashioned with a black, steel gate that I pulled to lock. The experience not only taught me responsibility, but how to be polite and patient to white customers, even when they were mean.

After a semester, I found that I was beginning to like college. I had teachers who paid attention to my work and talents. My grades were good; I even got an A in my favorite subject, forensics, a form of debate. It was in my forensics class that I released a lot of the passion and emotion that I had been suppressing.

The forensics instructor, a white man, allowed me to be myself, although it was hard for me to genuinely believe in his support since I didn't have positive white role models growing up. My instructor was open to discussing the only two subjects that I felt comfortable debating: track and civil rights. And he enrolled me in the Michigan Junior College Speech League, a statewide competition of junior colleges like Alpena, Concordia Lutheran, Grand Rapids, Kellogg, and Macomb County. There were three categories to speak from: oral interpretation, extempore speaking, and original oratory. I went for the original oratory.

We traveled in cars to Central Michigan University, where the competition was held. It was snowing, I was cold, and the hundred or so folks in the auditorium were all white. I was the only black person there.

I was an intense observer at the competition. What I saw lacking was energy from the speakers. They chose boring historical and political subjects. When my turn came, I was nervous, but my instructor told me to focus on maintaining a slow rhythm with my breathing. As I moved to the center of the stage, my legs felt like Jell-o, and I was breathing not slow but hard, as if I'd just finished the 440. I thought about Dad Harry, the eloquent preacher, and my real father, Robert, who was a gifted actor. Suddenly, I got courage. I thanked God.

I began with a quote, and then gave my topic, which was "The Wonderful World of Sports," not a mainstream choice for a woman in 1967. I talked about athletes like Al Oerter, who threw the discus in the 1964 Olympics. He arrived at the Olympics severely injured, with bandages dressing the torn cartilage in his ribcage. Doctors warned him against competing. They told him that the exertion could cause internal bleeding, but he ignored their advice. I revealed, "On his last throw, he reached back as far as he could and, roaring like a lion, he threw the discus two hundred and six feet to win Olympic gold." There was an audible reaction from the audience, which was hanging on my every word. Not once did I have to refer to my note cards.

When it came time for the judges, who all had doctorate degrees in education, to announce the winners, I had no expectations. My experiences had taught me not to. I was stunned when I heard, "And the winner in persuasive public speaking is...Gloria Ewing." My peers and instructor were thunderously applauding. All eyes were on me. When I finally got over the shock, I was able to walk across the stage and accept my award.

I had accomplished something equal to whites. I never fathomed that a small, junior college in Lansing would be the catalyst to restore my pride, would give me a fresh start on life's journey. But it did. It was then that I resumed track with my first coach, Vonda Gerow. She knew how to coach distance and believed in my running ability. Staying active in track gave me the outlet I needed to vent the rage I harbored against whites. The rage wasn't what it was when I graduated from high school, but, nonetheless, it was still there. Track allowed me to momentarily escape into a world that didn't judge me by my color, but by my ability. It took me away from my past—the molestations, abandonments, and failures.

We began with cross-country to build my stamina. I won medals that put me in the top contingent in the state. By the time track season came around in the spring, I was competing in the 880, which had become a race. Not many women in Michigan ran it; sometimes I was the only competitor entered and many times the only black competitor. My coach wanted me to run the 1,500 meter event because I had more stamina than speed. The 1968 Olympics wouldn't have the 1,500 for women, only for men. The longest Olympic race for women was 800 meters.

For speed work, I trained with Coach Jim Bibbs and the Detroit Track Club. This was the best team in Michigan, Ohio, and Illinois. In track meets, Coach Bibbs would have me run the 440 and sometimes the 4x440 relay. Every Saturday, I was running in an AAU meet, whether it was in Detroit, Toledo, or Chicago. The more I ran, the faster I became. The faster I became, the harder the competition got. I usually managed to walk away with a medal or ribbon in the 440, and occasionally in the 880.

My parents were so proud that they told the pastor of our church about my achievements in track, and he would announce them to the congregation every Sunday.

"Gloria, please stand. Sista, we so proud of you. You gonna be great one day. We gonna look up and see you in those 'lympics. Just keep the Lawd wif you," Pastor Robinson would say in his Southern dialect.

"Thank you," I'd respond softly, humbly, bowing my head.

Lansing Community College ran an article about my track wins. As I entered my second year there, my counselor wanted me to apply to four-year universities in Michigan. She felt I would do well at a school with a minimum of twenty thousand students. She said I could get the academic attention I needed to maintain good grades. I applied to Farris State College, Eastern Michigan University, Western Michigan, and Wayne State University. I was accepted at Eastern Michigan, which offered more sports for women than the other colleges. They didn't offer track, but with the plethora of other women's sports there, its addition was imminent.

It was the summer of 1967 when my acceptance letter came. It read something like this: "Dear Gloria Ewing: You have been admitted to Eastern Michigan University for the fall of 1967 under our affirmative-action program. Due to your average grades, we are required to place you on probation for one year. Within that period of time, you are expected to maintain a C average or better. Again, welcome to Eastern Michigan University."

Since Dad couldn't afford to send me, I would receive grants and college loans. It was a major accomplishment in the black community to attend college, so when folks from my neighborhood found out, they sent money and cards and stopped by our house to wish me well. My church even took up an offering. Folks had seen the articles about me in the *Lansing State Journal* and the Lansing Community College newspaper. They knew I wanted to make it to the Olympics one day.

Eastern Michigan was located in the small town of Ypsilanti. Students called it Ypsissippi because the whites who lived there were from the South; they were poor and spoke with a heavy Southern accent. Some even belonged to the KKK or the John Birch Society. Blacks didn't bother with them and instead lived on the outskirts in cities like Willow Run and Detroit, which were a hop, skip, and a jump from Ypsilanti.

It was my first time living in an apartment, and my first time having two white roommates. The university didn't match according to race, only the availability of student housing as it was a rare commodity.

Our apartment was located across the street from the campus. My roommates were from affluent families and possessed attitudes of privilege and entitlement. They would leave their clothes on the floor and dirty dishes in the sink. Their stained sanitary napkins lay in the wastebasket for days. They never washed the tub after showering, so I had to clean their long, blond hair from the drain. Their boyfriends would spend the night and eat my food the next day. To avoid conflict, I was gone much of the time, mostly training.

On Sundays, Reverend James Whitehead, the pastor of Willow Run Church of God in Christ, would pick me up. He was about sixty-five, and kind-hearted and patient. His long, black Cadillac had a special steering column to accommodate his paralysis. When he wanted to turn his head, he'd have to turn his entire body, at the same time looking over his thick, black-rimmed glasses. I was overwhelmed by the scent of cologne and Listerine when I stepped into his car every Sunday.

Reverend Whitehead's church was built by its members. It was located on a bumpy dirt road in the black community of Willow Run. The paint that covered it was chipped and bleached from the sun. The front stairs were crooked and squeaky. But once you got inside, you forgot about the exterior. Folks greeted everyone with a kiss and a hug, which was common in black churches. The pulpit was covered with colorful square strips of carpet remnants. To one side of it, there were drums, tambourines, an organ, and a piano. On the other side, there were wooden high-back pulpit chairs for the pastor, assistant pastor, and a visiting minister.

Just like my home church, folks who went there didn't have a formal college education, and many didn't even have a high-school diploma. They were from the South and had come north to work in the factories or homes of white folks. For many in the Church of God in Christ, education wasn't a priority; it was seen as worldly. But I could see a shift in my generation.

The pastor's son, Reverend Jack Whitehead, Jr., had a master's degree from a theology school called Interdenominational Theological Seminary in Atlanta. He was single, smart, articulate, and somewhat handsome. Although Afros were in style, his hair was closely shaven, a style ministers often wore. Each time I saw him, he was well-dressed in a three-piece suit and bow tie. He would always flirt with me at the end of the service, although nothing developed between us at the time. I felt obligated to attend church, but I had nothing but the Olympics on my mind.

Once I settled in at Eastern Michigan University, I met with the men's track-team coach, Coach Bob Parks.

"Coach Bibbs said that I should talk to you about training with the guys. I'm training for AAU track meets," I told him.

I had no idea how Coach Parks felt about the idea, so I was a little tentative with my proposal. Coach Parks was a thirty-nine-year-old white man who was about five-foot-eleven and quite slim. He wore a silver whistle with a black string around his neck and traditional coach's attire—a white knit polo shirt, long khaki pants, and white Adidas running shoes.

"My friend Jim is one of the best women's coaches around. He was a world-class sprinter in his day. You're welcome to work out with the guys. You'd be the only girl for now, but there's talk about getting a women's team. I'd like to see that happen soon."

"Why is that?"

"My daughter, Susan, loves to run. She'll be following you in a few years. She does distance, so I want to make sure she goes to a college that has track for women."

"I look forward to meeting her one day. Thank you so much, Coach Parks."

Word spread quickly that I was going to run with the men. People came just to watch me—students, especially the guys, and other athletes sat in the bleachers in amazement. The men got teased whenever I beat them, but it didn't go to my head because the fact was most of the time the guys outran me.

I began cross-country with the men's team, and in November when the snow fell and the ground froze, I trained on the indoor track, which was my favorite because it generated more speed. Some of my fastest 440s and 880s were done inside. Still, one afternoon, I decided to run on the back roads. I did it all the time with the guys, who had gone to a meet out of town. It was about three in the afternoon. I was dressed for the snow and ice: wool running pants, a lined parka, gloves, and a skullcap.

About six miles from the university on my way to Ann Arbor, a dark blue Chevy truck pulled up beside me. The driver and passenger were white. They wore crew cuts, were about twenty-something, and were chewing tobacco and laughing. A shotgun rested on hooks in the cabin of their truck. People referred to people like them as "hillbillies."

"Sho' like to catch me one of them niggers," I heard the passenger say.

I ran faster. They accelerated to keep up with me. An image of my body lying dead in a ditch entered my mind. I quickly turned and ran in the opposite direction. The truck turned, too, and sped up so that we were neck and neck. I couldn't maintain my speed for ten miles back to Ypsilanti.

When I slowed down to catch my breath, the driver revved the truck's engine and inched closer, nearly running me off the road. I didn't stop going. It was getting colder. The sun was going down, and I had to get back before dark. I prayed for a car to come along, but none did.

The crazy hillbillies began to laugh and smirk. I prayed, believing I'd surely die on the icy road between Ypsilanti and Ann Arbor. I recited the Lord's Prayer to myself. Finally, I turned and looked into the men's faces. Their eyes were red as the devil. They looked sloppy drunk. Then they began laughing at me like hyenas.

I glanced at the gun; it was still mounted. Suddenly, several cars passed. Then another car, and then another. They just kept coming down the two-lane highway. The men sped off like they were driving the Indy 500. I made it back to campus safely, but I was scared. I never ran on a desolate road alone again.

My intense training was paying off. I had become a full-fledged member of the Detroit Track Club. My best winter event that year was the State AAU track and field meet. Hundreds of girls from Michigan and Ohio competed. I ran the 440 several times to qualify for the finals. By the end of the day, I ran a fast 68.0 and took a medal for sixth place.

In the early spring of 1968, I competed in the AAU Junior National track meet in Maryland. It was my first time running the mile in a large national meet. The first place winner would advance to the nationals. The three winners from the nationals would go to the United States Olympic trials, then off to the 1968 Olympics in Mexico City.

Coach Bibbs told me, "When the gun goes off, get out like a rabbit the first 100 yards, but not as a front-runner; you'll fade. Settle into third or fourth, with a stride that feels relaxed. Stay there until the last 200 yards. Then attack. That's where endurance and speed pay off."

This worked well until the final 100 yards. I tried with every muscle in my body to catch the first-place runner. I just couldn't get my legs to go as fast as I wanted. I came in second place and got a round, silver medal that hung from my neck on a red, white, and blue ribbon.

I didn't advance to the nationals, but I was happy I'd done as well as I had, and Coach Bibbs was proud of me. I knew there would be another Olympics in four years and that by then there would be a women's mile run.

While I focused on running, the 1960s were playing out in all their madness and glory. From "Flower Power" to the British invasion to civil disobedience, there was never a dull moment. In spite of my straitlaced upbringing, the rebel in me was fascinated by and even drawn to the movements I was reading about in newspapers and watching on TV, although the first time I entered the fray, it was entirely by accident.

In August of 1968, I experienced my first live protest, during the National Democratic Convention. A few months before the start of the Olympics in Mexico, I'd gone to see my biological mother in Chicago. The protests against the war in Vietnam were peaking. Dr. King had been assassinated that April and Senator Robert Kennedy was gunned down in June. The nation's nerves were raw.

When I arrived at the Greyhound bus depot downtown, my mother met me in a taxi. I noticed the stoic faces of the Chicago police and national guard as they held their guns upright, prepared to shoot at the thousands of protesters lining Michigan Avenue and holding signs bearing slogans like: "Out of Nam NOW!" "Give Peace A Chance," "Make Babies, Not War," "War Is Not Healthy for Children and Other Living Things," "America Murders Innocent People."

The protesters were people in their twenties like me, but they were liberal white folks, commonly known as hippies. They proudly wore long hair and layers of colorful plastic beads coiled around their neck. There were flowers, usually daisies, in their hair. The women wore long cotton dresses, and the men wore white cotton dashikis with embroidered necklines. Leather sandals were essential footwear because they believed in walking instead of driving—driving caused air pollution. There weren't many blacks among the protestors. The black men were on the front lines fighting in Vietnam. The few whom I saw protesting in Chicago wore multi-colored dashikis and wide Afros.

"Can't we ask the driver to go faster, Mama? I just know those cops standing there ready to fire at any moment are going to, like they did to those other civil rights protestors. I don't trust them. This scene gives me the creeps."

"Now, now, honey. They wouldn't dare do anything like that. We can't go any faster," she replied.

"Yesterday the crowd had a big scuffle with the national guard, and they turned tear gas on them," the cab driver informed us as he cautiously navigated his car through the sea of people.

"Cops are pigs, Mama. They use violent tactics toward innocent people, just like most of white America does. Anyone who voices any sort of opposing view is beaten, gets the dogs called on them, gets hosed down. They even beat women and children sometimes, with billy clubs. Some cops are even members of the Ku Klux Klan, involved in public lynching."

Mama was unconvinced. In her calm, unassuming tone, she tried to do some convincing of her own, telling me that not all cops were bad and not all white folks were evil. Then she changed the subject to the hot August weather. Mama always felt uncomfortable talking politics. She said I was the radical, outspoken child in the family. I appreciated that she was okay with that, even if I couldn't get her to share my passionate views.

It took about thirty minutes to move five blocks to the Dan Ryan Expressway, which eventually took us to my mother's home. Her four-level, red brick building was neat and cute. It sat back from the street, sequestered by elm trees. Her one-bedroom apartment was on the second level. As inviting as the building seemed, it was in Blackstone Ranger territory. The Blackstone Rangers were the most violent gang in Chicago, aside from the mob. They marked their territory with graffiti; it covered the subways, the stores, and the schools in Mama's neighborhood. I had another reason to worry.

About a year before, Mama had been raped after being dropped off at her home. She told me it happened under the bottom apartment; she'd exited the taxi and decided to use the building's back door. The perpetrator was never caught because it was nighttime and too dark in that space for Mama to identify him. I couldn't stand the thought that my own mother had been violated. I wanted justice.

"There's not much a woman can do in Chicago when this happens," Mama explained. "Just report it to the police. But they couldn't care less when this happens to a black woman."

It bothered me intensely that in America women had to fight to get decent care after they'd been so horribly victimized. That night, as we were sitting on her bed together sharing an intimate mother-daughter moment, I voiced my concern for her safety.

"Mama, I'm worried about you going out at night in this neighborhood," I confided. "Especially after what happened."

"Well, I try to be more cautious now," Mama said. "I carry a knife and I don't use the back door at night. If I moved someplace else, my rent would double. I like where I am. It's close to the subway, and my neighbors are nice."

I didn't want to spend my precious time with Mama arguing, so I dropped that particular line of conversation. We had so much to catch up on. Mama had divorced Harold, her second husband, when they got back from Africa in 1964. I never had the chance to spend time with him. Mama explained that they fell on hard times when his family found out he was married to her. They disowned him and cut off his inheritance. He couldn't find work.

After the divorce, Mama went back to surviving the way she did when she first came to Chicago after divorcing my natural father. Mama had a few select male friends with whom she kept close company in exchange for money. "You know, Gloria, your mama has to make a livin', right?"

"Yes, Mama," I said, squeezing her hand in mine and managing to match her smile with a small one of my own.

"I can tell you this because you've always been the only child I could talk to. I always knew you'd understand. Things didn't work out for me when I first came here from Mt. Pleasant. I experienced a lot of prejudice trying to break into modeling. I worked minimum wage as a seamstress and did some interior design work that just didn't pay enough," she said. "These men are just friends who help me out. When they come over, you watch TV in the living room. Okay?"

Of course I would oblige. She was my mother and I loved her. At random times during my visit, white men who were mostly in their sixties arrived at Mama's apartment to "keep company" with her. When they greeted me they'd tell me that I was pretty like my mother.

I promised I'd keep how Mama supported herself a secret from the family, as she'd asked, so I could return every summer to spend time with her. But I did keep praying for her to get out of that business. I was afraid she'd contract a disease, or turn up dead in an alley. When I was with her, I tried not to think about what she did with these strange men and instead focused on cherishing our time together. There was too little of it. Mama always sent me back home, but she made sure I never left empty-handed; she generously gave me one of the crisp, new one-hundred-dollar bills that she had earned during my stay. It would have been insulting to her not to take the money.

I had to make my peace with who my mother was in order to have a relationship with her. I understood that she'd had her dreams, and that they hadn't come true. I wasn't going to let that happen to me. I was obsessed.

For two weeks in October of 1968, no one could unglue me from my black-and-white television set. I ate and slept the Olympics. I watched every event from track and field, swimming, kayaking, and volleyball, to basketball and gymnastics. I studied the athletes' every technique.

I especially felt a kinship to Madeline Manning because she was a Tigerbelle. She won the 800 meters in 2:00.9, becoming the first American woman to win this distance. Then there was Tommie Smith and John Carlos. They had courage to stand on the Olympic podium without shoes, heads bowed and black-gloved fists raised in the air in a Black Power salute, in protest of the injustice that blacks had suffered in America. I would have done the same thing.

American reporters had no empathy for them, though. They claimed it was the most disgraceful Olympics ever held. The consequences were dire. The Olympic committee ousted Tommie and John from the Olympic Village and, when they returned to America, there was no million-dollar endorsement from Wheaties waiting for them, as there was for many other Olympians. Instead, they found themselves jobless. Whites threatened their lives, and they lost their families to divorce.

Tommie and John's protest occurred at the height of racial turmoil in America. Dr. King's assassination led to an outpouring of violence in almost every major city across the country. Blacks were tired of being treated like second-class citizens. Whites tried to keep us down with police brutality, water hoses, and fire bombings.

Two camps emerged: one that believed in Dr. King's method of civil disobedience, and one that followed Malcolm X's edict of "by any means necessary." Personally, I believed in negotiating with the white man, but not if he was slapping blacks around. Still, it was hard watching my people burn our neighborhoods. There had to be another way to retaliate against white suppression and the wrongdoings we had endured for generations. Burning our own mom-and-pop stores was the wrong strategy, and it was hurting the wrong people.

CHAPTER EIGHT

I'd been vehemently opposed to the Vietnam War since it began. I saw on television too many innocent young people being slaughtered, especially black soldiers, who were the ones most frequently placed on the front lines. My prom date, Boyd Lewis, was among several young men from my high school who lost his life in the war. And those who were fortunate enough to survive couldn't buy a house, get a job, or access social services. My cousin Teddy didn't feel the need to sugarcoat his experience in Vietnam when he returned in the summer of 1968.

"You know I had no choice, Cuz. I was drafted. You think I wanted to go? Hell, no!"

Teddy apologized for cursing. He knew it was against my religious beliefs, but I told him it was okay. His language might not have been appropriate, but his anger was.

"Nam ain't about gettin' rid of communism. It's 'bout control," Teddy said. "The Vietnamese didn't ask for our help, but we got five hundred thousand soldiers there anyway. This year, US Army soldiers of "Charlie" Company went into the village of My Lai and killed over five hundred unarmed villagers who were just hanging out eatin' breakfast. And meanwhile us soldiers are all getting jacked up. You know about me, right?"

"Yeah, you told me. I'm so sorry, Cuz."

"I got one of my freakin' balls blown off! And so they give me some weed to take the pain away. It's a joint here and there. Some Jack Daniels. You know what I mean?"

"I hear you. The government should be held accountable for this war," I said.

"When I got back from Nam, this country wouldn't give me a pot to piss in or the time of day 'cause I was a black man, a Vietnam vet. This country just pushed us out in the cold, told us to make it the best way we could."

"You can't let the government get away with this, Teddy. You need to make them pay what they owe you. Can you get the VA to help you?"

"Come on, Cuz, be real. They ain't gonna help, and I ain't gonna ask Uncle Sam for a dime. I don't trust 'em."

"Now you be real, Teddy. You're not working. You don't have health insurance. You're hurting yourself by not getting what's due you. Think about it."

"It'll come together, Cuz. I just don't want any part of this government. Socialism is better."

"Socialism might work for us black folks and the poor. But, Teddy, rich folks won't buy it. They're sitting pretty, not paying any taxes. They're not gonna part with a dime to ensure everyone can have enough food to eat, a decent education. Is that why you started the Black Panthers in Flint? Because you support socialism?"

"I can't talk about that, Glo. I don't want to discuss that."

I wasn't clear as to why he didn't want to discuss the Panthers, but I respected Teddy's wishes. The Panthers had a bad rap for getting into shootouts with the cops, but they had done many good things in the community. Years later, I learned that there may have been a rift between Teddy and leadership in the party.

I felt a little guilty that as poorly as things were going for Teddy in 1968, they were looking pretty good for me. In the fall of that year, I returned to Eastern Michigan University. I was running faster in the 440 and the 880. Although the AAU still hadn't sanctioned the mile for women, I ran it in the meets that allowed me to. I was getting Bs in courses like physical education, English, psychology, and sociology. The university lifted my academic probation.

I was also dating a white guy for the first time. His name was Roger Tremblay, a French Canadian. He looked more Greek than white. His skin was a light olive color, and he had thick, dark brown hair. Although he was small boned and only stood about five feet, six inches tall, his muscles were built up from running.

Roger was one of the best distance runners at the university; our courtship began on the track. We trained together on weekends. In the evenings, we went to Bible study at the Campus Crusade for Christ. We'd sit around with a bunch of white students talking about our trials as Christians, searching for scriptures to help us cope. I enjoyed the camaraderie, but the songs were corny. They were campfire songs as opposed to the gospels that I preferred.

Roger and I were the only biracial couple in the study group and, to my knowledge, on campus. No one ever bothered us. Maybe we'd be the recipients of a curious glance or two, but otherwise, folks kept stepping. As a Canadian, Roger knew nothing about racial discrimination, which was healthy for our relationship.

My feelings for Roger were strong. I was in love for the first time. He was such a gentleman. He asked permission to kiss me for the first time. His lips were soft, but his pointed nose got in the way of me getting to them until I learned to make adjustments. No matter how much we kissed, we promised never to have sex. We both felt that was something that should be reserved for marriage. Still, I was caught off guard when Roger proposed.

"Gloria, I love you. I want you to marry me."

"I can't," I said quietly, turning away for fear of seeing any hurt in his eyes. "I've got my education ahead of me. I've got the Olympics. You know what my dreams are. I can't have children now."

"We can wait on kids. You can still run. I'll train you, but I can't lose you," was Roger's response.

"Roger, I'm sorry. I can't marry you now."

I loved Roger, but I loved my dreams more. Our relationship ended shortly after I turned down his proposal. Roger later married a black woman.

I met Tom Jackson during my last year at Eastern Michigan, in the winter of 1970. Tom was a big-time wrestler on campus. For months, he'd been watching me from the bleachers while I practiced track.

"Hello, there," he said when he finally got the courage to approach me. His voice was trembling. I was so shy myself that I could only manage a quick glance into his eyes as I shook his hand.

"Hi to you," I said.

"Was wondering if I could invite you for a pop or maybe get your phone number? I've been scared to ask since word is you're one of them holy rollers. But I like you."

We smiled at the same time. Tom was a handsome black man with protruding muscles in his neck, shoulders, and chest. He stood over six feet tall and weighed about two hundred and thirty pounds. His face was full, as were his lips. He had a light brown, chocolate complexion and slanted, dark brown eyes. Tom was one of the university's best heavyweight wrestlers and a football player, too. His dimples only appeared when he blushed. And he had beautiful, straight, white teeth.

I picked up from the gymnasium floor a basketball program for the previous night's game and scribbled my number with the pen Tom pulled from behind his ear.

"I'll call you," he promised. He was true to his word.

I started going to Tom's wrestling matches and football games, and then accompanying him to basketball games and the movies. He never went to church with me, but he said he believed in God. I didn't push the matter since it would only feed the stereotype he had of me as being a holy roller.

We began hanging out with Tom's best friend, Tommie, who was also a football player. Tommie's girlfriend, Juanita, was nice. She was mixed race and gorgeous, with a fair complexion and thick, curly hair that had the same texture as white folks' hair. She looked like Cleopatra. Juanita's hips were shapely, and her jeans fit like a glove. She wore tight blouses that accentuated her large breasts. Tommie and Juanita were always spending the night together. Tom wanted us to do the same.

"Ah, come on, there's nothing wrong with it when two people care about each other," he'd say.

"I'm a Christian, a virgin. I can't do that," I told him.

I did tag along with Tom and his friends to house parties. These parties opened my eyes to a lot of realities. Like the fact that all of Tom's friends, and the whole world aside from me, it seemed, smoked pot. I learned that white kids took LSD and blacks from the ghetto did heroin. But black college kids like Tommie, Tom, and Juanita were just potheads. They smoked all the time: after games, after football practice, in their apartment. They drank Budweiser beer while they got high. I despised the smell of marijuana. The odor made me think of the stench of urine that rose up from the bottom of my grandparents' outhouse.

Tom was driving us home from a party one night and he, Tommie, and Juanita were all as high as a kite. Tom kept swerving into the opposite lane. I prayed so hard to get home safely and made a deal with God that I would never do that again. Once I got out of the car, I felt light-headed. Tom said I had gotten a contact high and laughed so hard, he cried. I didn't smoke marijuana. Making it to the Olympics meant more to me than doing drugs. I tried to convince Tom to leave the stuff alone.

"Twenty years from now, you'll wake up and you won't have any brain cells. Pot is poison."

"Maybe so, maybe not. There's no proof. It's just an herb. Nobody says it's harmful," Tom defended.

"Drugs will keep blacks enslaved and destroy us. They're white folks' way of exterminating us. And 'cause you're always high, you won't have the energy for the struggle."

"Yep, you're probably right, Glo. But it sho' is good now."

I continued to tolerate Tom's drug use because he accepted me and my religious beliefs. Shortly after we started dating, I met Marvin Gaye, the Motown singer. He wasn't as famous in the late '60s as he was after his death. Marvin's dream was to play pro football, so the coach let him practice with the Eastern Michigan University team. That's how Tom and Marvin became good friends. Marvin didn't stand a chance as a football player because he was skinny and only stood about six feet tall, but he believed he could make it. Marvin offered Tom, Tommie, Juanita, and me a ride home on a day I'd stopped by to watch Tom practice.

"So you're Tom's girl? Heard good things about you," Marvin said, smiling shyly and shaking my hand.

"Good to meet you," I said.

We rode in the back of Marvin's black limousine, which had a large inventory of wine and assorted liquor stored in its cabinets. Marvin was a kind and generous man, but I think he, Tom, and his friends were doing more than playing football. They tried to speak in code, so that any talk of marijuana could only be picked up by reading between the lines, but I understood what was going on. Shortly after meeting Marvin, I broke up with Tom. He did too much partying and smoking for me.

That spring was a historical time for Eastern Michigan University. A few months before I graduated with a bachelor of science degree in sociology, violence broke out on campus. I was coming back from class one afternoon. I'll never forget the date: May 8, 1970. I saw twenty white students sitting on the sidewalk with their arms interlocked. They were dressed in bell-bottoms, tie-dyed tee shirts, green army jackets, and brown combat boots. Their hair was long and shaggy; some wore plastic beads, and some wore leather chains with a silver peace symbol. They were sitting in complete silence.

As I walked deeper into campus, toward Forest Avenue, I ran into about five hundred white students who were walking and chanting: "One, two, three, four, we don't want your war no more!" Their anti-war chants got louder as they snaked toward Washtenaw Avenue, which was the main artery through Ypsilanti.

These students were protesting the invasion of Cambodia and demanding an end to the war in Vietnam. They were also expressing their anger over the recent killing of four Kent State students. The protest activities were spearheaded by SLAM, the Student Liberation Action Movement. The group was predominately comprised of white students. They demanded student representation on the University Board of Regents. There was another movement on campus called the Black Students Association (BSA), of which I was a part. The BSA wanted the university to increase black enrollment to eighteen percent. We also demanded black studies courses.

These two separate movements polarized black and white students, in an "us against them" sort of way. Black students called SLAM the *white radical hippy protest* and to whites we were known as the *small black movement.* Whites had the upper hand because their movement was larger, due to higher white enrollment numbers. The BSA was perceived as the stepchild of SLAM because our demands were always mentioned last on SLAM's list. During several negotiations, only once did we have the opportunity to sit down in the board room to articulate what we wanted.

When SLAM's negotiations failed, they wanted to take their movement to the streets. The BSA didn't. We knew a strategy like that would make us a target of police brutality. Instead, we watched and waited.

The protest SLAM coordinated was peaceful. Hundreds of students sat and chanted for hours. Harold Sponberg, the president of the university, was uncomfortable with the large size of the protest, so he summoned the

City of Ypsilanti and state police forces onto campus. The police charged the students and exploded tear gas into the crowd. They dragged students into headlocks, choking some of them.

The next day, students retaliated. They broke the windows of businesses along Forest Avenue. They set fire to several campus trucks and pelted passing police cars with bottles, jeering at the cops all the while. Police again threw canisters of blinding, suffocating tear gas into the crowds.

I refused to participate in the boycott of classes the white students organized because of my Dad's harsh warnings.

"Gloria, we're tellin' you," he said, "if you're down there protesting and you get arrested, you'll have to sit in jail 'til you rot. We're not gettin' you out! We don't have bail money. I didn't send you to college to protest. You hear?"

It was the same message many black students had gotten from their parents. The fact was most black parents feared their kids would die at the hands of police.

The day of the retaliation, I got into a heated political debate with an Italian friend, Ed Mattos. Ed was a leader of the white student movement. He was extremely militant. He wore a black beret, espoused the teachings of Mao Tse-tung, and proudly boasted about his affiliation with the Socialist Party.

"Ed, if you get violent with the cops, they'll get violent back. And they won't listen. Passive resistance is better. Even if they handcuff you and take you to jail, eventually they'll have to listen," I explained.

"We tried that, Gloria. The pigs disrespected us. They came at us while we sat quietly on the streets. We got to protect ourselves. Pigs represented the guardsmen who shot the Kent State four. They were the military in Vietnam. And now they're here. Pigs are on us like white on rice."

Ed was gesticulating wildly with his hands as he spoke. His emotions were running so high that I decided it was best to leave the matter alone. Besides, it soon became clear that Ed was right. The campus was so blanketed with cops it was worse than the Chicago protest.

I had just finished track practice on the fourth night of the student protest. I only had ten minutes before the 8:00 p.m. curfew that Governor Milliken instituted took effect. The punishment for violating the curfew was jail. I ran to catch up with my neighbor, Sharon. Together, we ran the hundred yards on the warm tar to our Ambassador North apartment.

I was wearing bell-bottom jeans, platform shoes, and my arms were full of textbooks. Helicopters were shining their watchful beams down on our heads. Hordes of students were running frantically in the same direction as we were, all of us panic-stricken as we struggled to get home in time. About fifty yards from my apartment, I began counting the myriad of "pigs," but there were too many. They were lining the sidewalks and streets. Sharon was convinced they were going to shoot us.

National guardsmen were all over the place, too, standing at attention beside their squad cars, holding their rifles upright. They had been given orders to arrest any student who violated curfew. I scoured each guardsman's face, hoping to find a black man whom I could turn to if I didn't make curfew. But all the faces I saw behind those helmets were white. I reached the front door of my complex and did the best I could to unlock the outer door. A loud baritone voice with a heavy Southern accent shouted at me through a bullhorn.

"This is a warnin'. I repeat, a warnin.' Your eight p.m. curfew starts now. Anyone on the streets will be arrested and booked. I repeat, arrested!"

I'd thrown my books to the ground and was battling with the door.

"Sharon, my key is stuck! I can't turn it!"

I could see the cops out of the corner of my eye. I was petrified. I kept jiggling the key until it moved, and I felt the lock release. Sharon and I charged through the door and fled to my apartment on the second floor, which faced the street. We could see all the action from my balcony.

The announcement that came across the bullhorn this time was much louder than before.

"You got your warning. Go back inside. You'll be tear-gassed."

A few cops looked in my direction. One of them hurled a tear gas canister straight at my balcony. A thick, white cloud engulfed us. I gagged and began coughing and choking. Sharon sought refuge in her apartment down the hall, but I remained on the porch and hid against the brick wall to conceal my presence.

I could make out the faces of a few frantic students who were gasping for air as they attempted to run inside the Ambassador East apartment. Among those trying to escape was my friend Joe. He was the most popular guy on Eastern's wrestling team. It looked like he and his friends had managed to get inside the hallway, but just before they could shut the door the cops dragged them back into the street by their Afros. Joe was attempting to pull his head out of the choke hold the pig had him in, but the cop squeezed his neck tighter.

"Please stop...stop, this isn't right!" I screamed. The noise of police sirens and helicopters drowned out my cries.

I watched as Joe was handcuffed and shoved into the back of a patrol car. I could see, thanks to the illumination of all the red flashing lights that he was slumped over.

I had a sick feeling that something terrible was going to happen to Joe—that he was going to be beaten or killed. Word of his arrest spread like wildfire among black students. We organized ourselves and prepared to press charges against the police. We were surprised when during one of our planning meetings Joe walked in. He was almost un-recognizable. His eyes were bloodshot, and his face and lips were swol-len. A patch of hair had been yanked from his scalp. Almost every part of him that was visible was swollen, and black and blue. The attorney at his side told us that Joe had been beaten in the police car on the way to the station.

"We're bringing Joe's case before the City of Ypsilanti, charging the police with a violent and cruel act. The cops are accusing Joe and his friends of starting a fire between two apartments and throwing bottles from win-dows. We all know racism is involved. I'm asking for your help."

The attorney paused for a moment and looked around the room, meet-ing each of us in the eyes to make sure we were listening.

"If anyone witnessed what happened that night," he continued, "we need your testimony. You should see me after the meeting. It's going to be difficult to find witnesses with so many students leaving for the summer, and so many having fled the scene. I'll need names and numbers of anyone who saw anything."

I immediately stepped forward. The attorney said he'd contact me soon and that I'd be considered a key witness for the trial, which was scheduled for that summer.

The details of the riot were published in the *Eastern Echo,* the school's newspaper. The headline read "Students, police clash in four day protest." Excerpts of the meeting the students had with the president were also pub-lished. President Sponberg was quoted as saying, "I have no qualms about expelling any students who are menaces to the University and referring them to the proper student boards..."

According to the paper, President Sponberg's office had been flooded with phone calls from angry Ypsilanti residents. They felt intimidated by a curfew imposed because of the actions of "stupid hippies." The article went on to say that city and state police had arrested 170 students with injuries incurred from law enforcement. Property damage was in the thousands, and several university vehicles had been burned. An angry resident of Ypsilanti had even run his car into protesters.

A month before Joe's trial, I was offered an internship by the student aid office to work for the all-white Ypsilanti Police Department. The school had no idea I was a key witness for Joe, and I wasn't going to show my hand. This was my chance to get what I could for Joe's defense.

My job was boring—filing and typing. When a female was arrested, I would search her for any contraband. My work area was the reception room, furnished with two gray metal desks, one at which I sat; the other space was the jail cell. There were no women police officers, just clerks who were polite. They had heavy Southern accents and made the same weary speech to me day in and day out.

"Well, we just can't believe you are twenty-three. You look like a little girl."

The Southern policemen were loud and always laughing. They would nod at me instead of saying "good morning." Their hair was styled in military-type crew cuts. Their shirts fit tightly around their protruding stomachs. I was never able to get any information about Joe's beating because they never talked about the riot. What I did find out was that the Ypsilanti police were white, conservative, and closed-minded. My internship ended just before the summer did and just in time for Joe's trial. But it turns out my services as a witness weren't needed. Joe's attorney called and gave me the news.

"We appreciate your willingness to be a witness, Gloria, but the charges have been dropped. Our case has been dismissed. You were our only witness."

"Isn't there anything we can do to hold them accountable for what they did to Joe?" I asked.

"We can't have a trial with one witness, Gloria. I'm sorry."

There was some positive news in the coming weeks. A commission had been formed to investigate the circumstances of the violence, including excessive use of force by the police while arresting Joe and thirty-nine other students who were sitting-in peacefully. Also, students would now be represented on the Board of Regents. Black students would have black studies, and there would be an increase in black enrollment.

But my time at Eastern Michigan was over. I was proud to be the first in my adoptive and biological family to go to college and finish. Brother Robert had gone off to the navy. Sister Bobbie went to TSU, but didn't finish. I hadn't heard from Sister Ethel since I left Eudora all those years ago when I was five.

A year later, in December of 1971, I was accepted into the master's program at the University of Michigan School of Social Work. My acceptance was largely based on a passionate position paper I had written about how I wanted to facilitate social change for poor and oppressed blacks, so they could become more self-reliant.

UM was a part of the new Affirmative Action program, which meant that, in order for the school to receive government funds that year, more blacks and Native Americans needed to be admitted. I was offered a full scholarship if I maintained a 3.0 average, but I'd be on probation for the first semester because I didn't have a B average when I graduated from Eastern Michigan. They said if I didn't excel, I'd be expelled, and there would be no exceptions.

There would be no advantages given to students of color, although we were at a disadvantage in society. There would be no extra academic support for those of us who needed it.

I was on my own.

CHAPTER NINE

I drove away from Ypsilanti, where I had been living since graduating from Eastern Michigan, in a dark green 1965 Volkswagen Beetle. All of my worldly possessions were crammed inside that tiny car. My books on black history, religion, sociology, psychology, and Marxism barely left room for the two Samsonite suitcases that were bulging with my bell-bottom jeans, platform shoes, t-shirts bearing Black Power axioms, a worn Bible, and Afro Sheen hair-care products. I had also packed my church dresses and sensible wool sweaters. Some of these items typified who I had become, an independent-minded intellectual and concerned radical. Others represented the conservative, God-fearing young woman I'd been raised to be.

While I was growing up, I hadn't received the kind of encouragement that allowed me to believe I would one day be steering my car toward graduate school. Most of my teachers and the white majority who made the rules were always trying to place limitations on me. That was the past. Never again was I going to let others decide what I could do and where I deserved to be. I had proven myself, and I was going to keep on proving myself.

As I drove, my radio blasted the words of Martha Jean the Queen, the most popular black talk-show host in Detroit. Martha was the daily fix of Detroit's black factory workers, single mothers, and church folks. She would send the soulful vocals of Reverend James Cleveland's song "Peace Be Still" out over the airwaves and accompany them by saying, "Honey, now you hold your head up and be proud of your blackness!" and she'd get a steady stream of calls encouraging her to play the same tune again and again.

My parents weren't in the car with me, like when I set out for Tennessee State University. Mom Frances was forty-six and Dad Harry was sixty-six years old. They were busy with the church and rearing my sisters Eva and Lydia. They were also taking care of my grandmother Violet, whose right leg had been amputated due to complications from diabetes. A year before that surgery, she was diagnosed with breast cancer and had to have a mastectomy. Although their hands were full, my parents always found time to send a dose of their particular wisdom my way, especially Dad.

"Keep God first, like we raised you. You see most black folks, when they get a little educated, they forget Him. They don't go to church. They put the Lord on the back shelf. He's been too good to you for that kind of treatment. Understand?"

"Yes, Dad, I won't forget Him," I replied dutifully.

But Dad was right. The world I was moving into was different from the one I'd known. Blue-collar factory workers and holy rollers didn't share the progressive, liberal views the University of Michigan was known for. My experiences had taught me that highly educated people, especially professors, seldom believed in a God, let alone attended church.

As I drove through the streets of Ann Arbor that December of 1971, I marveled at how flat the land was. The university was composed of gray, brick buildings about six stories high with Gothic columns in the style of popular eighteenth-century architecture. The grass was green that spring, and the aroma from the campus's plentiful elm, maple, and pine trees was reminiscent of the scent found in the lingering smoke of a campfire.

I saw white students walking slowly and talking in clusters. The piles of books they carried against their hips forced their bodies to tilt a bit. The men had dark brown beards and long hair, and some even wore frizzy Afros, which shocked me because I had never seen whites trying to emulate blacks. The white women I saw had curly, puffy hair that flowed all the way down their backs. Everybody was wearing either a pea coat or a trench coat that fell to their knees, left unbuttoned to reveal embroidered silk shirts from India and layers of colorful plastic beads, which symbolized support for the peace movement.

The few blacks I saw were flaunting wide Afros and wearing loudly colorful dashikis over turtlenecks. Some were also wearing skullcaps knitted with red, black, and green yarn, the colors of Black Nationalism. Red represented the blood that was shed for liberation, black stood for the black race, and green stood for the millions of acres of land tilled during the time of slavery.

I was curious about the crowds gathered at the Diag in the center of campus, which I would learn was a popular place for students to meet, socialize, and organize protests. I parked, put a dime in the meter, and followed the brightly colored signs that communicated sentiments like, "Give Peace a Chance," "Legalize Marijuana," and "Power to the People." About twenty students were sitting in a circle on the hard concrete, smoking pot and laughing heartily with each puff they took. I picked out one of the friendlier-looking of the white, cackling faces.

"What's going on here?" I asked him.

"The best way for you to find out is to join our family, sister. Our movement's 'bout intimacy. You dig?"

"Go on."

"We believe in livin' in communes…sharin' our food, our weed, our love. We want free stores, free clinics, free kitchens. We want to establish a new value system where everyone is loved and accepted based on who they are, not what they look like or what they have. We want a life without violence. We demand a media that tells the truth. Right on, my sister!" He raised his fist high in the air, waiting for my response.

"I agree with securing freedom for the oppressed. I don't agree with your views about marijuana. You keep smoking like this, and you'll be brain dead in a few years."

"Come on, sister, it's just an herb. It's natural, and it feels good. If it feels good, do it," another student said, smiling.

There was no mistaking that these students were hippies, as were most of the white student protesters. I agreed with some of their ideas, like protesting the Vietnam War, starting an ecology movement, ending sexual stereotyping, and questioning the country's obsession with materialism. But I couldn't get behind the pot smoking.

Besides, my first love was for my people. I couldn't justify joining a hippie movement that wanted to idealize a society that didn't provide black folks with jobs, decent housing, and health care. Instead, I wanted to see more whites joining our movement. I wanted to see folks like President Richard Nixon and the masses of whites who voted him into a second term taking a stand against inequality. Instead, in the media, I saw school busses in Charlotte, Boston, and Denver getting bombed by whites, as black kids tried to integrate into public schools.

As I turned to leave, one of the students followed me.

"Listen, why not come to the Free John Now rally on the tenth? That's this Friday, at Ann Arbor's Crisler Arena. John Lennon and Yoko Ono are gonna be there."

"Who's the John you're freeing?" I asked.

"John Sinclair, our leader. He just got a law passed that if the pigs bust you for marijuana, you'll only get a five-dollar fine, like a parking ticket. Meantime he's serving a ten-year sentence for possession of two marijuana cigarettes."

The student's words were met by a blank stare from me, so he continued, "He's co-founder of the Detroit Artists' Workshop and one of the best teachers, poets, editors, and organizers around. He cofounded the White Panther Party, a leftist, anti-racist, political organization that's in solidarity with the Black Panther movement, but they're white, you dig? The White Panthers demand free food, clothing, housing, equal access to the media. They embrace a classless society. It's all about a culture of liberation."

"Ummm…thanks for the info. I'll think about it," I said, managing a polite smile.

"Cool, sister, hope to see you on Friday."

It was an eye-opening introduction to the University of Michigan. While their ideas intrigued me, if those kids represented the student population, I wasn't sure I was going to be feeling at home any time soon.

I acclimated quickly to my new apartment and was settled in by the time classes began in January. My new place was on Fuller Street in a complex with fifteen units. It was located on a hill across from the Ann Arbor River in a rustic environment with lots of pine trees. The School of Social Work was only six blocks away. My roommates were black and also seeking degrees in social work.

Pam was an outgoing intellectual from an affluent family. Her father was a prominent businessman in Indiana and her mother was a teacher. She was a few inches taller than I was and, at about one hundred and ten pounds, a little thinner. The freckles across the bridge of her nose mirrored my own. One of the first things I learned about her was how much she hated her hair.

"I can't stand it. It's too fine and too short," she said.

"It's cute. It's like the model Twiggy's," I reassured her, hoping to make a fast friend.

My other roommate, Marilyn, was kind and soft-spoken, from a working-class family like mine. She had a smooth, copper complexion, and took pride in dying her hair the same color. She was always tugging at the front of her shirt, self-conscious because she thought she was too chubby. When she was feeling insecure, she giggled nervously. I got along well with Marilyn, but it was Pam who became my best friend and confidante. She was also my first black Catholic girlfriend; she taught me that Catholics believed in Jesus, the Father, and the Holy Spirit, just like I did.

Pam and I became so close that our professors and colleagues called us "The Radical Bobsey Twins." Our talk, our walk, our presentations, and our lives revolved around organizing and creating change within systems that oppressed people, primarily black people. This line of thinking was encouraged by our professors. They challenged us to create social programs that were outside the box, as opposed to indoctrinating us to maintain the status quo. Instead, we were instructed on how to organize the poor, so they could revolutionize the systems that oppressed them.

I revered my professors: Dr. Jack Rothman, Dr. Madison Foster, Dr. Gail Perryman, and Dr. Howard Brabson. They had us reading and applying techniques from *Pedagogy of the Oppressed* by Paulo Freire, *A Manual for Direct Action* by Oppenheimer and Lakey, *Rules for Radicals* by Saul Alinsky, *Promoting Social Justice* by Jack Rothman, *The Autobiography of Malcolm X* by Alex Haley, and *Bury My Heart at Wounded Knee* by Dee Brown.

One of the most important things I learned during my first semester at Michigan was that I wasn't a slow learner, as my white teachers had led me to believe. I was a creative learner who needed to be challenged. If I could feel it, touch it, and sense it, then I could learn it.

After my first semester, I was removed from academic probation. I had worked hard for my close to A average and had taken nearly twenty credits. I had even found the time to stay connected to my religious roots. I attended Willow Run Church of God in Christ, a sanctified church just outside Detroit. Most of the folks at the church were poor and worked in the auto factory at Willow Run. They reminded me of the folks at my church back home. Every time I attended the Willow Run Church, someone would say, "Sister Gloria, we proud you ain't forgot God. We know it's hard being with them sinners in college and tryin' to serve Jesus. There ain't many young blacks in college who keep comin' to church."

"Thank you," I'd say, but I didn't feel I deserved the compliment. After all, I was changing, too.

As I became more enlightened I questioned the status quo of not just my society, but my religion. I wanted to know why Mom Frances and other women couldn't preach in the holiness church. And what was wrong with women wearing make-up and pants? Why did white Christians use the Bible to endorse slavery and oppress blacks? Why weren't holiness churches on the front line opposing injustice and racism, like a few other churches?

In full creative learning mode, Pam and I began to change our own status quo. When Thanksgiving recess came around, we couldn't justify celebrating the holiday when we knew that it wasn't Columbus who had "discovered" America. Instead, we mourned the annihilation of the Native Americans who were forced to go to the concentration camps more commonly known as reservations. At Thanksgiving dinner, we prayed with our families for God to forgive the hypocrisy of our country.

On some Saturdays, I would go to Chicago to join Reverend Jesse Jackson in the fight against racial injustice by helping with his Operation Breadbasket. My uncle Fredrick was Jesse's best friend, and he played the piano at his church and helped direct the choir. Because of Jesse's charisma, he could organize the masses in a heartbeat. A few phone calls and members of the National Association for the Advancement of Colored People, the Urban League, the National Council of Negro Women, and even liberal whites were united, marching for equal housing and employment opportunities for blacks.

As Pam and I grew more politically conscious together, we also began to share more about our lives. This kind of intimacy came easily to Pam, but I found it difficult.

"I've shared my secrets, Glo. What about yours?"

"I am what you see. I love the Lord, and I want to work on behalf of my people," I said, trying to convince her that I wasn't hiding anything.

"Yeah, I know all of that, but who are you? Sometimes you seem like you have such sadness inside, even though on the outside you're pretending everything's okay. What's goin' on? You can talk to me."

I had never had a friend like Pam before. Her directness made me feel exposed, naked even. It was as if she could see inside my heart, where I hid all the secrets of my childhood. As close as we were, I wasn't sure she would accept me if she knew those secrets, plus our family backgrounds were so different. I didn't want to be judged. I wasn't ready for Pam or anyone else to know who I really was or to dig up the years of pain I'd worked so hard to bury—the abandonment, the molestation, and my hidden rage. I wondered why Pam didn't focus on her boyfriend, Mike, the way she focused on our friendship.

I never gave up my evasiveness, but Pam never gave up pursuing a close friendship with me. She wrote me letters, whether she was living with me or home with her parents; she said it was like keeping a diary. One of my favorite letters was one she wrote me in 1972:

> *G—As I've stated to you in previous conversations or letters, I cannot be completely happy if someone close to me isn't. I'm not saying you are not happy or that I have more than you; what I'm merely saying is that every time I experience happiness, I want so much for you to experience it also, and to the same degree or to an even greater magnitude than I. I've really put you on a pedestal. The beautiful thing about it is that I am aware of your weaknesses and shortcomings, and, of course your immense beauty, and I can still put you up on that pedestal and rejoice that God has sent me another gift so full of marvel and joy and wisdom...I just want you to be happy, Gloria, more than anything else in the world. There are few people aware of my weaknesses, especially to the extent that you are, which leaves me quite vulnerable and insecure at times. But I'm glad I can let my defenses down with you—it makes me appreciate life and love more and more, and also appreciate God.*

No one had ever said things like that to me before. Receiving those letters made me feel special and loved. I suppose Pam knew, even without me being able to tell her, that was what I needed. I wrote letters back, and although I loved her, too, I couldn't give to her in the same measure. The one aspect of my life I was able to talk to her about was my desire to find my biological father, something I had wanted to do since I realized when I was about seven years old that he wasn't coming to find me.

Almost two decades later, I wanted to know whether I'd grown up to look like my father, Robert. Did I get my intelligence from him? I wanted to ask why he abandoned me, and invite him back into my life by asking if he'd come to my university graduation. I wanted to know if he'd proudly say, "That's my girl," when he saw me or if I'd stopped being his girl when he dropped me at the bus station in Eudora all those years ago.

I told Pam how I began the search in November of 1971, just before I started at the University of Michigan. Mom Thelma was helping me; I'd pleaded for as much information as she could provide.

"I heard he moved from Eudora to California, maybe Los Angeles," she said. "He was in the Korean War. Maybe you can check with the VA hospitals in California. They should have a record of his injury."

"I didn't know any of that. What happened to him? Is he okay?"

"He never talked about it. All I know is a typhoon hit his ship and somehow he lost an eye. But I swear you can't tell the difference," Mom Thelma told me.

The majority of blacks who migrated to the state settled in Southern California, so I got addresses for veterans' hospitals in that area from the reference section of the library. I wrote respectful letters to strangers whom I hoped had more answers than my mother did.

> *Dear Sir:*
>
> *I would like your assistance in attempting to locate my father, Mr. Robert D. Twiggs, Jr., whom I have not seen since age three. I am now twenty-four. His approximate age is 45–50. He migrated from Eudora, Arkansas, to Los Angeles in the 1960s.*
>
> *He graduated from Tennessee State University, did graduate work at the University of Iowa, and served in the Korean War in the 1950s. I realize it is not a policy of the hospital to give out former patients addresses; however, I wrote to the VA Wadsworth Hospital and was informed that a Mr. Robert D. Twiggs, Jr., was discharged from the facility on December 31, 1968, and that in order to procure his address, I would have to contact your office. Any information as to my father's whereabouts would be appreciated. Thank you in advance.*
>
> *Sincerely,*
> *Miss Gloria Twiggs Ewing*

For weeks, when I walked to the mailbox I prepared myself for disappointment while at the same time, my heart pounded in anticipation of the good news that might await me there. I received a letter from the San Fernando Hospital. They had called their regional office, but couldn't find contact information for my father. Then I received a typed response stapled to my original letter to the Los Angeles VA Hospital:

Dear Miss Ewing:

We have a Mr. Robert D. Twiggs, Jr., who was discharged from this facility on December 31, 1968. For information with regard to his address, it is suggested that you contact VA Regional Office at 11000 Wilshire Boulevard, Los Angeles, CA 90024.

Sleep wasn't a possibility that night. Instead, I toiled to find the right words for the letter I composed to my father. As the sun rose, I finally sealed the envelope. I'd requested that the Los Angeles VA's regional office forward the letter to the last known address they had for Robert D. Twiggs, Jr. Then I applied a ten-cent stamp and sent the letter off with a prayer that it would be received by my dad.

By the time the letter reached my father I had started graduate school; it took several months before I received a reply. He said he was glad to hear from me and that he, Mother Dear, and my sister Ethel were well. They were living together in Mother Dear's house in south central Los Angeles. The letter was brief, but friendly. I responded with brief letters to him, and our correspondence continued this way for a while.

One letter I received from my father contained a copy of an article about a book he wrote called *Pan-African Language in the Western Hemisphere*. It gave credence to black people's dialect and redefined it as a mainstream language. I couldn't believe the accomplished black man the article talked about was my father.

I gave information about dad's book to the University of Michigan library; they said they would order it. It was a good feeling to brag about him to the white folks I knew. Still, his letters never addressed my more personal questions. I was hoping he'd come to my graduation in May 1973, but he wasn't working and said he couldn't afford the trip. Despite his difficulties, he sent me sixty dollars as a graduation gift.

Even without my biological father present, my graduation was a proud family moment. Mom Frances, Dad Harry, and my sisters Eva and Lydia were there cheering me on in their Sunday best. Mom Thelma was there, dressed in her second-hand designer clothes. As I walked across the stage to collect my master's of social work degree, I could hear them oohing and aahing over me. And when the diploma was placed in my hand, my family broke into a loud chorus of "That's my girl!" I clutched the document to my heart as I walked off the other side of the stage. I couldn't hold back my tears.

I felt like that diploma was proof to society that I was just as good as anyone else. My education was something I'd accomplished on my own, and something that no one could ever take away from me.

This was a sad time for me, too, though. Even though Pam and I would both be living in Detroit, it wasn't going to be the same. Pam would be living with Mike, whom she had married, and I would be working in the inner city. At first, we made an effort to see each other at least once a week, but when Pam decided to pursue her lifelong dream of attending law school it became difficult to keep up, and we eventually lost touch.

Years later, I saw Pamela Fanning Carter's photograph in a history book for young adults. She was the first African American woman in the United States to be elected attorney general of Indiana. I felt just as proud of her as if we were still best friends. Seeing Pam's picture made my heart ache a little. I regretted not telling her my secrets. It was so hard to keep them locked inside and, after all those years, I realized she had been a true friend, someone I could have trusted.

A few months after I received my master's, my dad sent me half the airfare for a flight to Los Angeles; I'd saved up for the other half. I'd never been on a plane as large as the 747 Delta jet I boarded the day of my trip. I thought of the airliner as something like a time machine, taking me to face my past. A lot of thoughts percolated in my head during those hours in the air. I was a grown woman, but inside I felt like the scared and curious little girl I'd been all those years ago. I wondered if my father would still appear tall to me, now that I was all grown up. If his skin was still smooth and caramel colored. If there was still that familiar sparkle in his slanted, brown eyes. More important, would he be proud of the person I'd become? And would he tell me everything I wanted to know?

When the plane landed at Los Angeles International Airport, I walked determinedly down the exit ramp and plunged myself into the sea of waiting bystanders, looking intently at each one. I spotted my father almost immediately. He was the tallest man in the crowd, standing with his head held high and his shoulders back, proudly waiting to see his baby girl. When I got close to him, I quickly glanced into his dark brown eyes to see if I could tell which one was glass, but both matched perfectly, like Mom

Thelma said. Dad's short, kinky hair gave him a scholarly look. The only physical characteristic I seemed to have inherited from him was his high cheekbones. Otherwise, I looked more like my mother.

Dad's long arms opened to me the same way they did when I was a child. He wrapped them around my small waist, as I stood on tiptoe and gently kissed his forehead. Mother Dear was standing close by. She was as beautiful as I remembered, and her Chanel perfume tickled my nostrils just like it did when I was a little girl. My sister Ethel was there. As children, we had looked like twins and were still quite similar to each other. She was the same height as I, with the same pattern of brown freckles splattered across her nose. Her miniskirt revealed that her legs were shapely, like mine, and, when she giggled, it was like hearing my own laughter.

Ethel's six-year-old son tugged at the hem of her skirt and spoke in a small, sweet voice. "Hi, Aunt Gloria, my name is Ricky," he said as he'd rehearsed. I melted as I embraced my first and only nephew.

Dad had driven the family to the airport in his 1970 beige Cadillac, which was as long as a limousine. We put my luggage in the trunk and piled in for the ride to the house. We kept the conversation light, choosing our words carefully.

"How was your flight?" Dad asked.

"It was pleasant, nice."

"We're so proud of your recent degree," Mother Dear said.

"Oh, thank you. Wish you could have been there."

I blushed at the attention, but I was also distracted by the legions of tall palm trees I saw out the window. The trees' trunks reminded me of giraffe necks; I'd never seen trees like that up close.

"They're good for shade," Dad explained. "They're our best friends around July and August, when it gets up into the nineties."

The entire family lived in a modest, white bungalow on Third Street in South Los Angeles. The front yard was small and freshly manicured. Mother Dear may have left Eudora, but it seemed she took her red and pink rose bushes with her. I looked for a tree like Big Berry to confirm that I was really home, but nothing like it seemed to grow in the area.

There wasn't a lot of room inside the house, but it was cozy. There were three bedrooms, a bathroom, a kitchen, living room, and dining room with a large oak table and a breakfront. Piles of paper cluttered one corner of the living room, and Dad's teaching books from California State Los Angeles took up the space of another. Littered about the room were old newspapers and pictures of the family, including me; there were no pictures of Mom Thelma, I noticed. Although Big Berry was absent, there was something else there to confirm I was home—Granddad's two taxidermied deer heads.

"Mother Dear, I can't believe you brought those with you!"

"Couldn't leave them behind, sweetie. They were your granddad's prized possessions."

"I'll just pretend they're not there," I said, laughing. I was no longer afraid of those glassy eyes, like I was when I was a child. I looked into them, then into the eyes of my father. I still couldn't tell which one was real. I decided it was being alive that made the difference, not what parts you had.

Mother Dear hadn't lost her knack for cooking. Just for me, she had labored over her mouth-watering crispy fried chicken, corn bread, greens, and yams. She remembered that it had been my favorite meal. Even though I shied away from eating meat, I couldn't refuse this gift. I felt my grandmother's love in each bite of greasy chicken I took.

Ethel was two when she and I had last seen each other, but we got along so well it was if we'd never been separated. The words flowed freely between us, although only when we were discussing more superficial matters. My sister was passionate about being a Buddhist. But Ethel grew shy when I asked her serious questions about her life, about our life.

"Do you know what happened between Mom and Dad?"

"I wondered about it as I got older, but I never asked," she said.

"Did you ever wonder why you were left behind?"

"In the back of my mind. I knew Dad and Mom divorced, and that's all I knew. I heard Mom was pretty. Sometimes she would call, but eventually the calls stopped. Mother Dear was my mother."

Trying to get Ethel to share her feelings with me was like pulling teeth. It must've been how Pam felt, trying to get me to open up to her.

"What do you want to be?" I prodded. To my surprise, Ethel's face brightened.

"I want to be a Hollywood actress. I've done a lot of community theater. I'm in school, studying theater and dance now. Dad and Mother Dear help me raise Ricky while I attend college."

"That's right, sis. Reach for the sky! Go for it!"

I'd been hoping Ethel was someone who would understand, someone I could connect deeply with. But I didn't want to scare her away. I didn't make any overtures into uncovering the past after my first day in Los Angeles, and instead focused on having fun with my family, which included a trip to Disneyland, shopping on Olvera Street, and walking down Hollywood Boulevard taking pictures of the stars' names embedded in the concrete.

I waited patiently for Dad to tell me about my childhood. Surely, he knew I must've had questions—not just about my life, but about his. Instead, he engaged in intellectual chatter about black history, politics, his new book, and the issues he was having with the department head at Cal State. I didn't want to push and alienate my family just as I was getting to know them again. Still, it seemed strange to me that that family matters were all so hush, hush—as if there was a dark family secret they were trying to conceal. Then again, I had my secrets, too. But I couldn't open up to a family who wouldn't open up to me. I hoped that would change when Dad and I made our goodbyes at the airport, that he would reveal more of himself to me.

"We're so happy you came, darlin.' Let's keep in touch. I love you," he said as we hugged.

"I love you, too, Dad."

That was the sum of our exchange. I believed that my father loved me, and despite everything, I'd never stopped loving him. But where had the man been for twenty years? Wasn't he at all curious about the children he abandoned in 1950? After all, I was the one who sought him out, not the other way around. He loved me, but why didn't he want to be a father to me, or to Robert and Bobbie?

I returned to Michigan with more questions than I'd had before I left. Although my family members were now known to me, who they really were was still a mystery. I was frustrated and disappointed. After waiting so many years to see them again, my family wasn't able, or wasn't willing, to give me the answers I so desperately needed. While my father was proud of my education, I sensed that he was also threatened by my thirst for knowledge. He knew I was his most relentless child, and that eventually I'd find the answers I was seeking. I certainly wasn't giving up. If it took writing, calling, and showing up at my family's doorstep over and over, I was going to find out what I needed to know. But this was only one part of my life's journey; I didn't just need to come to terms with my past—I needed to build a future.

Gloria Ewing Lockhart

Photo 1

My maternal grandparents, Violet
(1893-1982) and Earl Young (1891-1971) of
Mt. Pleasant, Tennessee.

Photo 2

My biological mother, Thelma Young Twiggs, as
a young woman, Eudora, Arkansas.

Photo 3

My biological father, Robert De Leon Twiggs, II,
as a young man, Eudora, Arkansas.

My adoptive parents, Rev. Harry and
Frances Ewing, as a young couple,
Lansing, Michigan--late 40s.

Photo 4

Photo 5

Mom and her second husband, Harold
Hoffenkamp, came to see me in Lansing,
Michigan, 1958.

Photo 6

Eva Marie Ewing, my adopted sister and me,
Lansing, Michigan, 1959.

Photo 7

Santa and me, around eight years old, photo
courtesy of Knapp's Department Store,
Lansing, Michigan.

Photo 8

The beginning of my track career, Sexton High School, Lansing, Michigan, 1963.

Photo 9

Aug. 16, '63

Lansing Girl To Try-Out For Olympics

Gloria Ewing

Gloria Ewing, 16, is now training for the Diamond Jubilee Year Track and Field meet, junior division, to be held at the University of Detroit Stadium on August 24.

Gloria is being trained by Jerry Young, a student teacher in history at Jackson Junior High School. Training for the AAU meet has taken place at Michigan State University.

"I enjoy track very much," Gloria is quoted as saying. "And I wish there were other junior girls interested enough to participate in track."

She said that she became interested in sports when she was 13 years old, but didn't think about competing until she was 14.

In 1962, Gloria won two gold Young American Awards in the 50-yard dash and the 100-yard dash at Comstock Park during Lansing's Centennial Celebration.

Miss Ewing also won the 100-yard

"Lansing Girl To Try Out for Olympics," photo courtesy of *Lansing State Journal*, August 16, 1963.

Photo 10

Girls Enter Flint Meet

Lansing Lightningettes entered the Olympic Development track meet at Flint Northern high school last week.

Thirty-six girls entered the 100-yard dash, and Gloria Ewing of the Lansing team placed third with 12.4. Martha Ruffin was fourth with 12.6.

The 440-yard dash was won by Martha Ruffin in 63 seconds, and Sue Phelps came in third with 64.7. Mary Dorne was fourth with 65.2.

The next meet for the girls will be another Olympic Development meet Sunday, July 26 at Navarre Field in Monroe. The next U.S. Federation meet will be August 1, at 1 p.m. at Detroit Catholic Central high school.

"Girls Enter Flint Meet," article courtesy of *Lansing State Journal*, July 1964.

Photo 11

TALENT FROM SEXTON 1964

The "Big Red Review" was the theme of Sexton's talent show recently. Applause, laughter, and cheers were heard from the auditorium as Sexton High students displayed their talents.

Getting the show under way, a girl's chorus line presented its version of a selection from South Pacific. Next Gretchen Goodrich sang, followed by a reminiscence by the Sexton Players.

Diane Rivett, pianist, played a medley of songs from West Side Story. Gloria Ewing's rendition of "Stopping in the Big City" filled the auditorium with laughter. Bill Geller presented an interpretive dance highlighting the entertainment and was a skit put on by four faculty members depicting a classroom day.

Mike Crnos played the piano, followed by Jim Cool singing. Mary Jo Landry displayed her coordinating ability and Roslyn Abrams presented a 3D skating skit.

Wrapping up the Big Red Review were songs by "the Chandlos." This group consists of leader, Don Krueger, Terry Miller, Tom Wharton, Jesse Orta, and Dan Albert.

Who knows? If the talent displayed is a sample of their ability, some of these talented sons may seek a career in show business.

"Talent From Sexton," article courtesy of *Lansing State Journal*, 1964.

Photo 12

CHEERS BY EAR—"The loudspeaker system at Sexton High School has found a special use besides routine school announcements. The school's cheerleaders Thursday turned the loudspeakers into a way of leading a pep rally without the students leaving their classroom chairs. The cheerleaders yelled into the central microphone in the school office and the student body responded with yells. The pep rally by wire was designed to urge the Big Reds basketball team on to victory in their state basketball tournament game with Everett Thursday night. The Big Reds reacted on the air and whipped Everett 52-50. The cheerleaders are (clockwise) Donna Holquist, Pat Kelley, Connie Inkes, Sue Suding, Gloria Ewing and Kris Turk. (State Journal Photo)

"Cheers By Ear," article courtesy of *Lansing State Journal*, March 5, 1965.

Photo 13

THE ZODIAC

"The Signs of the Times" at Sexton High School

1954 NATIONAL BELLAMY AWARD WINNER

J. W. SEXTON HIGH SCHOOL, LANSING, MICHIGAN, TUESDAY, MAY 25, 1965

Popularity Poll

Best Personality	Sue Giroux	Gary Rossman
Most Popular	Sue Giroux	John Holms
Most Talkative	Nancy Adams	Tyrone Fletcher
Most Likely to Succeed	Rosalie Hudnut	Morgan Carter
Best Dressed	Lee Park	Mike Saul
Best Figure and Physique	Dotti Ferle	Ed Toomey
Most Studious	Margaret Rodgers	Jay Petersen
Nicest Hair	Shirley Poll	Mike Saul
Nicest Eyes	Shirley Poll	Greg Hardy
Best Disposition	Cindy Sanford	Greg Black
Best Athlete	Gloria Ewing	John Holms

"Popularity Poll," voted Best Athlete, article courtesy of *The Zodiac*, Sexton High School, May 25, 1965.

Photo 14

My senior prom date, Boyd Lewis, photo courtesy of Sexton High School, 1965.

Photo 15

Huron Girls Compete In Track

by Scotty Wainright

Gloria Ewing, Alma Outley and Karen Turner are a few of the names of a group of young ladies that are very rare in this part of the country. These are members of Eastern Michigan's track team. This group—through pain, devotion and personal sacrifice—is making women a moving force in the sport of track and field. Through desire and talent they are showing that inter-collegiate track for women can be a rewarding investment for the school and the individuals involved.

In this state alone, with such athletic powerhouses as Michigan State University and the University of Michigan, Eastern Michigan University and Central Michigan are the only schools that have a women's track team and this is truly a tragic occurrence.

Miss Coeun, the faculty advisor for this group, talked of why there is such a lack of interest in women's track. "Girls haven't been brought up in physical education. They are caught up in so many other things. They haven't been brought up to go all out past their natural ability. Many don't understand the reason behind the hard work and the significance of the results. Women as a whole just aren't ready."

The reasons they aren't ready, in many instances, are the lack of instruction and spirit displayed on the elementary and high school level. It takes a young lady with a lot of natural talent and funk to be picked up by a track club. While men are en-

couraged to be good in sports, to women it is something to be admired but avoided. The old line "it isn't lady-like" is a perfect analogy of the thinking of many.

Gloria Ewing, a transfer student from Tennessee, certainly knows what it is to run with and to be good and the results are shown in her great showing this season. All the girls who lay around and worry about too much exercise ruining their figure should take a look at Miss Ewing. Her running is only excelled by her beauty. She was second to the mile in the Junior Nationals in Chicago on April 6. During the coming weeks besides running for Eastern she will be entering some AAU meets as a member of the Detroit Track Club.

Alma Oatley is an outstanding sprinter on the team. She has run the 220 in 24 seconds and if that isn't good take a look at the times for the intramural 220 this year. She also runs the 50 yd. and 100 yd. dashes. Karon Turner is another outstanding performer who works very hard with very favorable results. She runs the 440 and 880.

Miss Coeun says, "we plan to go as far as the needs of the girls dictate." The girls just mentioned work very hard and no one acknowledges their devotion and success. These girls deserve nothing less than solid support. Maybe someday students can talk of Eastern Michigan being a power in both men and women's track; listening in Coach Parks???

"Huron Girls Compete In Track," article courtesy of *The Eastern Echo*, May 24, 1968, Eastern Michigan University.

Photo 16

"Students, police clash in four day protest," photo and article courtesy of *The Eastern Echo*, May 8, 1970, Eastern Michigan University.

Photo 17

My family attended my graduation from Eastern Michigan University, 1970; received Bachelor of Science degree: (back row) Mom Frances, Me, Eva, Dad Harry; (front row) Lydia.

Photo 18

My love for children and the community began at Carstens Elementary School as a
community organizer, Detroit, Michigan, 1974.

Photo 19

Chief Nana Boafo Asiedu, II
(oldest Chief in Ghana)

First of three trips to Africa; I
was honored to spend time with
the oldest chief in Ghana, Nana
Boafu Asiedu, II, 1975.

Photo 20

One of the first African American women to reach the summit of Mt. Kilimanjaro, 19,340 feet, 1976 in Tanzania, E. Africa.

Photo 21

After my climb to Mt. Kilimanjaro, I received a citation, 1976.

Photo 22

I was proud to have Mom Thelma and Mom Frances walk me down the aisle, June 1977.

Photo 23

A special moment with my daughter, Tiombe, at Disney World, around two years old.

Photo 24

My daughter, Tiombe, interviewed the legendary Rosa Parks for a school project; around 1987, Atlanta, Georgia, photo courtesy of Gloria Ewing Lockhart.

Photo 25

My performance of "Miss Johnson's Story", a one-woman show at the famous Ebenezer Baptist Church, Atlanta, around 1988.

Photo 26

I marched against the Ku Klux Klan in Jonesboro, Georgia, 1988, photo courtesy of Gloria Ewing Lockhart.

Photo 27

My daughter, Tiombe, age 11, sang *Lift Every Voice* at a mass rally for the Honorable Nelson Mandela, Bobby Dodd Stadium, Atlanta, 1990, photo courtesy of Gloria Ewing Lockhart.

Photo 28

I finished 26.2 miles of the LA Marathon, 1997, photo courtesy of MARATHONFOTO.

Photo 29

The Los Angeles City Council passed an ordinance restricting alcohol and to-bacco billboard advertising 1,000 feet from schools and public venues in 1998. The initiative began in 1996 with the Los Angeles County Alcohol, To-bacco and Drug Policy Coalition. I was a part of this city-wide group, and photographed this billboard that overlooked Santa Monica Elementary School in East Hollywood, CA. Our efforts demonstrated what happens when a com-munity organizes, and how much they can effect change. Photo courtesy of Gloria Ewing Lockhart, 1996.

Photo 30

I worked with a host of community partners to organize the first "Peace March" in Hollywood, CA while working in violence prevention at Children's Hospital Los Angeles, Adolescent Medicine, 2000.

Photo 31

In 2006, I was appointed by Los Angeles Mayor Antonio Villaraigosa to serve as a Commissioner of the Harbor Area Planning Commission. This appointment was the result of my work as Executive Director of Toberman Neighborhood Center.

Photo 32

I received the honor of *Woman of the Year*, by former California Assembly member Betty Karnette and former Speaker of the California State Assembly Karen Bass, Sacramento, CA, 2008, photo courtesy of Russel Collins Stiger.

Photo 33

A proud moment with my daughter at her film debut of *Inside A Change*, Manhattan, NY, 2009.

CHAPTER TEN

I continued to maintain a relationship with my relatives in California, particularly my sister Ethel, but I was determined not to be consumed by unanswered questions about my biological family; I had to move forward with my life. In the summer of 1973, that meant getting serious about finding a professional job. My dreams of making history as an Olympic athlete had been supplanted by a desire to make history as a force for social change.

Looking back, I had long been on the path to that place, but it was witnessing my friend Joe's abuse at the hands of the police that made it impossible for me to go in any other direction. In my heart, I would always be a runner, and I believed the strength and determination I learned during my athletic training would serve me well in the race to save children from the lasting effects of social injustice.

My job search began on the bulletin board at the School of Social Work. It didn't take much effort to get my first interview, which was with the administrator of the State of Michigan Department of Social Services, whom I knew through my parents in Lansing. Robert Little was a handsome, dignified black man—eight years my senior. His wooly, dark brown hair was closely cut to his pear-shaped face. I reached out to shake his hand, slightly intimidated by the extreme eloquence with which he pronounced his words and the serious way he looked out at me from his scholarly glasses.

"Hello, Mr. Little. Pleasure meeting you."

"Hello, Miss Ewing. I see you're from Lansing," he said, smiling in what I took to be an effort to relieve my nervousness.

"Yes, I am. My father, Reverend Harry Ewing, and my mother, Frances, know your parents well."

He paused. "Oh—my, yes, yes...the preacher. There weren't many of us blacks in Lansing. Everybody knew everybody. I assume your father knew my brother, Malcolm?" The brother of which Robert spoke was Malcolm X.

"Yes. He once told me Malcolm went to the Lansing Church of God. Dad said he was like a worm in hot ashes, always yapping in church and picking on kids."

"That was my brother," Mr. Little said, chuckling.

"How are your mother and the rest of the family?" I asked.

"Everybody is fine. My mother still lives in Lansing with my brother. Since you live nearby in Church Hill Downs, you should stop by and see us."

After our exchange of pleasantries was over, Mr. Little asked a series of questions about my group work courses and my experience as an intern at Ypsilanti State Mental Hospital. I also talked about my experience at Ann Arbor Community Center.

"You're the kind of social worker we need here at the state level," Mr. Little said, nodding. "You're sharp. You have experience as a community organizer. I think you can change the lives of children and families. You'll be working in our new foster-care program placing adjudicated delinquents, twelve to seventeen years old, in suitable foster homes. You'll have to work closely with the foster parents and the kids' families since our goal is to reunify the teens with their natural parents."

"I won't disappoint you, Mr. Little," I said, accepting my first professional social work job. I'd be making about twenty-eight thousand dollars a year. I wasn't going to get rich, but it sure beat working on the assembly line like Dad Harry.

I was assigned to delinquency services at 13131 Lyndon Avenue in Detroit. My supervisor, Bernice, was a tall, soft-spoken black woman in her thirties. Bernice had a strong work ethic. She started early in the morning and stayed at the office until the job was done. She navigated me through the bureaucracy she'd become so familiar with over the years. Everything needed to be recorded—I mean everything we did except going to the restroom had to be written down in a log.

What I liked most about the job was also the hardest thing about it—finding homes for older black kids and poor white ones whom nobody wanted because of their troubled past. Most of these kids had had run-ins with the law. They were society's "throwaway kids," meaning everyone had given up on them.

Almost every day an adolescent said to me, "I want to be loved. I want someone to care for me." It didn't matter if the child was black or white. They all wanted the same thing, and I was passionate about getting it for them. But the reality was placement was nearly impossible for black adolescents. If you were a white kid, even if you had a strike against you, foster placement was a thousand times easier.

When I'd been on the job for only a few months, there was a shooting at our headquarters on Temple Street. Some clients got fed up with being disrespected. So they strapped handguns to their bodies and strong-armed their way into the building. They were after the social workers, but they shot at anyone and anything in sight. After that, metal detectors were placed in the buildings and more police were hired to guard them.

While I certainly never condoned violence for any reason, I understood the rage that gave rise to the shootings. Many of my colleagues treated their young clients like they were nothing more than the case number in their file. They had no faith in these kids' ability to change the course of their lives and were just waiting for them to age out of the foster care system, after which they would enter the prison system. I always treated my clients with respect. I wanted the best for them, to give them the tools they needed to change their lives, tools that would get them out of the welfare system permanently, not just get their file off my desk.

I worked beyond the required eight hours a day to find safe and caring homes for these kids. I spoke at black churches. I appeared on black radio stations, like WJLB. The most exposure I got was from the *Detroit Free Press*. They ran a feature story entitled, "Willing to Accept a Challenge... With Love" with my picture right alongside it. The feature was so successful in calling attention to the need for quality foster homes that for weeks after it ran I was receiving calls from blue-collar families who wanted to help. Their homes were small and cluttered, but these folks were caring foster parents.

After working in social services for about a year, my attitude began to change and just as I had understood why those gunmen were so angry,

I grew to understand why my colleagues were so disillusioned. I came to see the system as a trap, a revolving door for the poor. Once a kid got into the system, it was hard to get out. They'd go from foster care to welfare, then into the juvenile justice system, and more often than not that led to incarceration in an adult prison. There were no programs designed to take clients out of the system and put them into jobs or send them back to school, and the system, of course, was controlled by whites. The bigotry enraged me.

I wanted more for my people—more than I could give them working for the county foster care system. Yet, when I saw the sorry state of Detroit, which was 45 percent black, it became clear why the welfare system wasn't working.

Mayor Roman S. Gribbs and the Detroit Police Department had started a program called STRESS: Stop the Robberies, Enjoy Safe Streets. They essentially turned Detroit into a police state, with undercover decoys marching through black neighborhoods, regularly knocking to the ground then frisking black men who were walking innocently down the street. News programs broadcast images of white policemen beating blacks mercilessly. In two years, they had killed twenty-two people. All were black except one.

Despite my frustration, I stayed at my job one more year, until 1974, when I got a new one with the Detroit public schools. On paper, I was a school community agent, but in action, I was organizing economically disadvantaged parents to become active in their children's education. This was the kind of position I'd wanted when I graduated. It was a government-funded job and my pay was a little more than working in foster care at about thirty thousand dollars per year, which was decent money back then.

I was assigned to Carstens Elementary School on the lower east side in a neighborhood called the Jefferson-Mack. There were other agents assigned to inner-city elementary schools, but Carstens was located in the largest, poorest neighborhood, the one white folks scurried past to get home to the wealthy, adjacent suburb of Grosse Pointe, where not one single black family lived. Jefferson-Mack had one of the highest school truancy rates, the highest crime rate, and the most families on welfare than any other community in the city. Fortunately, I was up for the challenge of motivating parents to serve on the school advisory council, and to make decisions about hiring a new principal.

I listened to people from the community, like Mrs. Baker, the attendance officer with whom I shared an office. She was a fifty-year-old, soft-spoken, eloquent black woman who always walked with distinction, with her head up and shoulders back. The pinhead-size moles on her face and her salt-and-pepper bubble curls reminded me of Mom Francis, and I immediately took to her. Mrs. Baker knew every parent and all two thousand children in the school by name, and she agreed to mentor me on life in the ghetto.

"Black parents want the same for their children as white parents want for theirs, but they don't know how to change being poor, okay? Their children come to school malnourished with snotty noises, wearing urine-smelling clothes, underwear that ain't been changed for days. Many of the parents are alcoholics or dope fiends. You got to start where they are. Okay?"

"Okay!" I always responded when Mrs. Baker shared her wisdom with me, letting her know I'd heard what she said, and that I understood.

I started by knocking on doors, handing out flyers explaining who I was and why parental involvement was so important. My first recruit was Karen, the mother of a happy third grader who happened to be a slow learner.

"Please come in, Miss Ewing, have a seat," Karen said when I knocked on her door. I enthusiastically accepted her invitation and took a seat on her faded gray couch.

"Thank you. I see Michael in my office almost every day. He's such a charming boy," I told her.

"May I get you a glass of water?"

"That would be fine, thank you," I replied politely.

I looked around at the sparsely furnished living room. There was a recliner that showed a lot of wear on the head and armrests. Instead of a television stand or coffee table, a small portable black-and-white television was positioned on stacks of yellow pages. The bright morning sun pierced the white sheer curtains that were only long enough to reach halfway down the bay window. My eyes caught the interesting pattern running along the dingy beige wallpaper. I couldn't figure out what the design was until I squinted and realized I was looking at hundreds of baby cockroaches moving slowly across the wall. I remained calm. I didn't want Karen to feel embarrassed.

"Michael is doing poorly in school," I said to her when she came back with the glass of water. "We'd like you to get involved so you can help him do better."

"What can I do? I can't even read. Can't get no job."

"When you join the parent council, it's your ideas that will count. We can also help you get services that will help improve your and Michael's situation. There are lots of parents dealing with the same problems as you. The council meets once a month at the school. I can give you a ride."

"Well, I don't see much point, but this is the first time I've been asked to do anything. I want better for my boy than what I got. I'll try."

It took a while to convince people, but eventually the community came out: teachers, parents, ministers, small black business leaders, and a block club president. It was through this work that I met Horace Sheffield; his family called him Skip. He was a fine black man, over six feet tall and nothing but muscle. His wavy hair was cut close to his head. He was humble, not stuck on his looks like a lot of mixed race people were. There was something militant about him, too, though. He said he was like his father, a famous union organizer in Detroit who had been a friend of Dr. Martin Luther King, Jr.

"Glo, I'm on a mission to change the plight of black folks in Detroit. We got to stop letting white folks sell them a bad bill of goods. I see what you're doing in the Jefferson-Mack community. If we work together, we can change things," he told me.

From that moment on, we worked as if the revolution was coming tomorrow. We became allies committed to ending oppression among our people. We also promised each other that, to preserve our friendship, we'd never get involved sexually. It was hard, because we had a crush on each other from the start.

We started by organizing the parents to get them the crossing guard they wanted at East Vernor, a high-traffic street where too many kids had been hit by cars headed to Grosse Pointe. For years, the school board had said there were no funds for a guard or a light. The city needed to understand that was no longer an acceptable answer.

Every day, parents marched in front of the school carrying signs that read: "Our school needs a crossing guard," "Children need safety," and "Save our children, save our children." They chanted the same slogans that were on the signs. In a few weeks, the city found money to hire a crossing guard. Encouraged by this small but important victory, and no longer skeptical about their ability to make a difference, the parents brought new parents to the council meetings, where they demanded books with black people in them. They wanted cleaner and safer neighborhoods.

I felt good about my work, but I wanted to effect change on a larger scale. My passion led me to join the Detroit branch of the National Alliance Against Racist and Political Repression (NAARPR). The controversial organization fought to end racism and abolish capital punishment. The National Committee to Free Angela Davis, the American Indian Movement, and other small grassroots groups banded together to start NAARPR, and I heard that the government was keeping dossiers on all of the group's members, some of whom were known communists. But NAARPR wasn't built on communist principles; instead, the group used the principles of democracy as a catalyst for change, particularly the First Amendment.

We got millions of signatures on petitions to stop the building of Butner Prison in North Carolina. The prison was going to offer shock treatment among other outdated and barbaric punitive behavior-modification programs. The South was notorious for having the most blacks on death row.

Shortly after I joined NAARPR, I went on my first freedom march. I took a Greyhound bus from Detroit to Raleigh, North Carolina, where, on July 4, 1974, thousands of people mobilized from around the country to end the racism and political repression that pervaded America's penal system. We were marching for Jo Ann Little and the Wilmington Ten.

Jo Ann, a young black woman, had been convicted of stabbing a white prison guard with an ice pick as he raped her. We believed that, given the circumstances of her crime, she should be exonerated for the murder.

In the Wilmington Ten case, Reverend Ben Chavis, a popular young black minister from the United Methodist Church, was arrested with nine black students for allegedly firebombing a grocery store and shooting at police officers in Wilmington. City officials had denied black students' request to hold a memorial service for Martin Luther King, Jr., in January 1971. Violent demonstrations erupted, including the firebombing, and the ten men were given a combined sentence of 282 years; the white woman arrested with them was freed.

When our group of about a hundred arrived in Raleigh, we joined the thousands of people who had arrived before us. We looked like a rainbow—blacks, whites, Asians, Latinos, and Native Americans standing side by side, demanding an end to the injustice. We carried signs and banners through the streets of Raleigh that read, "Free Jo Ann Little. Free the Wilmington

Ten. Don't Build Butner." My shock at seeing whites marching in solidarity with blacks, arm in arm, made me realize that my bias toward whites was steeped in the bad experiences I'd had during my childhood. Despite how much the world had changed since then, too much had stayed the same; it was on that march that I saw the Ku Klux Klan for the first time.

There were hundreds of Klan members at the march, standing shoulder to shoulder in military fashion. Their faces were hidden behind white silk hoods with small holes cut out so they could see. I thought maybe there was something behind their eyes that would help explain why. But their eyes were hidden well behind the hoods so that they were nothing more than dark orbs, like the eyes of my grandfather's stuffed deer heads.

Most Klan members' robes were white with flowing capes of the same color, but some capes were red, black, or dark green. Stripes that matched whatever color cape a member was wearing and which seemed to signify rank decorated the sleeves of the robes. Everyone's robe boldly displayed on its front a red circle with a white cross. There were other emblems that I didn't understand, but the cross was clearly the Klan's trademark insignia. Hooded men and hoodless women proudly waved the Confederate and American flags, and the Klansmen at the front of the line carried a banner that said, "Peaceful Patriotic Protest Knights of the Ku Klux Klan."

The youngest Klan member I saw was a child who appeared to be about five years old. The kids were robed, but not hooded, like the women. They carried signs as tall as they were that said, "Nigger go home." A lady stood next to a boy, presumably his mother, holding an incorrectly punctuated sign that said, "White Citizen's Council." As I passed, she raised her fist and belted, "White Power!"

There was a national guardsman shielding each Klansmen. The national guard hadn't varied its uniform since my college days. The guardsmen wore helmets and face guards and held their batons close to their chest. Some favored their rifle, which they held stiffly upright. They had been summoned by the White House to protect the Klan, yet we marched with no assurance of our safety. Fortunately, there were no physical confrontations, no need for the protection that we didn't have.

Our peaceful protest was a success, bringing national attention to the injustices of the American prison system. Our actions led to the US Court of Appeals overturning all convictions in the Wilmington Ten case. The court found that the state had illegally withheld exculpatory evidence, and that the trial court had employed methods that denied the defendants their constitutional rights. It wasn't until 1981 that North Carolina dropped all charges against the wrongfully convicted men. Jo Ann Little was finally acquitted for stabbing the white prison guard, a landmark decision as it was the first time in the United States that an African American woman was able to assert her right to self-defense against white rapists. And Butner Prison was put on hold.

While my peers got high on marijuana and LSD, I was getting high on community organizing and protest marches. My efforts provided a momentary rush, but the satisfaction never lasted. Instead, each victory and small step forward produced within me the feeling that I needed to do more. I wanted to truly embrace my people and my culture. I hadn't succeeded in learning much about my immediate family, but I was sure my ancestors had stories to share with me.

In 1975, I began to save money for a trip to Africa. I needed two thousand dollars. While I was pursuing my quest, I met Kofi, who turned out to be an answer to a prayer. He was a Ghanaian of about twenty who was studying at one of the universities in Detroit. He had beautiful, straight, white teeth, and his face lit up when he smiled. His eyes were sunken, as he was far too lean. He wore his hair in a short, dark-brown Afro, and his skin was creamy, like chocolate. He wasn't handsome, but he was charming and kind. And he was crazy about me, even though he understood that we were just going to be friends. Kofi was supportive of my plans to visit Africa.

"When you go to my country, you can stay with my family," he offered. "Ghana is the friendliest country on the continent. It was the first African country to become independent. All of our ancestors came from there."

Kofi taught me Twi, one of the many tribal languages of Ghana. English had become the dominant language there, but Twi was often still spoken. It was hard to get the hang of. It sounded like French, Spanish, Italian, and Greek combined. Learning languages had always been hard for me, but I had never encountered anything like Twi. I was only able to learn about one word a day. Kofi assured me I'd do fine in his country with even my limited native vocabulary.

In the summer of 1975, I left on Trans-International Airlines for Accra, Ghana; it was a fourteen-hour trip. When I arrived at Kotoka International Airport, I saw an amazing sea of beautiful black people with smooth, shiny, eggplant-colored complexions. Their brown eyes were sunken into their skulls, like Kofi's, and they had broad noses and lips. Most women wore their hair in short, nappy Afros like the men, but those who were more Westernized donned black wigs done up in a bouffant style. The older women wore traditional African head wraps that matched their long dresses, the material of which was decorated with bold, African prints, while the older men were clad in colorful dashikis. The young people wore bell-bottom blue jeans, t-shirts, and platform shoes.

Kofi's parents, brother, aunts, cousins, grandparents, and friends were all anxiously waiting for me. They were bobbing their heads, searching for my likeness while holding a wallet-size photo of me and a large worn cardboard sign that read, "Welcome GLORIA."

I was surprised by how much they looked like Dad Harry's kin. One of them grabbed me, leading to a flurry of hugs and kisses on the cheek. Kofi's family spoke English with a heavy British accent.

"I'm Papa Ampudu, your African father. This is Mama Ampudu, your African mother, and Adofo, Kofi's brother, who's now your brother, too."

Papa Ampudu went on to graciously introduce Kofi's aunts, uncles, and cousins to me, but their names were too complicated to remember. Finally, it was my turn to say something.

"*Ma dasi,*" I said in Twi. It meant "hello."

"You know Twi, our language? You know it?"

"A little, I learned from Kofi."

"You're beautiful, like your picture. You're Nigerian, maybe half-cast," someone commented.

"What's 'half-cast' mean?" I asked softly.

"Mixed white blood."

As I attempted to respond, the women began running their fingers through my cornrows, something I hadn't expected. I was the first black American they had seen outside of pictures in outdated issues of *Ebony* magazine, and they were fascinated by me. They continued to stare as we walked to Papa's yellow car. The poor little Honda looked like a banana; seven of us squeezed into its four seats. The rest of my welcome party took taxis, or tro-tros, which were what the city's buses were called.

Those of us in the car were packed in so tightly, people were hanging out the doors and windows. If anyone shifted their weight, I was sure the car would have tipped over. I saw nothing out its windows that resembled what I saw depicted in Tarzan and Jane movies, or read in American history books. Adofo served as my personal tour guide.

"Take a look—this is Black Star Square. The black star on the arch stands for our independence from the British in March 1957. Ghana was the first country in Africa to be free. There's the University of Ghana. Students become doctors, teachers, and lawyers, like in America. Here's our new sports stadium. We love soccer so much, like you Americans love football."

Kofi's family's neighborhood was small, taking up only about a one-mile radius. The houses were only one level and built out of stucco; they were shaped like perfect square boxes. My African parents' home was just as simple inside. There was a living room with a couch and a few chairs. The bedroom contained a queen-size bed and a dresser. The kitchen had space for the table and four chairs it held, and nothing more. The cooking was done outside in a wood shed on a wood stove. Next to it was an aluminum shed for showering, with a plastic shower curtain draped over the doorway for privacy.

"We don't have hot water, only cold," Papa said.

The toilet was also outdoors. I couldn't help but be reminded of my grandparents' home in Mt. Pleasant. I smiled, thinking how my stay there had prepared me so well for my trip to Africa. I felt for a moment as if my life was unfolding exactly as it was meant to.

As the guest, I was given the main bedroom while family members slept on the couch or with other relatives in the community. Kofi's family made me feel as if their home was my home. The only difficult adjustment I had to make was getting used to the lizards that shared the house with us. On my first day, I noticed two small ones crawling on my bedroom ceiling.

"Will they fall?" I asked, trying not to show how afraid I was.

"No, no. They're like flies in America, harmless. They run from you," said Papa.

That first night I kept waking up to make sure those lizards stayed in their place. When I awoke the next morning, my reptilian roommates were gone. Mama and Papa had risen before me and prepared a wonderful breakfast of black tea, biscuits, and orange slices, which I enjoyed very much. The delicious aroma of freshly made food and the sounds of family made me feel as if I hadn't traveled all that far, and when I closed my eyes, it was as if I were in my real home.

We spent my first full day in Ghana shopping at Makola market in the ninety-degree heat. Because of how crowded the market was, the tro-tro, a van, was the best way to get there. What a wonderful experience I had shopping! And I was treated to all sorts of delicious smells—sugar cane, yams, cassava, potatoes, and body oils. Not all the smells were good, though. The hardest one to get used to was the stench of body odor. People showered in the morning but, by the afternoon, their armpits reeked. Costing about five dollars, deodorant was too expensive to buy.

The market was bustling with Africans of assorted colors—caramel, dark brown, blue-black because people came from miles around to shop there. I soon became lost in the large crowd, moving in whichever direction the pushing and shoving of the masses carried me. People were bartering with merchants for colorful cloth. Some stopped to purchase dried fish being sold on small, weather-beaten wooden tables. Some merchants sold Colgate toothpaste, Dial soap, bleaching creams, and perfumes for triple the price the items sold for in the States.

I was amazed by the women I saw. They had round, protruding hips and strong backs. They could carry heavy porcelain bowls on their heads and at the same time balance a baby on their back. The bowls were filled with pieces of handmade, black soap used for bathing, which the women sold for ten cents. The women moved gracefully, like ballerinas, as if the bowls and babies they carried were light as a feather. It made me proud to see how much my curvaceous hips resembled theirs.

At the end of the outing, after I reunited with my host family, we walked along the gravel road together back to the tro-tro, passing a row of women crouched in a sitting position with babies tied to their backs. They begged us to buy the dry beans that were rationed into small piles in front of them. They were Ghana's poor, and they were the majority. Their nails were split and tattered. Their clothes were clean, but thin from wear. It appeared, from their dry skin, lips, and hollow cheeks, that they were malnourished. I reached into my purse, which was strapped across my chest to keep it safe, and gave several of them peswa, Ghana's main currency.

"You American?" one of the women asked.

"Yes, I'm black American. We are the same," I told her.

"We are not the same. You are rich," another woman said.

"Gloria," Adofo interjected. "Most Ghanaians don't see black Americans as their sisters or brothers. To them, you're just an American with money. I hear it goes both ways...that black Americans are ashamed of their African heritage. True?"

"It's true for some. Whites tell us that Africa is wild and savage. Those of us who know the truth need to do a better job of educating the world about the real Africa," I replied, the outline of a plan already beginning to take shape in my head. "I know if more black Americans came here, they'd see the true Africa and be supportive of the needs of their motherland."

On Sunday, I went with Adofo, Papa, Mama, and about fifteen of their relatives to a Pentecostal church. It wasn't that different from my church in the States. We prayed and sang, sometimes in Twi and sometimes in English. The congregation performed many tribal dances. They spoke in tongues, or maybe it was just another tribal language I didn't understand. The service lasted six hours; I was exhausted by the time it was over.

I couldn't visit Ghana without visiting Elmina; it was the only reason most people visited the country at all. Elmina was a small coastal town, three hours from where I was staying. It was where the slave castles were, although some called them slave forts. I was anxious to stand in the same place my ancestors did before they were forever ripped from their homeland and forced into strange, cruel worlds.

It was a perfect day for travel to Elmina, sunny and about eighty degrees, with a light wind coming in off the Indian Ocean. Papa drove all of us there. Despite his protestations, I paid for the petrol, which even back then was an outrageous three dollars a gallon. The gravel road was filled with potholes from the rains the night before, making riding over it tough. The worst part was having no lines to divide traffic coming from the opposite direction.

Seeing Papa wander onto what I considered the other side of the road was a little scary, especially because the hills prevented us from seeing oncoming cars. Thankfully, we got to our destination in one piece. Aside from a few elderly people who waved at us in slow motion as they cast their worn and patched nets into the Indian Ocean, the place seemed deserted.

At first glance, the castles that lay clustered in the distance appeared like something out of a fairy tale, but the closer we got the more real they became. The structures were surrounded for miles by double walls that stood more than thirty feet high, making it virtually impossible for the slaves to escape. Humongous black cannons were positioned on every rooftop, aimed in the direction of the ocean and poised to shoot any runaways.

We walked slowly up the cobblestone path to the fort's entrance. A black steel gate stood in our way. The air felt thicker than it had before. It was as if the place had an aura all its own, as if there were unsettled spirits looming around it.

"I will be your guide. I know this place well," Adofo said. "History was my major at the university. These forts were so strong, nothing could penetrate them. The Portuguese who colonized Ghana around 1482, and the Swedish, Danish, Dutch, and British who came after, all helped build these castles. They built them along the oceanfront to make exporting slaves easy."

"Adofo, tell me about domestic slavery in Africa, and the slave trade when Africans sold their own people into slavery." I was curious as to how he would respond to my raising these issues.

"Yes, domestic slavery was common in Africa before European slave buyers arrived," he proceeded. "It flourished as early as the year 869, mainly between Muslim traders and western African kingdoms. Muslims sold goods like gold, copper, salt, and dried fruits to the African kingdoms. Traders brought these things because they appealed to the kings of those tribes. The kings sold their own people to the traders in exchange for the goods."

I listened intently as Adofo continued.

"As for the triangular trade between Africa, Europe, and the New World, I'm ashamed to say that the vast majority of slaves taken out of Africa were sold by African rulers, traders, and a military aristocracy. These rulers grew powerful. It was a lucrative business. Any time a trader wanted slaves he had to go through an African ruler first. And then he was paid through imported goods like textiles, gold, brandy, salt, and guns."

I was speechless in the face of these hard truths, and had only one more question: "So, how did African rulers capture their own people?" I asked.

"They were captured through raids or betrayal."

Adofo used all his weight to pull open the heavy steel gate. As we stepped into the courtyard, and the gate slammed behind us, the spirits grew even more present. They began to dance around me. I could feel their sadness, their anger.

"You're standing in the place where African slaves were sold. They were put into shackles and forced in there," Adofo said, gesturing to the room in front of us. Its entry was blocked by a set of ten-foot, double doors made of steel and decorated with a checkerboard design. Carved above the doors in wood was a chipped and weather-beaten image of a white man's chubby face.

I walked up to the doors and cast them open, then walked softly into the dark, mildewed room. Adofo explained that as many slaves as could fit would have been cramped so tightly into the small, boxy space that they wouldn't have been able to move. I couldn't imagine that it was possible to fit more than thirty people into the room. I became aware of a strange odor, which grew stronger as we moved farther into the room.

"That smell, it's sickening," I said, taking short, shallow breaths. "It's the smell of dry blood. Like death."

"That smell is the blood of our ancestors. The slaves who were forced into this room were obstinate. They were beheaded here."

"I just can't believe the atrocities," I said, nearly in tears. "That it's been centuries, yet the smell still lingers."

Just like the spirits, I thought.

I leaned against the wall to compose myself. I knew it was against my religion, but at that moment I couldn't help hating the white people who sanctioned slavery. A soothing hand touched my shoulder, guiding me out of the room. It was Mama Ambudu. Her gentleness calmed me.

The next room was similar, but it had an altar where someone had just finished libations. There were puddles of palm wine, scraps of yellow squash, animal blood, and white candle wax.

As I walked quietly into the room adjacent to that one, which was shaped like a half moon, I noticed that I had become nauseated. The smell of sweat and blood was heavy in my nostrils. I couldn't stop thinking about the story Adofo told me; even though I had read it many times in black history books, it wasn't real to me until now.

"This room was the last stop before the ship. About a hundred slaves would have been packed in here together, like cattle. As you see, there are no windows for ventilation. That heavy wood door," Adofo explained, pointing, "sealed them in until the slave owner released them into the narrow tunnel, which led to the waiting ships."

As we shuffled toward the entrance of the narrow passageway, I imagined I felt what my ancestors must have during their final moments of captivity in Africa. I pretended I was one of them.

My hands and feet are anchored to heavy metal chains, which are also attached to my sister, Adowa. We are of the Akan tribe in Ghana. The earth below our feet is cold, and we go slowly, very slowly, taking baby steps through the dark tunnel. I am careful not to stumble for fear of tripping Adowa. If either of us falls, the tight chains will pierce our skin. The early-morning air is thick and muggy, making it hard to breathe. But as we get closer to the middle of the tunnel, I find some relief. We are closer to the ocean.

Sometimes the ocean breeze chills the air too much, making me shiver. The white linen that the white people draped around my breasts and hips is too thin. I tune out the cold by listening to the rhythm of the waves beating on the shore. They make soothing music, like the ceremonial music of my tribe. I want to scream, but no one will hear me. Everybody is moaning; we are all confused. I turn and speak softly to my sister in our native tongue.

"Adowa, where are they taking us? What have we done for this? We have lost our family, our children. Will we find them again? What will happen to our land, our homes?"

Adowa answers as softly as I asked. "We have done nothing. These people are evil. Remember, our family taught us to be strong. We must stay together and be strong for one another."

The shore is now in sight. Our captors are white men wearing big hats, black boots, and beige trousers and coats. Their language is strange, and their voices are too happy and too loud. Some have long pipes made of elephant tusk in their mouths. Maybe their smoke will send signals to nearby tribes and they will come help us.

"Move it, you monkeys—move!" is what I would hear one of the men say, if I could understand him. He has a leather whip in his hand, coiled in the shape of a sleeping snake. He unravels the whip and beats my people until they bleed. I watch as my people are shoved into a small boat that will take them to wide ships with billowy white sails. Some of them jump into the ocean. Others cry out to be rescued. I am soon face to face with the white man.

"Where are you taking us? Why are you doing this?" I ask. He laughs. He does not understand me. I want to run into the bush, but where can I hide? I cry in silence.

Suddenly, I felt something on my shoulder. It was Adofo's hand, shaking me out of my trance and saving me from my thoughts.

"Gloria...Gloria, my sister, come. We will return to Accra. We are done."

This visit to Africa, to the slave castles, changed my life forever.

CHAPTER ELEVEN

When I returned from West Africa in the summer of 1975, I accepted who I was without reservation—my soft, dark-brown fuzzy hair, the brown freckles across my broad nose, my full lips, my shapely hips and legs. All of what I looked like was part of my history, of my heritage.

I had come to understand my rage. It ran deep, like still waters. I thought it stemmed only from my childhood, from incidents like when I had to ride on the back of the bus with Mom Thelma on our trip from Arkansas to Tennessee. Even though I was young, I knew there was something terribly wrong with having to use separate washing machines at the Laundromat. By the time I started school, I was old enough to realize that it wasn't right for white teachers to treat me like I was cursed.

But now I understood my rage started much farther back than I first realized—that I carried within me the rage of my ancestors and all those who came before me. Their sadness and loss was my sadness and loss; their pain was just as much a part of me as my own.

Every now and then Dad Harry would talk about the injustices he suffered from his white bosses at the factory. We were limited to sharing stories about racism within the black community. Blacks couldn't seek counseling as victims of prejudice or discrimination, mainly because there were no black counselors or therapists, so who would understand? The closest thing to help black individuals could get for their mental anguish was in an asylum where they'd dope us up or deliver shock treatment.

We had to adjust to racism by laughing at white folks' behavior and taking everything to God in prayer. While that could be cathartic, black parents never knew the true impact prejudice and racism had on a child's psyche until years into adulthood.

It was hard admitting my feelings because my Christian upbringing told me it was wrong to hate. My parents always reminded me, "Jesus never hated, so neither can you."

But I did, and I never learned what to do with those feelings that were bottled up inside me. Becoming an activist against white oppression helped, but my trip to Africa was the closest thing to therapy I'd ever had. I knew others needed the same experience to change their lives.

Shortly after returning from Ghana, I started the African Study Program (ASP), an organization that educated inner-city black high school students about the African continent and gave them the opportunity to live with African families during the summer. Although it was unpopular in the 1970s to take inner-city kids to Africa, it became my passion.

Skip, still my best friend, readily bought into the idea. Together, we immersed ourselves in recruiting a small board of community folks that included pastors of small store-front churches, black mom-and-pop business owners, and members of the Detroit Youth Association, an organization founded by two young inner-city men, Billy Holcomb and Stanley Black.

Billy had been in prison for a crime he said he didn't commit. All I knew about him was that he was passionate about working with the poor, and that was good enough for me. Billy and Stanley became my best friends in the struggle for equality in education for poor inner-city students, which meant getting black kids books containing images that represented them, ensuring they had qualified and committed teachers, and fighting for affirmative action. These guys were also the kind of folks I could depend on to raise money.

We decided to send eight students from Southwest High School to Africa. This was the only high school in the area where I worked and the poorest in the district. We asked the students to write an essay on the topic "Why I want to go to Africa." We got over fifty provocative entries, and narrowed the candidates down to the eight we could afford to take through an interview process.

The trip cost two thousand dollars per student. Our board and the community pitched in to help cover the expenses, which included airfare, food, and living arrangements in Africa for a month. Liberal white folks made donations, and a neighborhood McDonald's found money for our cause. Even the Detroit Board of Education pitched in. The students who were going did their fair share by raising money through car washes, talent shows, and teas.

But not everyone was supportive of black kids going to Africa, or, for that matter, any black folks going there. Surprisingly, the loudest opposition came from my own people —folks like George Johnson, the chairman of the Carstens Elementary School Parent Advisory Council. Mr. Johnson was a fireball of a man in his thirties who, every chance he got, spoke out against our work. I was convinced his short stature had resulted in giving him a Napoleon complex.

"Why are you takin' our black kids to Africa? It's not our home. Africans don't like us, and we don't like them. Three weeks is a long time to be tramping off somewhere folks don't want us. Just 'cause you went don't mean you gotta involve our kids."

"Mr. Johnson, this is a once-in-a-lifetime chance for our kids to discover their history, their roots. It's because Africa is viewed so negatively that we have to educate ourselves about it, so we can remove the stigma. And there are many similarities between Africans and us."

These exchanges between Mr. Johnson and me went on for a while, but eventually I realized that his ignorance couldn't be changed. He was grounded in personal experience either from his limited interactions with Africans in the United States or by what he had read. What I could change was the mindset of the kids who were going to Africa; they would find the truth. I had accrued the time off from work I needed, and I was going to use it as I pleased. For his part, Mr. Johnson kept on telling people not to support my program. I just ignored everyone who didn't believe in my vision. I knew I was doing a good thing. The *Detroit Free Press* came to my rescue once again by running an article and, as a result, people I had never met sent money and well wishes. With ten months of fundraising time left, we were close to our goal.

A few months after the article ran, in the summer of 1976, I returned to Africa on a teaching safari. It was an expedition to East Africa that included a mix of teenagers and adults, sixteen of us in all. The expedition was led by Professor Jeffrey Fadiman, a young and well-known professor of African history at Eastern Michigan University. Dr. Fadiman was white; his family was originally from the Ukraine. He had dark features and a short, dark brown beard. He was of large stature, over six feet tall, with a well-toned physique. I thought he was handsome. I met him through a flyer he'd posted at the university about the expedition.

During my initial interview, he said everybody would have to learn some Swahili before leaving for the trip. Dr. Fadiman could speak Swahili and Zulu himself. He wanted to make sure I was tough enough to adapt to the cultures I would encounter, like the Maasai tribe. He wanted to make sure I was tough enough, period. He told me we'd be traveling in a huge, dirty old army truck and sleeping in the bush in flimsy canvas Boy Scout tents. Our meals would come out of cans and be prepared over an open fire.

But the interview wasn't all about trying to scare me away. Dr. Fadiman praised my work in the inner city, something I had never expected a white man to do. When the meeting was over, he challenged me to go to Mount Kilimanjaro.

"Why?" I asked.

"I've climbed twice. It's a deceptive mountain, easy at the beginning. The higher you climb, the more the temperature drops. Then the air thins. That's when the headaches and vomiting begin," Dr. Fadiman explained.

"That doesn't faze me. If I put my mind to it, I can do it. When people tell me I can't, I prove I can." My research had already taught me that an average of eight to ten trekkers died per year climbing Mount Kilimanjaro, mainly due to heart attacks and acute mountain sickness. I knew I was in excellent physical condition, so I wasn't daunted.

"I like your spirit, Gloria. I won't be doing the climb this time, but others will. Bring warm clothes for Kilimanjaro, but pack light for the rest of the expedition. Keep working out, read the syllabus, and I'll see you at the airport."

It was at New York's LaGuardia International Airport that I met the rest of the expedition team, the folks with whom I'd share my life for three weeks. I immediately looked for individuals I could relate to, other black folks. There were only three of us, all women.

I was curious as to why white folks wanted to learn about African culture. Surely they weren't going to exploit African and its people as their ancestors had perhaps done. No, these white folks proclaimed themselves liberals who had no agenda other than enlightenment. I would wait and see what happened on the expedition before I decided whether that was true.

The youngest members of the expedition team were two twelve-year-olds who were tagging along with their parents. The oldest member was fifty. We represented several Michigan towns, including Grosse Pointe, Detroit, Ypsilanti, and Lansing. Some of us were teachers; others, former students at the university. One of us was a Vietnam vet. Some travelers were middle-class while others came from more affluent backgrounds.

Black or white, wealthy or working class, we were all victims of 1970s fashion trends. The guys wore long straggly bangs. The girls either had long, wild, curly hair or wore it pin-straight in a bob. Mine was in corn-rows for not just reasons of black pride, but everyday convenience. We all wore bell-bottoms, straight-legged jeans, or beige khakis, paired with plain bulky sweatshirts or sweaters, and blue jean jackets. Our brown, ankle-length combat boots were either brand-spanking new or barely worn— clearly purchased for the purpose of the trip. Although we'd certainly stand out in the African bush, we blended well with each other.

As we introduced ourselves and shook hands, Dr. Fadiman gave us departing notes. "You all look rugged, just the way you should. As I told each of you in the interview, this is a real expedition, not one of those luxurious safaris you see in travel magazines.

"When we arrive in Kenya, we'll pick up a sixteen-ton army truck. That truck will be our best friend. It'll take us over hundreds of miles of dusty red desert to visit the Maasais—I'm fortunate to know one of the leading elders of that tribe. Then we'll move onto Northern Kenya to visit the Samburu tribe. I hope that everyone brought bug repellant like I told you. The mosquitoes can eat you alive at night. And if you didn't take your cycle of malaria pills, you're not boarding the plane."

We all nodded, standing beside our army-green duffle bags that carried only the bare necessities: an extra pair of jeans, a few shirts, and warm clothing should we be planning to climb Kilimanjaro. We'd pick up our tents and other supplies when we arrived in Africa.

After seventeen hours in the air, we landed at Kenya's airport in Nairobi, East Africa. It was a clear sunny day, about seventy-five degrees. Since it was nearing the end of summer, it wasn't as humid as it had been in the months that had just passed. We summoned an old rickety white van that was waiting to board passengers. All of us piled in, sitting on each other's laps and stepping on each other's new boots. None of us cared; our focus was on the expedition in Kenya and Tanzania.

As we made our way into town, I couldn't help but compare Kenya to my first visit to Ghana in West Africa. There were noticeable differences in people's complexions in the two regions, with much more variety in Kenya, where people were multiple shades of brown and black, or tan like the sand, or blue-black like the sky at dusk. White folks were as pale as pale could be, and the Indians from Asia were chocolate brown.

Like Ghana, though, Kenya didn't fit the jungle image depicted by Hollywood. Downtown Nairobi was a bustling cosmopolitan capital city with tall elevator buildings. There was a building near city hall with a revolving restaurant that overlooked a pond with floating lilies. It was named after Jomo Kenyatta, the former president. Imperialism was at its peak. The American and European businesses that monopolized the economy were as diverse as the people. There was a Volvo dealership, and Shell, Mobil, and Esso gas stations advertising their inflated prices of three dollars per gallon. From miles away you could see a Ford Motor Company sign elevated high above the Kenya Commercial Bank.

Young black Africans were extremely westernized, sporting bell-bottoms and chemically treated hair. Older Africans strutted around the streets flaunting the colorfully embroidered dashikis and African wraps that covered their entire body. Kenya's businessmen wore dark suits and carried leather briefcases. Many women owned small, storefront textile businesses and were practiced in the skills of bargaining.

The one thing that was unique to Kenya was the presence of the Maasai tribe. The Maasai were a proud people who paraded through the downtown streets with spears, beaded necklaces, and earrings that hung from their ears and broad noses. The young tribesmen were all well over six feet tall and fine-looking, with high cheekbones and cat-like eyes.

Their muscular bodies were draped in pretty, bright red material, which complemented their reddish-brown skin and dreadlocks. The cloth flowed freely with each long step they took, revealing their well-defined thighs. I was curious as to what they wore underneath their garb—traditional underwear or a jock strap maybe? I wasn't able to get a look, though. The Maasais' goats followed them, distinguishing them as a nomadic tribe who wandered wherever the best grazing was. I noticed that their sandals, which would have to be sturdy enough to see them through miles and miles of walking, were held in place by a toe strap.

Our army truck was waiting at the shed when we arrived. "Hey, there's Big Mack," someone said, referring to the monstrous vehicle's resemblance to a Mack truck; the name stuck for the duration of the trip.

Our Kenyan driver, Steven, greeted us. He was neatly dressed in beige khaki pants that were meticulously starched and ironed. Steven's brown army boots were slightly worn, but had been well polished. He wore a beige safari hat with a small brim to protect his forehead from the sun and a bright red sweater; red was a color many Kenyans seemed to love.

Steven's slight stature was a good match for his gentle spirit and soft-spoken manner. I figured he was about forty, maybe fifty years old, but it was hard to guess his age because, as with most Africans, especially those with dark complexions, his chocolate skin had remained smooth and un-wrinkled. Steven was a family man, and these driving expeditions were how he supported his wife and children. I could tell I was going to like him.

"*Hamjambo,*" he said, greeting us with a British accent and a wide smile.

"*Hatujambo,*" we responded in unison, also smiling.

"I'm Steven. I've been waiting for you, and I will take care of all of you. Come, let us go before the sun goes down."

"Big Mack" needed a good wash. The front of the truck was splattered with red dirt, and the eggshell white exterior was chipped in many places, testifying to the vehicle's frequent use. A piece of thick brown canvas covered the roof and sides to protect those of us inside from the scorching desert temperatures. It looked like a relic from World War II, and getting into "Big Mack" was certainly a battle. I had to use all of my upper-body strength to lift myself into the back, while being extremely careful not to get splinters from the wood floor or the uncomfortable wooden bench that did little to cushion our bottoms from the many potholes we encountered.

It took us several hours to get to the campsite in the bush; we arrived just before sundown. Anyone who has ever been to Africa will tell you that the most tranquil part of their visit was seeing the magnificent, pale blue sky fold into the yellow and orange sunset every night. We were encroaching on Maasai territory, and Dr. Fadiman was going to pay his respects to the tribe's chief in the morning. We would follow him.

After we pitched our tents, Steven built a fire from the wood we gathered from the nearby bush so we could cook dinner: canned beef stew, potatoes, and white bread. Since I was a vegetarian, I substituted kidney beans for the stew.

The notes Dr. Fadiman gave us that night were hard to forget. "You'll hear sounds...the sounds of the African night—lions, elephants. Don't be alarmed," he said. "The animals are just as afraid of us as we are of them. They don't attack. Just stay inside your tents."

My tent-mate, Audrey, was a middle-aged black woman. She didn't even have a smile line on her beautiful, unblemished face. She was a school teacher from East Lansing, and we became the best of friends. The tents provided flimsy protection, and we all agreed that we may as well have been lying directly on the hard dirt, for all the comfort the thin mats we slept on afforded us. The ground needed rain, but it was the dry season, and the skies probably wouldn't release any water for months. I found it hard to fall asleep and, when I finally did, it didn't last long.

"Audrey, girl, wake up, wake up! Something's out there. Listen to that purring," I whispered.

"Shhh, we got to keep quiet," Audrey admonished me.

"Do you think it's gonna eat us?"

"Yeah, I'm sure it's gonna hunt down the only black women and eat us," Audrey said, laughing.

We remained quiet, listening, until the sound disappeared into the bush. The rest of the night I slept as well as I could with one eye on the tent's zipper door.

In the morning, we found elongated footprints around the campsite. Dr. Fadiman said that maybe it was a lion. We had to be calm about it because wild animals were a part of bush life; we were the visitors there, not the beasts.

We dismantled our tents and fueled up on orange juice, oatmeal, and dry biscuits before piling into "Big Mack" to resume our adventure. Steven drove the sharp twists and narrow turns of the back roads like the pro he was, eventually ending up in the region of the mountain of Ngong in the Great Rift Valley. We were greeted by everyone in the Maasai village, including the headman. Dr. Fadiman walked ahead of us as a chorus of women, men, and children broke out with the familiar Swahili greeting, *"Hamjambo, hamjambo, hamjambo!"*

Our response was, *"Hatujambo,"* which means "we are all fine." The Maasai ushered us into the manyatta, their village, which consisted of a cluster of eight small huts. We stood by a thorny fence that resembled barbed wire and protected the manyatta, goats, and cows from wild animals. We were in a valley surrounded by cone-shaped mountains. The tallest peak enthralled me. It was covered with snow, giving the impression of a scoop of vanilla ice cream with fudge dripping down its sides. I was looking at Mount Kenya, the tallest mountain in the country. I wondered if Kilimanjaro was as stunning.

I was anxious to meet the beautiful, mystic people who had greeted us so graciously. In an effort to preserve every bit of their culture, the Maasai traditionally didn't associate with folks from the Western world. We were honored to be there with Dr. Fadiman who, because of how respectfully he'd dealt with the leading elder in the past, was permitted back for another visit.

Dr. Fadiman paid homage to the elder with bows and words of gratitude spoken in the native tongues of the land, before introducing us. The elder was probably about seventy years old and, aside from his dress, looked as if he could've been anyone's black grandfather back in the States. He was adorned in a long red cloth and his ears, neck, and arms were decorated with bauxite and amber jewelry. I found him to be distinguished-looking. He was also polite, nodding distinctly to each of us. After the elder had been properly introduced, the rest of the Maasai flocked around, giggling and touching our arms and clothes. Everyone seemed happy to meet us.

Suddenly my eyes locked with the eyes of a handsome young Maasai. He stood a few meters from me, smiling to reveal picture-perfect straight teeth. He moved closer, speaking in broken English.

"My name Warrior. This for you," he said, removing a leather-beaded bracelet from his wrist. He then tied the bracelet to my wrist and said, "We same."

I responded in appreciation by bowing my head and responding, "Thank you, Warrior, it's beautiful. And, yes, we are same."

Warrior held a sword in his left hand, which was a tradition among the Maasai. He stood proud at six feet tall and crossed his legs at the ankles, another trait of the Maasai. Like his tribesmen, he had no body fat, and his arms and legs were well-defined. The Maasai claimed the source of their good health was a daily diet of cows' blood mixed with milk. I would venture to say that was also the source of their smooth, silky, brown skin.

I loved Warrior's hairstyle. His shoulder-length hair was twisted like rope, adorned with cowry shells, and saturated with oil and red clay. He wasn't that much younger than I was, and I would have loved to have him as my boyfriend.

I knew that Warrior had gone through a "rites of passage" ceremony to initiate him into manhood, as all Maasai males did when they reached fifteen years of age. Despite my interest in Warrior, it was the women who fascinated me the most, just as they were fascinated by me. They circled me, touching and caressing my hair, which had white pearls at the end of each of its braids. "Nice, nice," they said, using their limited English vocabulary. Then they turned to run their fingers through the hair of the white women who were with us. When the Maasai women giggled, it sparked laughter among all of us.

Like the Maasai men, the women also possessed a good deal of upper-body strength. They needed those muscles to do the work required of them. The women built the dung huts their families lived in. They milked cows and sometimes traveled miles to fetch water. Their skilled hands picked gourds from vines, cleaned them, and decorated them. The Maasai women designed jewelry using cowry shells, leather, colorful beads, and stone. They adorned various parts of their body with their creations—their head, ears, nose, neck, arms, and legs. Their shaven heads and generously jeweled bodies gave them a regal appearance, even though the Maasai were essentially cattle herders.

The women motioned for us to follow them into one of the huts. Once inside, we realized they wanted us to see how they constructed them. It was a difficult job that took several months. It was the intricacy of weaving the twigs and branches into tight squares that was the most time-consuming part. Each hut was a unique tapestry.

I had nothing but admiration for these women. Just like the men, as *ndito* (that means in the Swahili language "young girl"), they had to pass through rites of passage. When they reached puberty, they had to undergo the torturous practice of female circumcision, clinically known as a clitoridectomy, which was meant to prohibit them from feeling pleasure during sex. I learned this through my readings about the Maasai.

A feast is prepared and everybody brings milk and livestock. The *mwari* sits on a cattle hide. Women in the village hold her in place during the operation.

As the young girl is healing, she's seen as 'unclean,' unable to wash. She's restricted from leaving the village or speaking to a man outside her family. A headband is placed on her head, and her head is shaven. Afterwards, she enters womanhood.

Looking into the Maasai women's smiling faces, I couldn't fathom how they survived having their clitoris cut out of their body without receiving any anesthesia. Although I respect and often embrace the practices of other cultures, to this day, it breaks my heart to think that young girls are still undergoing this type of mutilation and violence.

Our time with the Maasai was fading with the sun. We were going to be treated to one of their ceremonies first hand. There was no surgery involved in the departure ceremony held in our honor. The men performed dances while the women assembled in a circle and encouraged them with rhythmic clapping. We stood beside the women and emulated them. The energetic dancing lasted about an hour. Although the Maasai didn't appear in the least bit fatigued, the time had come for us to leave. Before we left, everyone in the tribe, including the lead elder, bowed their head and thanked us for our visit.

Early the next morning, we began our lengthy trek into Samburu country, which was slightly above the equator, toward the base of Mt. Kenya. After traveling hundreds of miles, I finally caught a second glimpse of the mountain and its snow-covered peak. She favored Kilimanjaro, but Kilimanjaro was taller and wider, every bit of 19,340 feet. I was getting anxious to acquaint myself with her, but I was still hundreds of miles away in Kenya, and she was in Tanzania. Our meeting was days away.

Upon our arrival in Samburu country, a few Samburu women and young boys and girls gathered around us, curious. Dr. Fadiman greeted them in Maa, their native language. They giggled, and when they did they looked a lot like the Maasai. It's been said that the Samburu splintered off from the Maasai when the tribes of Kenya first came from the Sudan.

I handed a hair ornament to one of the girls as a friendship gesture. She examined it and carefully tucked it into the palms of her hands.

The young girls were about twelve years old and topless, their small breasts just beginning to bud. Their long necks were decorated with layers of beaded necklaces, which, piled from their chin to their collarbone, seemed to almost be strangling them. The number of necklaces they wore depended on how much a young warrior liked them. Before he gave a girl jewelry, a boy had to be circumcised and initiated as a warrior. Then he could add as many beads as he wanted to a girl's neck, as a display of whom he would choose as his future bride.

We stayed in the bush long enough to take in Africa's rich heritage—giraffes eating from the thorny trees, wildebeests sprinting to better grazing land and the lions who were stalking them, swamps of hippos spewing muddy water from their nostrils, and elephants shredding whole trees with their bodies. We also saw dried-up elephant carcasses scattered for miles over the red desert. The animals had been ruthlessly killed by greedy poachers for their ivory tusks. The tusks were sold for millions of dollars—blood money.

I captured everything on camera, even the things I didn't really want to remember, like a freshly slaughtered elephant whose ivory had been brutally slashed out of her body with a machete, leaving layers of bloody flesh hanging from her face for the flies to feast on. In remembrance of all the murdered elephants I saw during the expedition, I managed to bring back to the States an elephant's rib about three feet long, to be used for lectures on the illegal poaching of Africa's fastest dying species.

Later that evening, we sat around the campfire eating the beans Steven cooked for us. It would be our last dinner together as an expedition team. That night, all sixteen of us talked about climbing Mount Kilimanjaro, but when morning broke that August morning in 1976, only eleven of us chose to cast our fate to her. The others bid us farewell and returned on "Big Mack" to Nairobi, where they would wait patiently for our return.

CHAPTER TWELVE

From the time Dr. Fadiman warned me about the tremendous odds I would face attempting to summit Kilimanjaro, I became determined that nothing would stop me from succeeding. I prepared well, training rigorously all summer the way I had when my sights were set on the Olympics. I felt that the misfortune that befell other climbers on Kilimanjaro wouldn't befall me. After all, most deaths on the mountain occurred prior to 1971, before the government decided to institute a formally regulated system that included trekking permits and guides.

When I first laid eyes on Kilimanjaro, I saw only her beauty, not her potential treachery. Her smooth sides were void of jagged edges, which made climbing seem effortless. I was immensely attracted to her perfectly snow-capped peak, one of the world's "seven summits," and could understand why so many risked their lives to touch it. Ascending Kilimanjaro would take three days; it would take another two days to descend. Our Kenyan expedition driver dropped the eleven of us who had chosen to brave the mountain at a bus stop to catch the next ride to Moshi, Tanzania, located at the base of Kilimanjaro.

The faded white bus we boarded was overloaded, a common problem in Africa. Everybody rode the rickety, rusty buses—from tribal chiefs dressed in their traditional African garb to women carrying bowls of food on their heads. Even livestock used this form of transportation when it was necessary. We were crowded in like sardines in a can; from the sound of the bus's engine it was none-too-happy with the weight. Every time the vehicle jolted along the red dirt road, our bodies collided and the slick, funky sweat of our fellow passengers mixed with our own.

We spent three hours at the border of Kenya and Tanzania. Every parcel, purse, food item had to be checked for ammunition. The members of my expedition weren't searched, only the indigenous people traveling with us. When all was said and done, it took nine hours to travel the 175 miles from Nairobi, Kenya, to Moshi, Tanzania. We were about 4,000 feet above sea level.

We followed a single-lane dirt road to the base of the mountain. We were surrounded by coffee bean fields and sweet-smelling pineapple and coconut trees. At the edge of this beautiful landscape stood Kilimanjaro. It was unusual seeing snow on a mountain situated on the equator where the same crops were growing as were found in the tropics. We reached Kibo Hut, which would serve as our headquarters prior to the climb. I was disappointed to see that it was just a simple A-frame, two-story building made of wood that resembled a ski lodge. I expected something more authentic and native-looking. It was once a farmhouse and still had the original wood floors, which did afford it some charm.

Upstairs, there was a large room crowded with wooden bunk beds. Downstairs, in front of the large fireplace, there were old wooden chairs and a large table. The table could comfortable seat about ten people, but luckily we'd gotten used to things being a little crowded. The temperatures had dipped into the fifties, so we were anxious to sit around the fire.

A few climbers from Europe had already arrived. They greeted us with heavy accents as they sat around the table, eating soup and bread and laughing among themselves. They were in their twenties and thirties, and all of the men were lanky and bearded. There was only one woman with them. The group was going to start their climb before us, and was off to bed by 8:00 p.m.

Our dinner didn't appeal to the vegetarian lifestyle I'd acquired in graduate school when the cattle feed had become contaminated. The main course was beef stew, accompanied by homemade white bread and black chai ("chai" is Swahili for tea). I fished out the chunks of beef and drank the stew broth for sustenance, being careful not to make a fuss. Our breakfast the next morning was more appealing—oatmeal, toast, and chai again. I was cold and couldn't seem to get enough chai.

As we stepped into the fresh, cool morning air to begin our trek, several Tanzanian men, known as porters, greeted us. They were a gregarious and welcoming group, clapping and raising their fists in a Black Power salute as we worked our way toward them. They were about six strong and had been assigned to carry our canned food on their heads. The food was placed in a porcelain bowl, the base of which was wrapped in fabric for balance. We would carry our own backpacks, which contained warm clothing.

"*Jambo, jambo, jambo,*" the Tanzanians said in Swahili, the dominant language of the land.

"*Jambo,*" we said, nodding politely. I couldn't get over how straight and perfect everyone's teeth were in Africa. All of the porters were well-coordinated, although at about five-foot-seven, they were much slighter than the tribal men we'd met. They wore short wool jackets, dingy white t-shirts, beige cotton khakis, and black ankle boots. Their dark-colored skullcaps and gloves were stuffed into the pockets of their corduroy jackets for when the temperatures dropped. A soft-spoken Tanzanian scurried up to us and anxiously shook our hands, smiling widely. He spoke broken English with a British accent.

"*Jambo,* my name is Morgan. I will be your guide. This is Tony. He will help me. Call him Mr. T, like in America. All of you will make Kilimanjaro. Just be sure to go *pole, pole*—that's 'slow' in Swahili. I show you how, it's my job. I go up and down this mountain many times this year. I know what to do. Not easy, but you follow me, you be okay," he said, still smiling.

I speculated that, among the eleven members in my expedition team, eight of us would reach the summit. Most of us were in our mid-twenties and strong physically. Fred was a shoo-in. He had just come from active combat duty in Vietnam. In sizing up my companions, I realized my white expedition mates were different from the whites I grew up with. They didn't ask stupid questions about my hair, my features, or my culture, nor did they ever say anything derogatory about Africa. Knowing Dr. Fadiman, he only chose progressive, liberal-minded people for this expedition. Still, everyone had their quirks.

There was Dave, who was cocky, self-assured, and narcissistic. One day around the campfire in Kenya, he removed his t-shirt, flexed his muscles, and flung back his shoulder-length blond hair, saying, "Now how do you like that?" Maybe his bravado would get him to the summit.

Rod was a different story. "I'm a world traveler, got lots of traveling under my belt," he always reminded us in his laid-back, unassuming way. He was quiet most of time, hiding behind his silver, wire-rim glasses. He was also a hippie, who wore his reddish-brown hair down to his shoulders. I thought he had a sexy sparkle in his dark-brown eyes.

Henry I had serious doubts about. He was in his fifties and moved like a turtle. I did appreciate his sense of humor, but he'd need more than that to get him to the summit of Kilimanjaro.

Susan, Jennifer, and Laurie were best friends and all had vibrant personalities. I was just as sure as they were that they'd make the summit. They were a few years younger than I was and were always challenging the men when they made sexist comments like, "You women aren't strong like us guys—you won't make it."

"We'll prove it," they'd say. "We're just as strong as you are."

My connection to these women seemed so natural, maybe because of the struggles they had faced being Jewish. I had long held the belief that African Americans and Jews were bonded through the atrocities our people had suffered, mine during slavery, and Susan, Jennifer, and Laurie's during the Holocaust.

There were three other female climbers in the group, and I had doubts about all of their abilities. One of those women was Audrey, my tent partner. She set herself up not to make it. She'd say, "I just want to get to the first plateau so when I return home, I can say I attempted Kilimanjaro. I'm too old to go all the way up."

Piper and Wendy weren't athletic and had no drive to excel. They were just tagging along for the experience and to see how far they could go.

Of all the women, I was the fittest. I never doubted myself.

We were instructed to dress light for the start of the climb, but to stuff our backpacks with warm clothing so that we could add layers as it got colder. It was a crisp August morning, about fifty-five degrees, when our expedition team headed out. I was wearing khaki army pants, a cotton turtleneck, combat boots, and a bandana.

We all followed Morgan closely as he led us down a red clay road lined with banana and coconut trees, and into a small crowd of cheering village people known as the Chaggas. They were standing next to their wobbly fruit tables, making hissing sounds with their teeth. They waved exuberantly as though they knew us. Little children ran up to us and touched our hands. Some beckoned us to buy their fruit. A small transistor radio was broadcasting the music of Fela Ransome Kuti, who was to Africa what James Brown was to America.

"Jambo, habari gani, habari gani," the Chaggas said.

We smiled and responded, *"Habari gani, habari gani,"* which means "How are you?" in Swahili.

The Chagga women were clad in colorful, native-print cotton dresses tailored to fit their voluptuous breasts and wide hips, and over the dresses they were wearing lightweight cardigan sweaters. A few women ran into a huddle and began snickering. They pointed to me. I asked Morgan what it meant.

"You climb their mountain. They don't see black American women climbing, only white women," he said.

"Why don't they climb?" I asked.

"In our culture, women are not like American women. They care for family, work in markets. Their husbands work the land and in shops. They believe if you climb their mountain, you will be punished and cursed by angry gods that live inside. If you are cursed, you will get sick or die."

"Morgan, do you believe the curse?"

"I've seen strange things happen up Kilimanjaro. I cannot say. You will see. Come, let's go, *pole, pole.*"

Before I continued on, I turned and waved respectfully at the women. When I got far enough away that they couldn't hear me, I said, "I'm gonna make it. You'll see."

Morgan said Marangu was the least challenging route to take to Kilimanjaro's summit and therefore the best one for first-time climbers. It wasn't as steep as the others, and getting to our first rest stop would take only two and a half hours; it would be like an invigorating walk.

We hiked straight into the lowlands, where the clouds were so thick they blocked the summit. An onslaught of white African Colobus monkeys with thick black circles around their eyes turned flips onto our path and performed acrobatics through the trees. It was our first sign of animal life. I wanted to reach out and hug the amusing creatures, but Morgan quickly reminded us that they were wild and uncontrollable. We kept moving, *pole, pole.*

We soon became immersed in a heavy fog. The mist was so thick drops of water were falling into our eyes, even though it wasn't raining. Eventually, the thick fog of the rain forest consumed us, and we were unable to see a thing.

"Stay close to each other, single file," Morgan warned.

Our path grew steep and narrow; it took us to streams of cool, virgin water that we drank from until our stomachs ached. I was fascinated by the leafy palm trees that stretched to the sky with gray moss sagging from their branches. They looked identical to ones I'd seen in picture books of the swamps of Savannah, Georgia.

As we trekked higher, the terrain changed. We were confronted with a riverbed of thick, red mud that crept slowly to the top of our boots. We began slipping and sliding everywhere. I attempted to pirouette from one dry spot to the next, but that didn't work for long. Our path changed abruptly, shooting upward like a launching rocket, then it leveled off, leading us to a ravine about ten feet wide, much too wide to leap over. When we looked down, we saw a sparse stream of water and mud.

"Okay, we will cross over like this. Grab this vine, it is strong. I push," Morgan said.

The vine was long and thick. I gripped it tightly as Morgan had instructed, then he gave me an extra push. In the time it took to blink, I was on the other side. Piper, though, wasn't feeling as brave.

"I could fall. What if the vine breaks?"

"Come, you will be okay," Morgan said to her in a patient tone.

Piper coiled her body tightly around the rope and screamed so loud when Morgan pushed her that I'm sure the Chaggas at the base heard her cries. When her feet touched the ground, she was as white as a ghost. No one else was as afraid as Piper.

We were all drenched. The scorching temperatures we encountered on the next part of our trek dried us out quickly enough. It was about 115 degrees. Although I had been raised in cold weather, I always preferred the heat; I was a little anxious about the subzero temperatures that lay ahead. Sweaty and on the verge of heat stroke, we finally encountered a brook. It was the freshest and coolest spring water I'd ever tasted, even better than the fresh water at my grandparents' place in Tennessee. I freed my feet from the combat boots and soaked them in the stream. I couldn't wait to bathe when we returned to the base; it had been a week since I'd last showered.

We soon passed three of the five Europeans from base camp.

"How was it? Did you make it? What was it like?"

We were all asking them questions at once.

"It was rough, and…well, only two went before us. Good luck."

I wondered why they didn't go all the way. I was sure that as we got closer, we'd understand.

Our first rest stop, Mandara Hut, stood nearly 9,000 feet above sea level. My climbing buddies complained of fatigued muscles and tired feet when we got there, but I felt energized. Mandara Hut was a cozy wood house that resembled our lodgings at base camp, with a similar layout. Morgan and Mr. T prepared the same dinner we'd had the night before, and for breakfast we were treated to a biscuit with porridge, an orange, tea, and coffee. I'd gotten so used to the chai that I didn't care at all for the coffee.

People were already starting to take themselves out of the climb.

"Piper's head is pounding like mad. I'm not strong enough to make it. We're goin' back. You guys keep up the good work," Wendy told us at breakfast.

Maybe emboldened by the fact that she wouldn't be the only one dropping out, Audrey turned to me and said, "Honey, I'm nobody's martyr."

"Yup, that's it for me. I can't torture myself anymore. See you guys in a few," Henry said rather matter-of-factly.

All of the quitting made me a little nervous that maybe I wasn't being realistic about how hard the trek would get.

"Remember, the higher you go, *pole, pole*, less oxygen," Morgan advised the seven of us who remained: Fred, Dave, Rod, Susan, Jennifer, Laurie, and me. I took an inventory of my physical condition. I had no pain, no nausea, and my breathing was normal. I was good to go.

That day, we covered about ten miles of the most serene terrain on the climb. We were 12,000 feet above sea level, far above the clouds. We spent a few minutes enjoying the green grass that grew taller than we were and the yellow flowers that resembled daisies. The air was pure and fresh. The sky in front of me was an electric blue and seemed to gently kiss the ground. It was a strange place to be, like we were halfway between heaven and earth.

We walked with trepidation, one foot in front of the other, because it seemed we were going to fall off the cliff. But it was only an illusion. As we trekked on, we saw that there was plenty of land in front of us. Our steep path wound downward, then upward. Morgan stayed close, guiding our every step.

"Careful, there's an incline in front, a few kilometers steep. Lean, lean forward. Use your walking sticks. Take small steps."

Sometimes gravity would pull me backward. With the air thinning, Susan, Jennifer, and Laurie began to fatigue. They gasped for breath, making choking sounds. They stopped to rest often and complained just as much.

"I, I can't breathe," Susan would say.

"Feelin' dizzy, head's pounding like crazy," Jennifer would relay to us, while holding her head between her hands.

"How far, Morgan? I'm gonna throw up," Laurie would add, not to be outdone.

"Stop, let's all rest here. Drink water, good for sickness."

We rested on the thick, green grass while Morgan poured cool water from his canteen on a dingy white hand towel and gently applied it to Jennifer's head. I noticed a sign that read, "Last Water."

"Morgan, does that really mean there's no more?" I asked.

"Right. Fill your canteens here. In a few kilometers, we'll be at our second hut."

It was here, for the first time, that I began feeling the effects of the climb. It was getting colder. My feet and hands were numb. I just couldn't stay warm. I had already put on extra mittens and socks for protection. The higher we climbed, the more my fear of the cold was exacerbated.

Someone's desperate cry interrupted the internal dialogue I was having about my own health.

"Morgan, we're turning back. I can't breathe!"

It was Susan. Jennifer and Laurie wanted to join her.

"My sisters, you can't go back now. We've got to take the summit together. We don't want the guys to do it alone. Just walk, you'll feel better. We'll be at Horombo soon," I offered encouragingly, smiling through my own pain.

"We can't, we're hurting too much. We can't think about the guys now," Laurie said.

"Wait until after supper to make your decision," Morgan said.

As we moved toward our living quarters, it was hard to get excited about the puffy clouds that clustered below the cabin. I was worried about my sister climbers. They couldn't walk off their sickness like I would in track. Their symptoms were life-threatening. If their brains weren't getting enough oxygen, they could die. As we ate, I could sense from their silence that they were worried. Laurie issued the verdict for all three of them.

"Glo, we can't do it. You go. You gotta make the summit for us. Make us proud."

"I will. I'm so sorry you got so sick. I'll see you in a few days," I said as we hugged each other, not feeling our bodies touch because of the cold.

I was disappointed and sad. I had wanted to prove to the guys that women were just as capable of reaching the summit as they were. Nonetheless, at this point in the climb, no one could predict what would happen to the four of us who remained the higher we ascended. The guys knew better than to make any chauvinistic comments about Susan, Jennifer, and Laurie's return to base camp. As I watched the young women disappear into the clouds, I felt a heavy sense of responsibility to make the summit. I refused to believe that the women back at Marangu were right. We weren't being punished by the gods. Things like this, and worse things, happened on the mountain all the time; otherwise, reaching the top wouldn't be such a big deal.

Fred, Dave, and Rod were waiting for me by the outhouse. It would be our last time using one before the summit. We knew the bushes would serve us well, just as they had in Kenya. Morgan hurried us up so we would make the final resting stop before dusk. For the first time during the expedition, I felt like I was truly part of a team.

"Stay close, no matter what. We're stronger together," Morgan said.

The men nodded and made eye contact with me. We were all too cold to speak. I'd relinquished my gender; I was now one of the guys. The winds were hollering, the air was thinning, and the terrain was shifting upward, forcing us to shadow each other and walk shoulder to shoulder. We concentrated on staying close to each other, using our conjoined bodies as a barrier against the winds

"This...your hardest climb. Stay together. Go *pole, pole,*" Morgan instructed.

We suddenly found ourselves walking on fine pebbles made of gray and black ash, residue from Kilimanjaro's first eruption three hundred and sixty thousand years ago and another that occurred in the late 1700s. Our steps were small and slow as we navigated what felt like a ninety-degree incline. We were so close to the ground it felt we were parallel to it.

We arrived at the mountain's saddle, where Kilimanjaro's peaks, Kibo and Mawenzi, stood like granite statues. They were once a singular part of Kilimanjaro before, being separated by a volcano. Now they were her sisters.

After maneuvering several hours in gray ash and hard volcanic rock, we ascended into a zone where the air was so paper thin, we felt as if we were suffocating. I took short breaths through my mouth then exhaled slowly and rhythmically the same way, bypassing my nose. My years of running were certainly paying off. As for the guys, they were stopping frequently, especially Rod. His breathing was almost spasmodic.

"Remember, take your time. Americans are too fast. Breathe in slow, out slow," Morgan demonstrated. He was a well-trained leader. Going up and down Kilimanjaro was old hat for him.

Even with the extra clothing, the numbness penetrated my bones. I had to put on my third pair of wool socks and mittens. I noticed my right sock was stuck to my heel, and there was blood on it. As I gently peeled it away from my foot, I realized a blister had broken, and the pus and blood had congealed on the sock. My feet were in bad shape. One of my toenails had turned blue. Morgan didn't have Band-aids, so I was forced to put my shoe back on and leave everything as it was.

When we reached Kibo Hut, our final rest stop, we were 15,500 feet above sea level, and our team seemed to be falling apart.

"Morgan, got an aspirin?" Fred asked, holding his head.

"Yeah, I could use one, too," Dave said.

The guys were staggering around as if they'd just downed a bottle of whiskey.

"Here, this will help," Morgan said, handing them the aspirin.

Rod told Morgan how nauseated he was.

"We will eat first, go to bed, and get up at three in the morning. You feel better. I know you will. We must see sunrise over summit. The most beautiful thing you will see in your life."

Our final rest stop was a wooden shack that sat on brick stilts, like something out of the Wild West. Portions of the aluminum siding and roof weren't nailed down well, which meant a loud flapping sound accompanied each guest of wind. There were no windows, just a doorframe without a door. Inside were six metal bunk beds with faded mattresses. The decor brought back memories of my internship at Ypsilanti State mental hospital.

"Morgan, why are there fewer beds than at the rest of the stops?" I asked.

"Because most climbers don't make Kibo."

Morgan took the bottom bunk, since he would be the first one up in the morning. He wasted no time preparing our final dinner on an open fire he built with wood he carried in on his head. It was the lightest meal we had during the climb—broth with bread and tea.

We threw our fatigued bodies onto the beds, fully clothed. We hadn't had a change of clothing since we left base camp; we just kept adding more layers. All together I had on three pairs of mittens, a wool cap with a bandana underneath, a long-sleeved thermal t-shirt, thermal long johns, a red cotton lumberjack shirt, a navy blue cotton turtleneck, a wool dickey, a dark blue down jacket, and beige khaki army pants. Still, I was ice-cold. The sun had gone down around seven that night, and the temperature had dropped to about ten degrees below zero. I had no faith that I'd be feeling warm anytime soon.

The winds howled and knocked viciously against the shack. Morgan was sound asleep as the men and I tossed and turned and chattered nonsense. I didn't know who was saying what. I was barely coherent myself.

"Hey, guys, do you think I'll freeze to death before morning?" I asked.

I think it was Fred who said, "No way. It's too cold to die here."

My teeth were clattering. My lips had turned blue during the day, according to the guys. That was certainly a sign of hypothermia. But I still found the courage to hold on to my dream of going to the summit. We talked nonsense all night, just to keep our minds off how awful we felt and the demons that were stirring inside us. We never slept.

Morgan woke at 3:00 a.m. as promised and was anxious to go. We told him that we weren't able to get any sleep. He shook his head in sympathy.

"So sorry. I make fire. We eat and go."

I staggered to the doorway. My feet were numb. I pinched and pulled the skin of my face; there was no sensation. The guys staggered to the door after me, each listing his complaints. None of us was well. The guys grabbed the doorframe for balance, just as I had.

"No matter what, stay together," counseled Morgan.

"No pain, no gain," one of the guys said.

Morgan prepared our final meal of the climb—oatmeal, a biscuit, and hot black tea that turned lukewarm once it touched my lips.

Before we began our final ascent, I had to pray.

"Lord, give me the strength to climb this mountain. Please be with me, and don't let me freeze."

Over the next six hours, we were glued to each other, afraid of getting lost. Our Eveready flashlights illuminated our path only faintly. I felt I was in the darkest place on earth. The full moon was faintly visible behind the endless black sky, which was devoid of stars. We sunk into gray ash pits and stepped on shards that poked holes in the soles of our shoes. I had forgotten about the blister on my heel because I had lost all feeling in my body. The Lord's Prayer was my constant companion. The thinning air wreaked havoc with our brains, preventing us from being able to concentrate. Morgan stayed close.

"No life here, nothing grows; volcano ash all over. Keep going *pole, pole,*" he said.

We had to go slow; the higher we climbed, the less oxygen we took in. We began stumbling over each other's feet and falling down. Our equilibrium was off, and it got worse as the terrain shot upward like a roller coaster. We were forced to lean forward to walk, fighting the gravitational pull that tried to move us in the opposite direction. We had to poke around with our walking sticks before placing our feet, first making sure we were on solid ground. The more force with which we leaned forward, the more we sank into ash.

We frequently stopped to catch our breath. At least the pain from the shards let me know that my feet weren't frostbitten, about to fall off.

Yes, I can feel, I can feel, I said to myself.

"We're 18,000 feet above the earth. We've climbed five hours since leaving camp," Morgan informed us. "Come, let's rest inside this cave. Not for long, though. We want to see sunrise soon on the summit. We can't see anything now."

Morgan's calmness kept me centered. We rested inside a cave that was about twelve feet high, just big enough for the five of us to snuggle into. For light, Morgan leaned his flashlight against the entrance.

I was happy for this respite. The temperature had dropped to about fifteen degrees below zero. I glanced over at Fred. The mucus from his nose had dripped onto his upper lip and formed a frozen moustache. He had a terrible migraine and leaned his head against the wall, hoping to find some relief.

Morgan searched his backpack for another aspirin, but his supply had run out. He wanted us to drink water from his canteen, but it was frozen; he couldn't even get a trickle to come out.

"We got to get there. We can't stop long, or I'll turn back," Dave said softly.

Suddenly Rod's body thrust forward. He heaved and vomited up the broth and something green. He gagged, and then heaved again. His vomit turned to ice on the cave floor. Rod's pallor was whiter than white. Dave staggered over to help him, but he was in bad shape, too.

"Just keep breathing slowly. That's it. You will be okay," Morgan advised.

The men followed his instructions. As for me, I couldn't move. I leaned against the wall stoically, thinking about my warm bed in Detroit.

"Come, time to go. Sun coming, only half hour to summit," Morgan said.

Fred, Dave, and Rod pushed off the cave walls, propelling themselves to the entrance. Their steps were slow. Rod turned and spoke to me.

"Gloria, we'll wait for you."

"No, please go on. I'm not sure if I can. I can't feel anything again. I think I'm frostbitten. So, go," I said, trembling.

"You can't stop now. You're the strongest among us," encouraged Fred.

The men's eyes were closing as they drifted from consciousness to semi-consciousness.

"Thanks, guys. Go. I'll catch you. If you don't see me in a few minutes, I've turned back."

"I will stay with her. You go *pole, pole.* Follow that path ahead," Morgan told them, pointing ahead.

The three men walked slowly away from the cave, hunched over like old, wounded soldiers. If I wanted to catch up to them, I could have. I began to move, dragging one foot then the other. I stopped and leaned against the cave's entrance. I thought about the woman at Arusha. I turned to Morgan. "Was that lady right? Are we really cursed by the cold, huh? My feet are as stiff as a cadaver's."

"What is that?" he asked.

"A dead body. That's how I feel. I can't feel anything. I know I'm frost-bitten. When you're frostbitten, they have to amputate you," I remarked.

"I don't believe the curse. When people climb, things happen to the body and mind," he said, pointing to his head. "Bad things start going through your mind."

Morgan moved close to me. I stared into his soft, brown eyes. He gently pulled off my layers of mittens. He cupped his hands over mine and moved them to his mouth. He tenderly breathed the warm air from his body on my hands. The only thing I could feel were his gentle words touching my heart.

"My sister, you will make it. Remember, black Americans don't climb Kilimanjaro. Go *pole, pole* just half mile to summit. You will make it."

This time when I looked into his oval eyes, I saw my African ancestry, a rich lineage—a lineage that had suffered oppression, but had stood up and fought tenaciously to end it. I wanted to be proud like the person I saw in Morgan's eyes. That could only happen if I released the rage caused by the wrongs done to me and my ancestors. I had to let it go.

With Morgan's encouragement, I took small steps out of the cave. I had little oxygen, so I was forced to go slow. Eventually, I came to a narrow path wide enough to place one foot in front of the other. It was covered with snow, ice, and ash. Moving was problematic, as over and over again I sank into deep ash pits. Then, I fell. A sense of helplessness came over me. A litany of self-defeating thoughts ran through my mind.

Why can't I just do it? I'm an athlete; this shouldn't happen. Why am I here? Why am I torturing myself? Why didn't I just listen to white folks when they told me I'd never be anything?

I had learned how much harder Kilimanjaro was than I'd expected— more difficult than the pictures in nature magazines implied. Morgan reached for my aching arm and gently pulled me up.

"Gloria, you will not give up. Black Americans don't climb Kilimanjaro, but you will!"

I began to think about my female relatives and what advice they would give me if they were there.

My mother's mother would tell me, "We never gave up through hardships. We never quit."

Mother Dear would say, "Honey, you come too far, you must go on. I endured hardship. Now you're standing on my shoulders to make it in life."

Even Dad Harry's words found their way into my head. "A winner never quits, and a quitter never wins," he'd say.

I thought of my favorite scripture, which I evoked often during my college years: *I can do all things through Christ who strengthens me.*

Morgan was hovering over me. "Gloria, there, see Kilimanjaro. You go. I will stand here, I wait for you."

He pointed to the peak. It was less than a mile away, slightly to the right, yet it looked even closer, like I could throw one of the volcanic pebbles and hit it. That's one of the mystical things about climbing Kilimanjaro; your destination looks closer than your reality. I turned to Morgan.

"I'll go. I can't turn back now."

Suddenly, adrenaline kicked in. I quickened my steps, stumbling over my lifeless feet. My mind was in high gear, but my body was slow and fatigued. I found a less tedious way to walk, following the footprints my teammates had made in the snow.

As the sun's face pierced the horizon, I finally saw what Morgan had been talking about. It was so electrifying that when I looked directly into it. I was blinded. Somehow, I found strength to reach for my ski goggles.

The guys had made the summit only a few minutes before I did. They were basking spread eagle in the sun's warmth.

I hobbled on my numb feet through the crackling snow and ice. Just when I thought I was almost at the summit, the path narrowed. Morgan had me walk in front of him. He wanted to make sure I was okay. I began stumbling over small boulders, broken pieces of thick ice, and sharp pieces of rock. I had arrived at the rim of the crater. The sides were steep and filled with black cinder and pieces of ice. I was extra careful because there was no guardrail, and at any time I could fall over the sides and into a ravine.

It was eerily quiet. I had managed to create a rhythm with my walking stick, hitting every pile of ice and rock at the same "tap-tap-tap" interval; I used that rhythm to regulate my breathing. I was just steps from the summit as my cold body bent in two, so that I was walking the path like an old woman with a bad case of osteoporosis. I could hear Morgan's voice in my head.

"Go *pole, pole*. Make summit. Black Americans don't climb Kilimanjaro."

"Well, now they do, Morgan, 'cause I've just claimed my spot," I said so softly he couldn't hear from where he was waiting a few meters away. With raised hands, I looked upward to the heavens in appreciation. Then, I planted my stick in the snow next to a tattered European flag and a concrete plaque that read "Gilman's Point."

Although many say the actual summit is Uhuru—600 feet and ninety minutes farther away—most climbers stop where I did and consider their mission accomplished. More importantly, the government recognizes the place to which I climbed as the summit.

I felt a tremendous sense of accomplishment, finally being able to plant my feet on the roof of the world, witnessing the sun rising big and full against the backdrop of the blue sky. I noticed that even the puffy, white clouds were dancing in celebration of my feat, and the huge glaciers were sparkling like diamonds in the sun just for me.

"We did it," Fred said in a satisfying tone. We were all too exhausted to carry on a real conversation.

"Yeah, we did," was all I said.

What I saw and felt were different from what my climbing buddies experienced. When I saw the jagged boulders of volcanic rock that made gashes in the glaciers, I was reminded of how the racism and injustice imposed on me nearly destroyed my life. I had become bitter and consumed with rage. Whites hated me and my ancestors, which drove me to hate them and, worse, to hate myself: my hair, my nose, my skin, my language, and my intelligence. If it hadn't been for this climb, I'm certain my rage would have turned lethal. It would have killed my dreams.

I learned from this climb not to believe things white folks, nor any folks, say if it doesn't foster the goodness of human spirit, if it's contradictory to my belief system.

And climbing Kilimanjaro also taught me how to forgive.

My opinion of white folks changed. Not all of them had oppressive attitudes like I was surrounded by growing up. The whites who made the expedition with me were liberal and progressive, desiring the same freedoms that I did. Otherwise, they wouldn't have put themselves through the difficulties of the journey. They wouldn't have survived it.

Extending my hands to the heavens, I surrendered the rage, the bitterness, and the vengeance—all the painful prejudice and racism that had been inflicted on me. I forgave those who had harmed me. I forgave myself for believing harmful things. I was now free. I had met God on Mount Kilimanjaro, and I had been transformed.

I still needed to purge myself of the pain of my childhood molestations, as I had done with the pain of white oppression. I knew that because of the strength I'd found on that mountain, when the time was right I would find the strength to face all my demons. I decided that, when it came to going down such a scary path, I would follow the lesson Morgan taught me: *"Pole, pole."*

CHAPTER THIRTEEN

When I returned from Africa to my community-organizing job in Detroit, I had a new lease on life. I was changed and proud of it—proud of my ability to stand on the summit of Kilimanjaro and release my years of rage and hatred toward whites. In 1977, the government brought on certified guides to ensure the safety of climbers on Kilimanjaro; I liked the fact that, when I took on the mountain, it was still a little more dangerous to do so. *The Detroit News* published a front-page feature on my climb, but it didn't mention my new spiritual awakening; I wasn't ready to share that with anyone. I was ready to find someone to share my life with, though.

At the beginning of 1977, about six months after I returned from Africa, I met Henry, the most gorgeous, drop-dead handsome man I'd ever seen. It was as if he'd been conjured from one of my dreams, with his high cheekbones and caramel complexion, his wavy hair styled in an Afro.

I was smitten by Henry's intellect, his vocabulary, his radiant smile, and gentlemanly manners. It was a rarity to meet a black man from my church with a college education. The holiness, some call it Pentecostal, church placed little value on education because they felt it too worldly, and that once people acquired it, they soon forgot about God. It was nearly taboo for women to seek higher education. We were relegated to the house—cooking and rearing babies.

Henry was a minister in the Church of God in Christ in South Bend, Indiana. When we met, he had just been accepted into a theological university in Atlanta, where he was to begin studying for his master's degree that September. Although he was seven years younger than I, everyone said I looked younger.

We were inseparable when we got the chance to be together. We played tennis, took walks in the park, and, of course, went to church. On weekends when Henry couldn't get to Lansing, we were constantly on the phone with each other. He said he enjoyed our intellectual talks because there were so few black women in the holiness church who had acquired degrees, like I had. As hard as it was, we made a vow to respect our denomination's belief about abstaining from sex until marriage. I truly felt that we were meant for each other. After only a few months of dating, he popped "the question." He said that I was what he'd always wanted in a wife. "You're all I need," I told him with no hesitation.

The engagement ring I flaunted was from a previous relationship of Henry's, which didn't faze me because he promised to buy a new ring when he finished graduate school. I trusted him—whenever he said he was going to do something, he always did. He never broke a date. He was a good listener. He was compassionate about blacks and the poor. Most importantly, we accepted each other as we were. I was also impressed by how certain Henry was of what he wanted out of life. He dreamed of pastoring and starting a religious business. His qualities put him far above other black men I knew.

My parents liked Henry, too. Whatever made me happy, they were for it, as long as the man I married treated me with respect, worked to take care of his family, and had a college education. Henry's mother was nice to me—so nice it was like having another mother.

Despite how sure I was, how well I thought I knew Henry (and myself), after we were married I came to realize that I hadn't known Henry the way I thought I did. It's different when you're living with someone. I wasn't familiar with his temperament, his moods, and hot buttons. Because we were in a long-distance relationship, we were so happy when we got to be together that we were on our best behavior and overly respectful of one another. Something happened one month before our marriage that should have been an indicator of what Henry was truly like.

Henry had a classic black and white convertible that was twenty years old. The leather interior was in need of some repairs, as was the convertible top. The body was in good condition, a few rust spots here and there that could be fixed. The car ran well. Henry planned to restore it and sell it for a nice profit—at least that's what we had discussed.

One day Henry told me that once we married, he would simply retire his convertible and drive my Audi. I told him that didn't seem like a good plan, that I would need my car for work. Henry said he would drop me off at work and pick me up, and if I had meetings to attend, he would chauffer me back and forth to those, too. I couldn't understand his logic. The graduate school he was attending was down the street from our apartment. He would hardly ever even need a car.

I continued to debate the subject with him, but Henry failed to see my side. During our exchange, he raised his voice to me for the first time.

"I see you're stubborn, accustomed to your independence, having your way," he said. "Well, if this is an indication of what our marriage will be like, maybe we should call it off."

I was stunned. I loved this man; I didn't want to lose him because of a disagreement over a car. I carefully thought it over and decided to concede. "You're right, maybe I am stubborn and too independent from being on my own for so long." Then I apologized and said I would work on being more considerate of having a partner in my life.

When Henry and I told his mother about the argument, she agreed that I needed a car for work. Henry was peeved and accused her of siding with me. So that I wouldn't lose the good man I was convinced I'd found, I never disagreed with Henry again during our courtship.

On the day before the wedding, I decided to test my false eyelashes. Henry demanded that I remove them, saying, "You look like Jezebel. I'm not having a wife like that."

Eyelashes weren't worth calling off a wedding over—at least I didn't think so. On June 25, 1977, our nuptials took place as planned. I had five of my best friends as bride's maids and my sister Eva as my maid of honor. As the oldest by many years, I was the first in the Ewing family to marry.

The ladies wore light pink dresses that beautifully complemented my long, white satin one. The only make-up I wore was pink lip gloss, although it was barely noticeable under my long white veil, which also hid most of my shoulder-length curls. The men wore burgundy suits with pink shirts. Much of the ceremony is a blur because I was so exhausted from taking care of the arrangements.

I do remember how I proudly walked down the aisle, knees trembling, feeling so happy to share the most joyous moment of my life with my biological mother on one arm and my adoptive mother on the other. Dad Harry gave me away, although he was slightly oblivious to what was going on due to his failing health.

After honeymooning a week in Canada, Henry and I returned to Lansing to make our farewells before setting off for Atlanta, Georgia, in Henry's classic convertible, with my Audi attached to the U-Haul. When we arrived, our two-bedroom apartment was waiting for us. Before we could occupy it, Mr. Coleman, the manager, gave us a lecture about the rules: no working on cars; no clothes or rugs hanging from the exterior; no loud music; and no late rent payments. Mr. Coleman's in-your-face style irritated Henry. When my husband questioned him about a rule, Mr. Coleman became irritated. "Look, Reverend, if it weren't for your wife here, I wouldn't rent to you. I'm not going to put up with your attitude."

From then on, I got to deal with Mr. Coleman.

We were in Atlanta less than a month when Henry and I left for Africa, to fulfill my promise of taking the Detroit high school students there with the African Study Program. We had worked hard to raise the necessary funds. First, Henry and I flew to New York to meet the eight fortunate students and their chaperones. And then it was off to Ghana.

Since I had made this trip before, I was familiar with the sights that greeted us when we arrived at Kotoka International airport in Accra, Ghana's capital, where we were assigned our host families. The students, however, experienced a bit of culture shock, which was to be expected. Kids being kids, they quickly assimilated.

The students immediately took to dressing in the colorful native garb. The young men fashioned themselves in colorful print tops made from Kwame Nkrumah cloth (named after a former president of Ghana), and matching pants tailored to the ankle.

They eagerly consumed the local cuisine. Everyone agreed that the most delicious dish was ground nut soup—peanuts ground into a powder with spicy red pepper. There was also a consensus by the students that they could go the rest of their lives without ever again tasting fufu—a pounded cassava meal with a taste similar to flour dough, served with fresh, meaty fish from the Atlantic Ocean and a spicy curry sauce.

An experience that left the youth wide-eyed was shopping with their host families at Makola Market on Kojo Thompson Road. It was the largest market in Accra. Smoked dried fish, boiled peanuts, tomatoes, Colgate toothpaste, Ivory liquid soap, Listerine, and hair chemicals were displayed neatly on wood crates along the curb. Although some Africans still spoke their native Twi, and still others continued to embrace the six other tribal languages, nearly everyone spoke English with an eloquent British accent. Aggressive merchants shouted, "You American, my sister, my brother, come, this is American—buy."

But we weren't there to buy American. We stopped by every stall that proudly displayed the treasures for which Ghana was known: hand-crafted statues, brass jewelry, stacks of colorful fabric, and kente cloth, a beautifully hand-woven brightly colored cloth reserved for joyous occasions.

We were all in awe of how skillfully the indigenous people balanced objects on their heads: black soap, tomatoes, plantains. One of the host families tried to balance a wide pan on a student's head, but it quickly fell. African children hone their fine motor skills at an early age, so by adulthood they have excellent balance.

Our three-week stay didn't provide the students sufficient time to fully comprehend the richness and beauty of a country that had hundreds of years of history but, nonetheless, the visit did change their negative, Eurocentric perceptions of Africa. And we all forged friendships with our host families that we would cherish for years.

Shortly after returning from Ghana, I landed a job as assistant director of community services for the Atlanta Urban League, a position that required a master's degree and paid about thirty thousand dollars a year to start. I had to interact with other social service agencies, coordinate the membership drive, and attend meetings in the community. As I'd predicted, I needed a car, but Henry was so adamant about taking me to and from work that I didn't dare argue. It bothered me how much I couldn't think for myself at home in order to keep peace in the marriage. It was different at work—I performed duties that required me to make independent decisions. But at home, Henry wanted to make all the decisions himself. He often reminded me that he was the man of the house.

"I have the final word. God wanted the wife to be subject to the husband."

Even though I was beginning to see Henry for who he really was, I had hope for the marriage. I believed things would change; after all, this was a new situation for both of us.

Henry worked as a paid coordinator for a local Church of God in Christ, which was at the time the newest black church in Atlanta, with a membership of thousands. His role was to coordinate programs and to assist the pastor, Dr. Isaac Green.

Then, six months into our marriage, Henry decided to start a religious business that he called a ministry, an idea he never specifically discussed with me, but something he said God put on his heart to do. He told me it was something that was needed in the black church, and if I supported it, we would reap financial rewards later. It was an audio-visual ministry that addressed various needs in the church.

His first creation was "Blacks in the Bible" with a well-known black scholar. Henry excelled at script writing, securing actors, shooting the film, and marketing. It was ingenious—certainly a needed ministry. I felt I needed to support him. But at this point in our marriage, I was concerned about finances.

"Honey, how is this going to be funded?" I asked.

"Through our tithes. Your tithes, my tithes from my job. We'll get contributions from friends. I know a lot of people who will support this. Plus, the audio-visuals will generate revenue that we'll reinvest into the ministry." I wasn't sold on the idea, but I felt that I had no choice but to go along with what my husband wanted. I supported our church and this new ministry through tithes. That wasn't good enough for Henry.

"How is it that you're my wife and can't tithe one hundred percent to my ministry?"

"I don't feel your ministry qualifies as a church. I'm uncomfortable not giving to my church," I told him.

We debated for weeks. To avoid further conflict, I began tithing to his ministry exclusively. Henry was pleased.

"Babe, it means a lot for a wife to support her husband. You won't regret your decision. Trust me, this will secure our future. Just have faith in me."

I also gave beyond the tithe. Whatever was needed for this new ministry, I made it happen, whether it was a new projector or film, business cards, or brochures. Shortly after he started this business, Henry quit his job at the church to give it the full attention it needed, he said. He remained in theology school, but now there was only one check coming in. My income was supposed to cover household expenses, a car loan, groceries, overdue bills, and the needs of his business.

I grew exceedingly anxious about our finances. We were unable to save. I couldn't buy clothes for my job, although I found a way to proudly wear the same three dresses and one pair of shoes throughout the week. The dresses were simple shifts that covered my knee, something our church believed women should do. And I wore no make-up. Sometimes I felt like I was living in the stagecoach era. Yet it was better for me this way; it kept my husband from falsely accusing me of attracting men, something I had experienced early on in my marriage when I learned that Henry was incredibly insecure and obsessively jealous.

Henry and I had been invited to a large church banquet at a fancy hotel. A man sitting across the table from us stared at me through the entire event; I felt like he was undressing me with his eyes, as the saying goes. I tried to ignore him because I knew if I didn't, Henry would make a big deal of it later. It didn't work; when we got home, Henry scolded me as though I were a child.

"Did you think I didn't see you flirting with that man? I know what you were doing."

"Henry, I had no idea who that man was. I've never seen him before. I was uncomfortable with how he kept staring at me. I tried looking in the opposite direction."

For the rest of the night, I got my husband's cold shoulder.

I began to live my life as Henry wanted me to. Within a year of our marriage, I had cut all ties with my friends in Detroit, especially Skip, my militant civil-rights brother. Henry accused me of having an affair with him, which was never the case. I also broke ties with my girlfriends, including my best, best girlfriend, Pam. Eventually I had little to do with my family. Henry told me I was married to him and not to any of those other people. Mom Frances had real concerns. She felt Henry was neglecting his family.

"So if he's not bringing home a paycheck, how are you surviving?" she asked during one of our phone conversations.

"His new religious ministry will support us eventually. It's an investment. It's only in the start-up phase. It'll take some time and sacrifice, but it'll bring in money."

Henry overheard me and snatched the phone away. He confronted my mother in a hostile manner.

"Why are you prying into our marriage? Mind your own business. You don't know what I'm trying to do!"

Then Henry slammed down the phone. He told me Mom Frances was interfering in our marriage, and it would be best to separate myself from her. I was appalled at his behavior, especially since he was a minister. I had never seen Dad Harry treat Mom Frances the way Henry was treating me.

I still found ways to communicate with Mom. I would call her when Henry wasn't home or send a card to let her know I was fine. That wasn't really true, though. I hardly ever laughed anymore.

Although our marriage was a roller-coaster the first year, Henry and I both hoped it would get better. We planned to have two children, a boy first and then a girl, hoping this would make us more committed to each other. In order to emulate what I thought a good wife should be, I became a "yes" woman—not the woman that God made me, but the one Henry wanted. I was no longer the independent, vivacious black woman I used to be. Instead, I devolved into a submissive wife

I had gotten married at thirty, which was late. If I divorced Henry, I didn't think I would find anyone who would accept me, a fear Henry continually reinforced. I also felt the pressure to stay married because of our church. They believed in divorce exclusively under the conditions of adultery. Growing up, I saw my adoptive parents' lengthy marriage succeed, and I wanted my marriage to last like that, too. It was around the first week of December in 1978 when I awoke covered with hives from my head to my toes. I had swelling around my eyes, lips, hands, and feet. I was an unrecognizable monster. It turned out I was pregnant.

I was miserably happy. Happy to give birth at thirty-three years old, but miserable because there was no cure for what I had—urticaria and angioedema. In layman's terms that's acute hives; the pimple-sized blisters could only be relieved with Benadryl and nothing else, as other meds could endanger the baby. The Benadryl only worked for eight hours and then the hives came right back. My illness lasted the entire nine months I was pregnant.

Many nights, Henry would relieve the itch by gently scratching the hives with a bore brush. Sometimes when I would scratch, I would make them bleed. My doctor said my particular case was probably due to a hormonal imbalance. He was certain the hives would go away after the baby was born.

My husband was the most loving and gentle man during my pregnancy. We seldom argued. He said he wanted me to be stress-free so that our son would be healthy. "I've got to have a son to keep my legacy alive," he said constantly.

"But what if it's a girl?" I asked.

"Well, I just know it's a boy, so there's no point in thinking about a girl. It's time in my family for a boy. And if it's a girl, well, I'll love her anyway, as long as she's healthy."

Still, from early on in my pregnancy, Henry got me so revved up about giving birth to a boy that I didn't think much about having a girl. The only complaint I had during my pregnancy was that Henry didn't give me enough help. I worked all day and came home to find that I had to cook and clean the house. He would pitch in whenever I asked or on special occasions, but I continued to do the bulk of the work.

Although I was plagued daily with side effects from urticaria, my physical suffering became insignificant compared to feeling my baby jab its little fingers into my stomach and push his feet into my skin until I could see the imprint. The best part was feeling the feet and fingers move to the beat of music in church. Henry felt validated.

"You see," he'd say to me. "That's just like a boy drummer or musician."

Henry even got the doctor to say we were going to have a boy because the heartbeat was so strong.

I was still working at the Urban League two weeks before the delivery. My boss, Peter Wright, wasn't happy about my pregnancy.

"I thought you were going to give the League three years," he told me.

During this era, it was typical for men to not support working women with families. I paid Mr. Wright no mind. I was concerned about how we were going to survive with no paycheck and a new baby while I was on maternity leave. There wasn't enough money from Henry's ministry business. Whatever small amount came in from an audio-visual sale to a church had to be reinvested.

On September 25, 1979, I went into labor. After seventeen hours, I was only dilated two centimeters. If Henry hadn't coached me through the Lamaze technique, I would have yanked the baby out. Dr. Stanley Levine at Northside Hospital finally rendered his verdict: "Mrs. Lockhart, your cervix is the size of a young girl's. You can't have a vaginal delivery. We're forced to do a caesarean," Dr. Levine said.

I was too tired from pushing to ask how he hadn't known this before. And I was worried; the baby had a bowel movement inside of me, which was a sign of distress. I was given an epidural and was wheeled into the delivery room. Henry proudly walked into the room in his green scrubs, with a still camera hanging from his side and a portable tape recorder in one hand, while coaching me through the pain.

I was awake during the entire procedure to witness the delivery on September 26, 1979 at 6:13 a.m. of a healthy baby girl who weighed seven pounds and four ounces. My daughter wasn't shy. She kicked and screamed at the top of her lungs without having to be spanked in the traditional manner.

Henry and I weren't prepared with names for a girl; it took us a day to come up with a few. We wanted something that reflected our African pride. We liked that Tiombe was simple and had a nice sound. It meant "gentle"; our daughter's middle name, Anika, meant "kind."

The following day was worse than the labor pains. The nurses forced me to walk, but I moved so slowly Henry said he imagined Miss Jane Pittman, the legendary slave who lived to be 110 years old, would move faster. The pain from the caesarean was followed by the pain of trying to breastfeed Tiombe for the first time. My nipples were so sore I thought they were going to fall off. I couldn't touch them much less have the baby take milk from them. If it hadn't been for the coaching of the La Leche League, I would have given up. It took three weeks to toughen my nipples.

At home, I quickly acclimated to the regimen of washing cloth diapers in our stackable washer and dryer unit. We were too poor to afford Pampers or diaper service. Multi-tasking had become a habit. I cared for the baby, did the daily wash, kept the house, and cooked Monday through Sunday. Henry would play with Tiombe, but he didn't lend a helping hand very often. He felt his role was to continue to work on his ministry and finish graduate school. Soon, he had reverted to his old ways of not helping at all.

With no additional income and my final paycheck exhausted, we fell on hard times. The phone was disconnected. The lights were turned off. We had borrowed at capacity from Henry's mother and my uncle Fredrick. I couldn't allow things to get out of control. I refused to endanger myself and my baby.

I put on an old pregnancy outfit—I couldn't afford anything new—held my head up as high as I could, and stepped into the office of the Fulton County Department of Child and Family Services to obtain food stamps. We were so poor that they issued food stamps immediately and a small check that we would receive monthly until our case was reevaluated. Going to the county was humiliating. I had to produce bank statements, bills, a birth certificate, a social security card, and a driver's license. I didn't even have my car anymore; someone ran into Henry and totaled it.

What we received from the county wasn't enough for a family of three, so Henry had to take a job at a gas station. After a few months, he quit. He said it took too much time away from his ministry. So I was forced to return to work at the Atlanta Urban League. As a new mom, it was a painful decision. I just wasn't ready. My scar from the caesarean hadn't completely healed, which prohibited me from lifting. My stomach was bloated, and my breasts were always full of milk. I had no choice, though; we were getting deeper and deeper in debt.

In February 1980, I sent a letter to Peter Wright and to the executive director, Gary Jackson, advising them of my early return. After not hearing from them, I phoned my boss, Mr. Wright, and he gave me the news.

"Well, Mrs. Lockhart, your job has been filled. I'm sorry. Check back with us in a few months to see if we have any openings."

The League didn't fill my position until March 17, weeks after they knew I was returning. It was filled by a male employee who didn't have a master's degree, which had been a requirement of the position when I took it. There had been several vacancies between the time of my expected return and the time I actually wanted to return. I had just read the disability law, which also pertained to maternity leave, and knew I could return to the same position if it were available, or I could fill a comparable job.

I was desperate for money. I applied for unemployment with the Georgia Department of Labor, but it was quickly denied by the Atlanta Urban League. I appealed and won.

I then contacted the EEOC, the Equal Employment Opportunity Commission, to determine my recourse. The news that I wanted to return spread quickly at the League; so did my going to the EEOC. Several friends from the League called and told me under no circumstances should I report the agency's wrongdoings to the EEOC. They felt Gary Jackson was the most powerful and influential black man in the city; no one had ever opposed him. Other people had lost their jobs in a similar manner, but they quietly moved on. Mr. Jackson knew every person of influence in the city, including those at the EEOC, which was in the same building as the League. He also served on the board of MARTA, the rapid transit system.

"Gloria, if you sue, you'll be blackballed for life. You'll never work in Atlanta again," people told me.

My retort was, "I want my job back, and I want justice to prevail."

On May 13, 1980, I met with Richard Stone, a commission representative, in a fact-finding conference. I had charged the League with sexual discrimination under two conditions: my job was conveniently filled by a male when it was understood that I would be returning and, throughout my employment, I had encountered sexual innuendos from Peter Wright that were inappropriate. I was subjected to comments such as, "Lockhart, I should have married you instead of Henry. You just came a few years too late," and "Look out, Lockhart, hmm...look out, lookin' good today."

When Mr. Jackson first learned of my pregnancy, he stated, "We had some things in the making for you."

The commission representative listened, took copious notes, and later said, "You have a good case. We'll do what we can. If you're looking for money, we can't help you, but if you want to be reinstated, we'll take your case."

In a few weeks, the League reinstated me. As I returned to the Piedmont building, I walked down the long corridor not knowing what to expect. Most people were in disbelief. There was no fanfare surrounding my return, but colleagues secretly told me how noble I was to stand up for my rights against the most prominent black in the city. Neither Peter Wright nor Gary Jackson ever mentioned the case. The man who was in my position was demoted to another in the agency.

After two months back at the League, I resigned. A new position had been offered to me as coordinator of volunteer services for the United Way of Metropolitan Atlanta. Gary Jackson was so furious that he generated a memo to his entire staff, "Any staff seeking employment outside of the Atlanta Urban League must notify their immediate supervisor first." I found out he was upset because he served on the United Way board and he would have blocked me if he had known about my job offer in time.

United Way was a refreshing change. My supervisor, Mae Gilley, was a parent herself and embraced my role as a new mom. The people there were friendly and supportive. Unfortunately, things weren't going well at home. Henry and I were continually getting into arguments over finances. He said I put too much pressure on him to take a regular job so that we could pay bills and that I didn't validate his business.

I made several efforts to convince him that I believed in his dream, but I was under so much financial pressure I couldn't get around the fact that we needed two steady incomes. Our finances were in such bad shape that my paycheck was garnished. Henry relented and took a job as a drug rehabilitation counselor, but after about six months he was let go because he didn't get along with his supervisor. I didn't understand why he couldn't hold on to a job knowing he had a family to support. I was becoming bitter and unhappy.

To save our marriage, we began Christian counseling with Dr. Annenberg. He was a calm and understanding minister whose wife was also older than he. Henry and I went to about three sessions when the counselor began to identify the problem.

"Reverend, I feel your wife is overcompensating for you. It's time for you not to rely on her for everything. Take on responsibilities. She's protecting you too much," he said.

Henry got up, stormed out, and never went back. When we got home, he accused me of calling the counselor prior to the session and telling him about our relationship, which was untrue. From then on, the tension between us grew. I was afraid to say anything to Henry. I completely closed down.

Sometime in the winter of 1981, when Tiombe was about two years old, the three of us were walking back to our apartment, which was in the heart of the black community. We had just finished seeing a movie at the Omni, in downtown Atlanta. The three of us were walking across an overpass; I was on the far left, Tiombe was in the middle holding my hand, and Henry was on the right, by the curb.

At that moment, I contemplated jumping off the overpass. It was about three stories down. I wanted to end my life. I couldn't find a way out of my abusive marriage. I had no one to talk to and didn't think anyone would listen anyway. After all, I was a minister's wife, and no one expected us to have problems with our husbands, at least I had never heard of a minister and his wife having problems. Everything seemed to be a tightly held secret among this culture of wives.

As I looked over the edge, my entire body seized up. My legs got weak. *What if I jump and not die, but become paralyzed?* I thought.

Then Tiombe looked up at me and smiled, revealing her two front teeth. Her smile calmed me.

I can't have these thoughts; I must live for my child, not for my marriage, I told myself.

A few months later, something happened to me that no wife should ever have to experience. Henry and I had gotten into another argument over finances; this time I spoke up about how I really felt. Henry responded by slapping me across my face, causing my nose to bleed profusely. My face was numb for several minutes. It was hard to stop the bleeding. This brought back memories of when Mom Frances slapped me as a child for being "lippy," which meant talking back. I applied a small piece of brown paper from a bag under my upper lip, the same as she had done, and eventually the bleeding stopped.

Henry apologized over and over again. He was remorseful and, for the first time, I saw him cry. "Babe, I'm so sorry. I never meant to hurt you. I lost my temper," he said.

We prayed together for a better understanding, but weeks later, things worsened. It seemed every time I presented my opinion, we argued. Henry slammed the refrigerator and broke all the eggs, then turned to me as I stood by the closet door with my baby in my arms. He slammed his fist into the door's wooden slabs, causing them to bend inward. I ducked to miss his swing. As he walked toward me, I kicked him in the leg for fear that he would slap me again. He yelled as he walked toward the phone. He picked up the receiver and began shouting at me.

"Go ahead, call the cops! I'll tell them I have a wife who nags all the time. She doesn't appreciate the long hours I put in trying to build a future for my family. Go ahead! Go ahead! Call them!"

I took the receiver from Henry. I was shaking and mortified as I dialed 911. I couldn't believe I was being abused again. How could he truly be sorry yet continue to do this to me? It had to stop. In a matter of minutes, two officers from the Atlanta Police Department, a woman and a man, were in our apartment. Their response wasn't what I had anticipated.

They stepped into our dining room and listened carefully to both sides. Then the female officer said, "Now, now, Reverend. You're a minister. I'm sure you can work all this out."

I couldn't believe that a woman would side with Henry just because he was a minister. Couldn't she see what was happening? I wanted her to arrest him.

Then, as if reading my mind, the male officer turned to me and said, "Would you like to press charges? That means we'll remove him and book him at the station."

By this point, Henry had calmed down. As much as it was what I wanted, it was hard to bear the thought of my daughter seeing her father hauled off by the cops. I could feel Henry's eyes on me, but I couldn't look at him. I replied with my head down in a sheepish manner, "No."

"Okay, I know you can work this all out," he said.

I nodded in agreement and sat on the couch to gain my composure. As I hugged my daughter, I prayed she wouldn't remember any of this.

For about a week, Henry was remorseful and sweet. He blamed the argument on me and the fact that I didn't have faith in him to make his business work. Once again I acquiesced and agreed that I could be more patient. Still, in my heart, I felt he needed to work to take care of his child. It wasn't about him giving up his dream—it was about our family. During our few weeks of reconciliation, we even talked about having another baby, this time the boy he wanted. The relationship soon took another turn downward, though.

In January 1982, Atlanta experienced the worst snow and ice storm in its history. People were caught off-guard as in a matter of hours the city was blanketed with heavy snow mixed with ice. Cars were abandoned in the middle of freeways. Busses slid into opposite lanes as people jumped off and walked down the highway in an attempt to get home or pick up their children. No one owned snow tires. The city didn't have appropriate snow equipment and the city government was in disarray.

For several days, Atlanta was paralyzed. Schools, colleges, daycare centers, businesses, and other organizations had to close down. People depended on the United Way for services and I had to return to work. Henry's college was closed, so I asked for his help with the baby during the half day I had to be at the office.

"I was up late last night working on the business and need a break. I need to chill, go to a movie. Just take her with you," he said.

"I'll need to take the car then, since I'll have her with me," I replied. Although the roads were hazardous, I knew from living in Michigan how to drive in snow.

"That's okay, I'll drop you off."

Although it wasn't common to bring kids to the workplace, a few people did. At two, Tiombe was the best behaved child. She would sit for hours reading books, coloring, and playing with her suitcase full of Barbie dolls and also with her imaginary friends. At the end of my half day, I called Henry to pick us up. He didn't seem to want to be disturbed.

"I can't. I'm on my way to the movie. I haven't gotten to rest like I wanted yet. Just take MARTA. You'll be here in minutes."

"But, Henry, the sidewalks are covered with ice and snow. People can barely walk on them. Most people couldn't even get into work here today."

"All you have to do is walk a few blocks to MARTA, get on the train, and I'll pick you up at the Vine Street station," he said.

I zipped Tiombe into her pink polyester snow suit, placed the pink mittens attached to her coat onto her hands, tied her white wool scarf around her neck, placed her pink wool cap over her ears, and put on her white rubber boots, which would give her traction in the snow. With my briefcase in one hand and holding on to my child's hand with the other, I stepped from the salt-treated stairs onto the public sidewalk. It was then that I realized what I was attempting was nearly impossible with a child. Each step I took down Edgewood Avenue was tentative.

By the time I got to the corner, I had nearly fallen onto the hard ice several times. I knew the only way we would get to the station safely was if I carried Tiombe on my hip and alternated my briefcase from one hand to the other.

"Mama, Mama, are you okay?" Tiombe asked.

"Yes, baby, just hold on to Mama's neck real tight."

With each slow step, I had to do a lot of positive self-talk. I pretended I was climbing Kilimanjaro again, or running in a race. I never showed any signs of weakness to my child. Although the downtown MARTA station was about four blocks away, when I got there I felt like I had completed a marathon.

When Henry picked us up, I curtly greeted him, then said nothing. He had the audacity to ask, "Why are you so quiet? What's wrong?"

"If you can't see what I just went through to get here, then you're selfish." I was in no mood to be anything but blunt.

When we arrived home, I saw that Henry had thrown his underwear and other clothes on the floor; laundry was strewn from the kitchen to the living room. Dishes from the night before were piled up in the sink, and the bed was unmade.

"What's for dinner?" he asked.

I dropped my belongings at the door and began dinner, complaining timidly about the condition of the house. Messiness had been the norm for Henry since the beginning of our marriage.

After dinner, he wanted to participate in a game of backgammon. He hurled insults and belittled me. Unable to take it anymore, I threw the pieces down.

"Henry, I'm tired of your insults, your abuse. I refuse to take it any longer. I've taken it for almost five years, and that's long enough!"

"Well, what do you propose we do?" he asked with a note of arrogance in his voice.

"I want a separation. We need a break from each other."

"Now that's what you want, huh? I'm a minister with needs. What's the purpose in separation? You may as well file for divorce."

"We could try to work on our issues while we're apart. We have a child, and I would hate to divorce. I believe we can work it out," I said.

"There's nothing to work out. I'll find an attorney tomorrow, and we can end this," was Henry's response.

I sensed any further discussion was pointless.

It was apparent from how quick Henry was to dissolve the marriage that he had thought about divorce long before I proposed separation. He just didn't want to be the first to initiate it, so that he wouldn't be considered the "bad guy." First thing the next morning, he found an attorney to start the process.

Over the next month, a night didn't pass that I didn't cry myself to sleep. I dreaded having to divorce. It was too painful for me, and I wanted to avoid it at all cost for Tiombe's sake. I didn't want her to feel the same pain I felt when my biological parents divorced. I wanted Tiombe to be in the presence of a father. On the other hand, I wanted her to be in a home that radiated love, a home where she felt healthy and safe to express herself.

Henry immediately moved down the street with a friend. Several weeks later, he wanted to make amends. He constantly reminded me, "It's gonna be hard for you to remarry because you're thirty-five years old with a child. No man is gonna want a ready-made family."

He also told me how much he loved me and that he wanted to come back and make it work. I couldn't be convinced. How could you love someone and abuse them at the same time? It was preposterous. Enough was enough; I was finally ready to leave.

In May 1982, my divorce from Henry was final. I was a free woman. What surprised me most about leaving was the disbelief of the church folks. Many stopped me and asked what happened. Their comments were so naïve. "You were the most perfect couple I'd ever seen. I can't believe you're divorcing Reverend. He's such a good man," they'd tell me.

"You just don't know the truth. I'm happy to be free," I'd tell them, with a smile on my face for the first time in a long time.

CHAPTER FOURTEEN

"Free at last, free at last, thank God almighty, I'm free at last" was my daily devotion as I moved from my abusive marriage to single parenthood. It was 1982. I could almost fly like a bird, if it weren't for all the baggage I was carrying into my new life. I felt unattractive wearing long dresses like the holiness women, owning only enough of them to last a few days before I had to wear the same ones again, and going without make-up because it was prohibited in my church. I didn't think I would ever meet a man who would love me again.

"No man's gonna want you with a child," Henry would say.

Whatever he believed, I believed, too. I worried about everything. I worried about raising a kid alone. I worried about my social work job at United Way not being enough to pay debts incurred during my marriage. I worried about my daughter not having enough to eat. I worried about not being able to pay the four-hundred-dollar-a-month rent. I worried that Henry's obligation of $100 a month in child support, the minimum in the state of Georgia, wouldn't be enough for his daughter—if he even paid it.

Henry was consistent about fulfilling his financial obligations for about a year; after that, it was a hit or miss. It wasn't until he landed a professional job after graduating from theology school that we were able to count on him for a while. He became a chaplain at a military base near Savannah, Georgia, which was located over two hundred miles from Atlanta. On the weekends, he would come and spend time with Tiombe. When Henry came to Atlanta, we would usually have heated arguments about his visitations, which were scheduled for every other weekend. Sometimes he would come on off weekends, and other times Tiombe was busy with her budding modeling career.

"You're trying to keep her from me," Henry would accuse.

"I would never. It's just she's got such a promising future. It's what's best for her," I responded in my defense. Henry didn't understand the business.

At four years old, Tiombe was studying under a lady by the name of Michelle, a passionate teacher who taught black children modeling classes and self-esteem. This experience led to Tiombe's first modeling job, participating in a runway fashion show at the local Neiman Marcus. Everyone in the business said my child was a natural ham. By six years old, Tiombe had done print work for many national department stores. She was also active in the children's church choir. I didn't want to interrupt her schedule because it was rare that black kids had these types of opportunities, since the industry was still predominately white. Henry didn't understand.

"Your mom's pushing you into this, isn't she?" he would grill Tiombe.

Tiombe tried to convince her dad that she liked it, that she thought it was fun. But the situation didn't jive with Henry's conservative point of view. Instead of appreciating Tiombe's success, he felt slighted and betrayed. I never said anything negative about Henry to Tiombe. She loved her daddy so much. I wanted her to be an average kid who never got caught up in adult matters like I did after my parents divorced. I wanted to protect her from the pain of it all as much as I could, to shelter her from my hang-ups and issues about Henry. I wanted my daughter and her father to have a close relationship, so I did whatever I could to make that happen. Whenever she was busy and she missed seeing him, I tried to make it up.

One time, I nearly went to the end of the earth so Tiombe could see her dad. I didn't want him to think I was sabotaging their relationship, so I drove over 200 miles so she could spend a week with him.

I wasn't a fast, crazy driver, just one to keep within the fifty-five miles per hour speed limit. I was driving the eight-year-old Volvo that I held on to from the divorce. It needed repair work; I wasn't sure if it would make the trip, but I was willing to risk it for my child to see her dad. I also knew that Volvos were supposed to hold up under all kinds of conditions. My heart was prayerful.

The stretch of Highway 75 South and the five other highways we had to travel were the most monotonous and flat you'd ever want to ride over. At dusk, the sky and highway blended into one huge canvas of gray tones, making it impossible to see ahead. In minutes, the gray became pitch black. I found myself driving in one humongous open space with the only light coming from the few cars traveling in the opposite direction.

With only twenty miles to go before we hit Hinesville, my car broke down. All the panel lights lit up, and then the car slowed. Sensing that it was ready to die, I steered it off to the shoulder. I tried starting it again and again, but nothing happened. I took a deep breath as I surveyed my surroundings. Since the highway had no lights, there was nothing to see, just blackness. I was hours away from the urban city of Atlanta and stuck in a small Southern town. In the South, black folks had a saying, "If you ever travel outside of an urban Southern city, watch out. Don't ever stop. You're in Klan country."

I locked the car doors and sat nervously in the driver's seat, continually looking in the rearview mirror for the shape of a pointed, white hood, for the cloaked figure of Klansmen coming to lynch me and my child. I was doing some serious praying.

Realizing that panic wouldn't save us, I got hold of my emotions. I had to stay calm for my daughter, who was sitting patiently in her car seat in the back.

"Mama, it's gonna be okay. It's gonna be okay, okay?"

"Yes, honey, it's going to be okay. Someone will come for us soon," I reassured her.

I turned on my emergency flashers and gathered my courage to leave the car to tie a white rag on my antenna, something I had read about in the *Automobile Club* magazine. Instead, I rolled my window down, prepared to wave a white towel at the next moving car; all of them were going in the opposite direction across the median.

When several cars did drive by, none of them stopped. Some would slow down, but then they'd speed up again and keep on going. *Perhaps it's because I'm black,* I thought.

Just as my flashers grew dim, a semi-truck came to a halt behind me, its high beams supplying much-needed light. I always had faith in truckers because Dad Harry told me they were good folks who helped out on the road. This trucker, dressed in a uniform, with straggly, greasy hair, walked over to my car with what seemed like great trepidation.

"What's the problem, madam?" he asked in a Southern drawl.

"Don't know. It just stopped, and it won't start again."

The trucker gave me some instructions, which he thought might fix things, but the engine wouldn't budge.

"Okay, here's what I'm going to do. I'll radio a tow truck for you. It's the best I can do," he said.

I thanked my angel in disguise and waited and waited for another half hour. Finally a tow truck arrived. The driver favored the trucker in his appearance. He was white and wore a uniform covered in grease, like a mechanic's. He had a Southern accent and black hair styled like Elvis Presley. His appearance confirmed that I was in redneck country, Klan territory. I grew nervous again.

"Hello, madam, a trucker radioed me and said you needed help. If you could turn the car on, let's see what's goin' on here," he said.

"Thank you so much. It won't turn over." I was making an effort to say as little as possible. I didn't want to accidentally antagonize this stranger. I turned the key in the ignition, showing him how desperately I'd been trying to start the car and how stubborn the vehicle was being.

"Okay, don't worry. I have a mechanic shop in town. It's closed now... let's see, it's nearly nine p.m. I hate for you and your child to be stranded like this."

"I just need to get to Hinesville, to her father, and we'll be okay."

"Here's what I can do. I can tow you to my house. You can sleep on my couch, get up in the mornin,' and I can take a look at it," the man offered.

I must have turned the palest high-yellow caramel color a black girl could turn. My throat went dry. My heart dropped and raced at the same time. My lips became dry. I began to panic. *What if he takes me to his house, rapes me, and hangs me from a tree?* The same thing could happen if I stayed on the highway, though.

"Thanks so much. If you can tow me in, I'll call for help."

The man could see I was nervous.

"My wife and children is there. It's safe. We ain't got much, but you can stay."

I smiled. "Thank you so much," I said. At that moment, I felt that this man, too, was an angel like the trucker. I took a chance.

He hitched my car to his tow truck. Tiombe and I rode in the cab to his home, which was about ten miles away, just outside of Hinesville. Several dogs ran freely over his yard and jumped up and down at the sight of him. A myriad of cars were parked in front of the house on red dirt; there was no grass. As Tiombe and I walked into the house, we were greeted by the driver's wife, who wore a faded flower dress and slippers. Several children with stringy hair ran and jumped into their father's arms. Then they went up to Tiombe, who smiled sheepishly as the children set about getting to know each other.

"Please have a seat. Like some water?" the man's wife asked.

"No, I'm just fine. Thank you for letting us come to your home," I said.

We chatted until Henry picked us up. He was standoffish and uncomfortable when he greeted the family. Later, I assured him that it was much safer at a stranger's home than being stranded on a dark highway for over an hour.

Hinesville was only a few miles down the road, and Henry offered for me to stay at his place, but I stayed at a hotel instead.

The following morning, we searched high and low for a mechanic who was qualified to work on a Volvo, but there wasn't one to be found, so I ended up riding back to Atlanta with the tow truck driver. I soon discovered that I had to shell out a thousand dollars to fix the car.

It was around this time when a freelance job in speech writing came through, which helped pay for the car repairs. I wrote speeches for Hank Aaron, one of the greatest black ball players in the world. I was honored to know the man who had set the Major League Baseball record for most career home runs while playing for a league that at one time barred him because he was black. He became famous for surpassing Babe Ruth's record and hit a career total of 755 home runs.

Most of the speeches I wrote for him were inspirational and had titles that reflected that, such as "Building Toward One Society" for him to give to the NAACP, or "Keys to Success" for his presentation at Grambling State, or "Commitment," which he gave to the United Negro College Fund in Philadelphia. Hank paid me one hundred and fifty dollars per speech. He always paid me on time and was grateful for my work. I kept the speeches simple, funny, and factual. This working relationship lasted three years.

Just as I had begun to pay bills on time and crawl out of debt, my life was turned upside-down again. In the summer of 1984, my biological mom, Thelma, was diagnosed with multiple myeloma, a type of cancer in the bone marrow formed by malignant plasma cells. Mom had no early symptoms, other than being severely anemic, which was something she had dealt with all her life. When she felt aches in her bones and tired, she said it was her anemia, but she was actually experiencing the late stages of cancer.

She never called her cancer "cancer." She believed if you spoke negatively, what you spoke about would come to fruition. I never knew the magnitude of her suffering because she never talked about pain. It wasn't until her brother, Frederick, called that I got an inkling of how bad things really were.

"I think you should visit your mother soon. She's not doing well. I'll send the money for you and Tiombe to come to Chicago," he told me. I still thought that if Mom was that sick, she would have told me. After all, she had told me a lot of intimate things about herself. This was no different.

Mom didn't know Uncle Fredrick called me, only that I was coming to see her. She was ecstatic.

"I think you should know before you come, I've lost a lot of weight. You probably won't recognize me, so don't be surprised. I'm getting better, though," she reassured me.

When I saw Mom, I knew immediately that she wasn't well. Her weight had dropped to about ninety pounds. She no longer had her shapely hips or muscular legs. Her eyes were sunken, producing a haunting effect. Her high, sculptured, Cherokee cheek bones were cavernous; her face was hollow. Her steps were slow, dragging. Yet she tried to convince me that she was going to beat the cancer. I believed in her the same way I always had. I wanted to do whatever I could to preserve her life.

"Come to Atlanta, live with me. I want to take care of you. I'll make carrot juice every day, give you herbs for your immune system," I told her.

"You're so thoughtful, Gloria. You've always been. No, honey, I'm going to be all right. I can't leave Chicago. It's my home. My friends are here."

I spent as much time with her as I could that week. I took her to her radiation treatment at Weiss Memorial Hospital. She wouldn't have survived chemotherapy because the disease was too advanced. Doctors said it was one of the worst cancers because the symptoms didn't usually appear until it was too late for treatment.

One day, my mother's doctor pulled me aside and said he was glad I was with her; her time was short. My heart dropped. *What do you know?* I thought. *You're not God.* I didn't want to believe him. I wanted to believe in miracles.

On our way back, we stopped for our traditional lunch together, something we'd been doing since I started visiting her in Chicago as a child. This time Mom didn't hold my hand as we strolled down the street laughing like teens. This time, she clutched my arm tightly, afraid of falling. She could only smile, because laughing made her tired. We didn't sit long. She was too weak.

"I always regretted that I couldn't rear you, Bobbie, and Robert. Of course, Ethel was fine. She was with your father. Harry and Frances took good care of you, though. You got a good education. I always tried to do more for Robert and Bobbie than you because your father and grandmother didn't have all the means like you had," my mother confessed.

"That's all behind us now, Mom. You did the best you could. I hold nothing against you." I meant it.

"I'm glad," she said with a gentle smile.

"I love you," I said, smiling, too, so as not to cry as we held each other tight, trying to hold on to that moment for as long as possible.

Mom Thelma died on January 15, 1985—Dr. Martin Luther King, Jr.'s birthday. Mom freed her soul from the guilt of not raising us. Of course, it was a sad day for me because this was the end of the friendship I'd worked so hard to establish with her. There was a lot of unfinished family business that I wanted to discuss, but never had the chance, like my molestation. I wanted to know more about why Ethel stayed with Dad and not her, about Mom's life. I wanted to know whether her heart was right with the Lord. Mom Frances told me later that it was.

I didn't feel the impact of Mom's death until shortly thereafter. I'd pick up the phone to call and ask her a question about clothes or beauty; I'd get halfway through dialing her number before I'd remember that she wasn't there to answer. In terms of more practical matters, I'd come to depend on Mom for financial support to get Tiombe and me through tough times. Now I had no one to turn to when I had an emergency. I had to find a way to make ends meet on my own, so I began cleaning houses part-time with my friend, Ben. I was also close to his wife, Karen, whose father had been a well-known civil rights activist who worked alongside Martin Luther King, Jr., and their young daughters.

I was still part of the working poor, but with an extra sixty dollars a week, I could put more on the table and didn't have to serve the same thrifty meal to my child all the time.

"Mama, are we poor?" Tiombe asked me one night. "Every day, we eat beans and rice."

"Baby, we don't have a lot, but we have each other," I told her, trying as hard as I could to smile. I was embarrassed, wishing I could give her more.

I felt the weight of the world on my shoulders. Tiombe's acting and music kept her busy, and I was active in the PTA, Girl Scouts, field trips, and church. While this helped to keep Tiombe on the right path, it all required extra funds. It was a vicious cycle, trying to do the right thing, but driving myself into the poor house to do it.

Even after the divorce, Tiombe and I continued to attend West Hunter Street Baptist Church, the church Henry joined after we left the Church of God in Christ. I wanted to return to my roots, but my daughter had become active in the children's choir and was developing some valuable friendships. She needed stability after the divorce, and church gave it to her.

I also enjoyed the preaching of the pastor, Reverend Dr. David Ralph Abernathy. He was a world leader and the best friend of Dr. Martin Luther King, Jr. I admired his slow and deliberate Southern drawl and his fiery sermons. He was a down-to-earth, personable man who loved children. He took a liking to Tiombe when she interviewed him for an elementary school assignment on famous people.

Tiombe met him one Saturday morning in his office. He took time to tell her about growing up in the South and his life with Dr. King. Once he finished, he threw me a curveball.

"Mrs. Lockhart, if someone sitting in this room asked you to go to breakfast with him, would you?" he asked.

"I don't understand your question," I said. I knew he was married, so I hoped I was imagining what he was getting at.

He repeated himself slowly, gesturing to his heart. He kept the conversation light so my daughter wouldn't understand him.

"If someone who's sitting across from you asks you to go out, would you?"

"I can't believe you want to do that. I can't do that."

He smiled. "Okay, Mrs. Lockhart, you won't give me a chance."

I said nothing. I just maintained my composure, smiled politely, shook his hand, and told him how much we appreciated the interview. He didn't seem the least bit shaken by my rejection. For my part, I couldn't believe that I had just been approached by a married man, a well-known civil rights leader, and a man of the cloth. He had nerve! If I were a vindictive woman, I could have fallen for him and, in the end, destroyed his character and career. Why would anyone put himself in that position, unless he felt too powerful to be taken down that way? All I knew was that on Sunday mornings when he preached, I no longer felt a thing.

Tiombe continued to flourish. By the time she was seven years old, she was known among friends as the "little girl with the big voice." Once she got her first standing ovation, her life was never the same.

By the time Tiombe was eight, I had found Ted Borden, a print and television agent. Tiombe had sung for most black churches in Atlanta, something I attributed to her godfather, the Reverend Dr. Cornelius Henderson. He was a bishop in the United Methodist church and was noted in *Ebony* magazine as one of the most outstanding black preachers in America. He was well-connected and saw to it that Tiombe was compensated through free-will offerings. For churches at which he didn't preach, folks just said, "Thank you, it'll be good for your resume." We needed the money more.

It was around this time, when I often felt like I was barely holding on by a thread, that I became tangled in a dark web that nearly choked me.

One evening Tiombe and I were walking through Atlanta's Hartsfield International Airport. My eyes locked with the eyes of a man walking in my direction. He stood about six feet tall, had a flawless, milk-chocolate complexion, and a closely shaven head. His wire-rim glasses gave him a look of distinction, like a banker or an accountant. He paused in front of Tiombe and me and spoke a simple greeting. I nodded, and then my daughter innocently asked a leading question.

"Are you coming with us?"

"Sure would like to," the dashing man said, smiling coyly.

I blushed as he told me how pretty my daughter and I were. He said he wanted to have coffee with me one day. Without thinking twice, I gave him my number. I knew nothing about him, but I was thrilled that a fine-looking gentleman would be interested in me. If we were going to stay in touch, the best way was through his main business office, although he did have a home outside of Atlanta. I didn't question this explanation and was thrilled when he called a week later and made a date with me for that cup of coffee. When we met again, the first thing I did was ask about his personal life.

"So, Mr. Jones, do you have a girlfriend? Are you dating anyone?"

"No, none of those," he responded, more seriously than I would have liked.

"A nice-looking man like you, how could that be?"

"There's something you need to know," he replied. My heart was racing. "I'm married."

"You're married?" I was stunned. I expected him to have a girlfriend maybe, but not a wife.

"But we can still be friends. There's no harm in being friends, right?"

"Well, I guess not, but I'm surprised. Why did you ask for my number?"

"There's nothing wrong with friendships, that's all. My wife is a good woman, and I love her dearly. She's experienced illness, and I've been there for her. She's been in my corner often enough, too."

"But I can't date a married man," I said emphatically.

"You're not. We're just friends."

Kurt Jones was a convincing man; I accepted his friendship more enthusiastically than I should have. Over the next several months, we opened up to each other in ways I only had with my closest girlfriends. Kurt spoke in a gentle manner about his sons and about his wife's illness. It made me feel free to discuss my failed marriage and the financial hardship I was experiencing as a single parent. Kurt listened without judging me. He was one of the most caring men I had met since my divorce. I felt I had found someone who validated my self-worth.

As is almost always the case, I eventually got beat by this game. I fell in love with Kurt and our friendship stopped being platonic. For many years, Kurt was the only man in my life. He took away the pain caused by my abusive marriage and the pain caused by the abandonment of my biological father. Being with him even distracted me from the pain I lived with from having been molested by Dad Harry. I needed that so badly.

Our secret was well-kept, but a day never went by that I wasn't tormented by my actions, regardless of how good I felt when I was in Kurt's arms. I knew I was hurting myself and that I would eventually reap what I was sowing. He was married, after all; I was sharing him with someone who had more of a right to him than I did. I couldn't stop thinking about what would happen if his wife found out.

Yet, I had a difficult time breaking free. I had become addicted to Kurt's presence. I'd go cold turkey, eliminating him from my life entirely. I'd avoid seeing him for many months, until he'd call. Then I'd go back to my old ways—I couldn't help myself. Sometimes I would tell Kurt I never wanted to see him again.

"Okay, if that's how you feel, do what's best. I want you to be happy," he would say.

One time, I managed to put the relationship to an end for more than a year. When he finally called, Kurt said, "I don't want anything. I'm just calling to see if you're okay. Just checking. I miss you."

Those words, spoken by a voice husky with emotion, made it difficult for me to permanently sever our ties. It was around 1990 when I managed to take a quantum leap away from Kurt. I was sitting in church, listening to a sermon. I don't remember the title, but as I listened, a deep conviction came over me that left me so guilt-ridden I began to weep in my seat. I thought about how I would feel if another woman went with my husband. I also thought about how I was creating a bad example for my daughter. Kurt asked me out many more times after I broke it off, but my double life had officially ended.

Tiombe was finding herself, too. By the time she turned nine, she'd been a guest star on CBS's *In the Heat of the Night* with Carroll O'Connor, the actor whom everyone loved to hate as Archie Bunker on *All in the Family*. He was warm and kind to Tiombe.

In 1989, when she was ten, Tiombe got her big break on the famous national television show *Star Search*. Although she didn't win her category, she had opportunities that an average ten-year-old would never have had otherwise. She traveled to Italy to sing on *Lo Zecchino D'Oro*, a children's television show. She performed in *Porgy and Bess* at the Fox Theatre.

By the time Tiombe was twelve, she had sung at every major event in Atlanta. Every newspaper in the city had written about Tiombe's extraordinary singing voice. She was the talk of the town. Tiombe wanted more, though—more than she could find in Atlanta at the time.

"Mom, I'm tired of singing and singing with nothing happenin.' I want to make music and record it. I want to be in the movies. Let's go to New York or California."

She'd always had so much wisdom for her age.

"Let's look into what's best for your career," I told her. "If you're will-ing to make sacrifices, lose friends, and have to make new ones—if you're willing to start over, I'll be there for you."

Tiombe was willing. We looked into it, and decided on Los Angeles. The weather was good most of the year, the schools had high standards, and Tiombe would have more career choices. Moving to Los Angeles would also provide a chance for me to reconnect with my biological fa-ther. In terms of Tiombe's father, before we left Atlanta, Henry told me he was not happy with our move to Los Angeles. He didn't want his daughter living in a city that he called "wicked" with high crime and drive-by shootings.

Our friends, on the other hand, were very supportive of the move. They organized a host committee called "Friends of Tiombe Lockhart" and staged a farewell concert that included a celebrity silent auction. The event took place on August 3, 1991, at the Omni Hotel, which was at the CNN Center. Hundreds of people came out to support my daugh-ter. More than six thousand dollars was raised. I couldn't believe how much folks loved Tiombe and believed in her dreams. Folks like Zell Miller, the governor; the Hawks; her agent, Ted Borden and Associates; 11 Alive television; WAOK and WSB radio; and William Tolliver, the renowned artist who donated his popular silkscreen, *Jazz Reflections,* to Tiombe.

I couldn't believe I was finally leaving 444 Beckwith Court. I'd occu-pied that two-bedroom apartment for fourteen years. I was leaving behind joy, pain, and suffering, memories from my marriage and the birth of my daughter, and, hopefully, the pain of my divorce from Henry. I was looking forward to a new life on the West Coast. Tiombe and I were only taking a few necessary items.

My friend Ben was the last person I saw before leaving Atlanta. He made sure my car was properly stowed on the truck. In exchange, I turned over my housecleaning accounts to him. Ben and I had such a sweet and caring friendship. We were like sister and brother, and I was going to miss him.

Shortly after I left Atlanta, I got a phone call from Ben's wife, Karen.

"Since you and Ben were close, I thought you should know," Karen said. "Ben is dying of AIDS."

I was shocked. I thought Ben had shared everything there was to know about himself with me.

"It's a deep, dark secret he's kept for years," Karen went on. "I just found out he's bisexual. I had no idea. There were signs, looking back, but I didn't pay them any attention. I never imagined he was gay."

"Oh, Karen, I'm so sorry. What happened? How did he tell you?"

"He didn't tell me. Not exactly. I noticed every time we made love, he never wanted the lights on. But one time when I felt his back and his head, there were scabs. I freaked out and turned the lights on. He was covered with sores."

I had no idea what to say, so I just listened.

"Now looking back, he and I had the same friends come to the house. Some were gay. But I never thought he had anything to do with them. They're all dead today." Karen began to cry.

"Have you been tested?" I asked.

"Yes, almost weekly. I'm negative. The doctor told me not to come back for a while. He said I'm too compulsive."

"Karen, I remember him having a cold sore for months and a cough that lingered. He told me it was because his immune system was low," I said.

"That was one of the many symptoms I missed. He's been battling AIDS for some time."

"What about the children and the family?"

"I can't tell the kids. My father is distraught about it, but he's helping me cope. I just hope no one in the community finds out. I'm afraid someone will try to hurt the kids."

Before we hung up, I thanked Karen for sharing her hardships with me and assured her that, whenever she needed to talk, I'd be there. Karen revealed that she'd kicked Ben out of the house several times. He had no other place to stay and always returned. Then his health began to deteriorate. Since he was the father of their children, Karen wanted to do the right thing; she made arrangements for him to stay at the house when it came time for him to receive hospice care.

Ben died a few months after Karen told me he had AIDS. I found his death hard to accept. He was the last person I saw before leaving Atlanta, and we had shared a lot about our lives while cleaning houses. Apparently, I'd shared more than he had.

I was concerned about his wife's health. She had to raise their children alone and worry all the time about being infected. Karen was a beautiful, strong black woman and, thankfully, she was able to pick up the pieces of her life and move on. Within a year, she had released Ben and began a new life with her daughters and another man.

As for me, I was discovering that starting over in Los Angeles wasn't as easy as I'd imagined. I was held captive by bad memories. As long as they kept weighing down my wings, my soul would never be free.

CHAPTER FIFTEEN

The size of places like Detroit and Atlanta couldn't compare to the size of Los Angeles. I had visited LA in the '70s in search of my biological father, but I had no idea what the city was really like.

My daughter and I arrived with a few antiques I'd inherited from my grandma Violet in tow. I held on to my BMW, which had clocked more than 100,000 miles on its odometer, and Tiombe took her beat-up wooden trunk stuffed with toy animals, Barbie dolls, and cassette tapes. What we kept closest to our hearts was a lithograph known as *Jazz Reflections*, which the artist William Tolliver presented to Tiombe at her going-away celebration.

I hadn't secured a job before the move, but I was confident I would land one soon given that, as long as there was human suffering, social workers would be needed. What I didn't anticipate was not having a roof over our heads. I had arranged to live with a girlfriend, but we couldn't move in right away. A friend in Atlanta told me about a friend of his who had an extra room in Hollywood. In return, I promised to help with the rent using the three thousand dollars I'd generated from selling our things in Atlanta.

Stepping off the American Airlines flight at LAX was like stepping into another world. Los Angeles was much more diverse than anyplace I'd ever been. I saw Armenians. There were Latinos from Mexico, El Salvador, Guatemala, Nicaragua, Cuba, Puerto Rico, and Chile. They lived in segregated pockets of Los Angeles, East Hollywood, Pasadena, and Glendale. Los Angeles's wealthiest residents were tucked away in West Los Angeles and Beverly Hills, while white yuppies settled in the San Fernando Valley, Studio City, Encino, and Woodland Hills. The neighborhoods of Palos Verdes, Rolling Hills, Carson, and Torrance were also well-to-do. Small cities like Harbor City, Harbor-Gateway, Wilmington, and San Pedro were home to predominantly Italian, Croatian, Latino, and African American populations.

I desperately searched for a black community. I wanted to live where I could be involved in changing the system to empower my people, where I could patronize black businesses. Much to my chagrin, there was no pure black community. Blacks had migrated from south Los Angeles to cities like Inglewood, Hawthorne, Torrance, and Carson. My dad still owned his home in south LA, as did many older blacks.

The traffic congestion on the Los Angeles freeways lived up to its reputation. It was a car-dependent city where few people walked. Everything was sprawled out. A newcomer had to be a rocket scientist to figure out LA's endless freeways: the 110, the 405, the 101, the 105, the 170, the 5, the 134, the 91, the 210, the 605, the 10, and the 710. I learned the hard way to allow a few hours of travel time if I wanted to arrive anywhere when I was supposed to.

I was glad to finally be able to move in with my girlfriend Cassandra and Christopher, her son, who was a few years younger than Tiombe. They lived in a two-bedroom apartment on Fountain Street, just off La Brea Boulevard in Hollywood. Cassandra was as generous to me as I had been to her when she was looking for work in Atlanta years before.

Cassandra wasted no time getting Tiombe's career started. She was a music producer for several reggae groups. She helped me find the Bobby Ball Talent Agency in West Los Angeles and a good middle school for Tiombe to attend. I once again felt like a normal parent and enjoyed the daily routine of prying my kid out of bed, fixing her breakfast, and taking her a dreadful but expedient way to Walter Reed Middle School.

My job search lasted about eight months, much longer than I anticipated. Governor Pete Wilson had frozen the state budget; it took months of political arm twisting before it was approved. I had been offered a job with the county department of social services, but the day before I was to begin, the offer was rescinded. The department was told to hire from within be-cause of the budget situation.

By then, my funds had been depleted. I was destined to be homeless if I didn't work. Cassandra introduced me to a few wealthy blacks who were producers and writers, like Bee Bee and Fred Johnson and Samm-Art Williams. They sympathized with my plight and offered me housecleaning jobs. He produced *Martin*, the show starring Martin Lawrence, and *The Fresh Prince of Bel-Air*. Every week, he left a nice check for sixty-five dollars that helped with gasoline and food, but it wasn't enough to cover my car note. I had no choice but to seek public assistance.

I probably should have been embarrassed, having a master's degree from one of the country's finest universities and being on welfare. I knew it was only a pause on the journey to get me to a better place, though, not a permanent condition. Welfare allowed me to move into a two-bedroom apartment with Renee, a friend of Cassandra's. She was a singer who quickly took an interest in Tiombe's career. Renee coached Tiombe and introduced her to a hip-hop group who fell in love with her voice and gave her weekly choreography lessons.

Tiombe blossomed, and her vocal skills increased considerably. On November 19, 1991, she had her first performance in LA at the Roxy on Sunset Boulevard.

"Mom, ballads aren't my style. They're not me," she'd say.

"Sing what's offered. You can find your style later. Take what comes your way," I counseled.

I soon found a young and vivacious voice coach for Tiombe, but I couldn't afford to keep up with his weekly twenty-five-dollar fees. Besides, he wanted Tiombe to sing show tunes, which was a far cry from what she wanted. Our quest to find the right coach finally led us to Bill Thomas. He was experienced with kids and had been on the *Cosby Show* and in tons of commercials and musicals. He loved Tiombe's voice and knew how to chal-lenge her in a way that kept her interested. They were a perfect fit.

With this extra professional training, auditions quickly followed. It was tough for Tiombe because she had dual talents, acting and singing, and, unfortunately, Hollywood discouraged this. They wanted one or the other.

Tiombe was also a victim of her age and appearance. Hollywood pre-ferred young kids over teenagers. Agents often got calls for white kids with blond hair and blue eyes or for an African American girl with a dark complexion, or an Asian boy who looked obviously Asian. Tiombe looked like a regular kid, beautiful, but not stereotypical in any way.

I admired my daughter's ability to handle the rejection. She'd read the script as she was trained, would give it her best shot, then be off to have fun with friends—totally cavalier. I, on the other hand, was a nervous wreck after every audition, worrying if Tiombe was going to get the part, if she had the right look, wondering what had gone wrong when the disappointing phone call came. I had always hoped Tiombe would land a major role so she'd be secure for college. That was my true dream for my daughter.

I quickly learned that to be young, gifted, and black in Hollywood meant you had to work even harder than everyone else for your big break—that no matter how talented you were, you weren't guaranteed a thing from that town. We kept trying to get our piece of it, though.

In May of 1992, Tiombe got an opportunity to show off her musical talent. She auditioned for a stage musical called *TWIST: A New Musical*, inspired by Charles Dickens's classic tale *Oliver Twist*. The show was produced by Landmark Entertainment Group and Willette Klausner. Tiombe was selected along with twenty-four other talented young people. Although the show was the talk of Hollywood for having landed some of the most talented kids in showbiz, it didn't make it out of the city. Working on the production did provide Tiombe with new friends, including Brandy and Willie Norwood, a brother and sister duo who would later become America's top hip-hop stars.

Tiombe had enough work under her belt to become a member of the union. She landed a guest costar role on *Thea*, an ABC series. She then became the principal singer on ABC's *Rhythm & Jam*, a pilot that aired Saturday mornings; it was a fun, creative show that the network hoped would become a series. It starred six young teens who performed educational vignettes and sang jazz, blues, and soul. It had the flair of *West Side Story* and the erudition of *Sesame Street*. Unfortunately, the show didn't find an audience.

Tiombe landed feature film roles in *True Crime* by Trimark Pictures and *Sliver* by Paramount Pictures. These speaking roles put her into the Screen Actors Guild—American Federation of Television and Radio Artists; the membership dues were nine hundred dollars. Instead of these parts leading to bigger and better ones, the auditions dried up. Tiombe was entering adolescence, and Hollywood was more interested in the talent under the age of twelve. The more Tiombe saw Hollywood's prescription for success—youth, having a particular skin color, being a certain shape and size—the more disdain she developed for the place.

"Mom, I don't know if I want to do this anymore. I don't like it," Tiombe told me when she was fourteen.

"I can't believe you want to give it all up, after we've worked so hard."

"It's not about you, Mom. It's about what I want now. I'm tired of not getting anything. You're right, I've worked hard. I want to take a break."

I could tell Tiombe was tired of my asking, "Did you practice piano today? Did you go over your script? Did you finish your homework?" I knew she was on the edge. She was displaying certain resentful behaviors, such as rolling her eyes at me and sighing loudly. I was beginning to lose my kid to adolescence, to a world of loud music behind a closed bedroom door. She would much rather be serenaded by Mary J. Blige, Bone Thugs-n-Harmony, Xscape, Tu Pac, En Vogue, Notorious B.I.G., or Snoop Dog than go on auditions or listen to me.

My daughter and I were growing apart. If and when Tiombe decided to speak, it seemed to be about her dad. Once we left Atlanta, I had no contact with Henry; I couldn't wait on him to heal from the divorce. I had to move on with my life and do what was best for Tiombe and me. Even before we moved to LA, the visitations between Tiombe and her father had become almost non-existent. Once we were on the West Coast, Henry used distance as an excuse for not seeing his daughter. Tiombe didn't understand, just as I hadn't understood my father's absence.

"Why doesn't he call? I miss him. Why can't he send child support so I can do fun things with my friends? We never have enough money to go anywhere," she would say.

"I know it's hard for us now, but trust me, it won't always be like this," I'd try to reassure her, disguising my own uncertainty. I still never made a negative comment about Henry, although many times I wanted to. I couldn't destroy Tiombe's faith in her father. She loved him so much.

All I wanted was for Tiombe's pain to go away. I tried hard to compensate for Henry's shortcomings by not paying a bill so Tiombe and I could enjoy a matinee after church, or dinner at McDonald's on a Friday. During the week, I would gather loose change so she could buy food from the school cafeteria and not feel out of place unwrapping my homemade turkey sandwiches, which she later told me she often threw away. Instead she would eat cafeteria food from her friends' trays. Yet, it seemed the more I tried to compensate, the wider the gap grew.

I eventually came to realize that no matter what lengths a mother goes to make up for a father's absence, she can never fully take his place. Still, I couldn't stop compensating. I didn't want Tiombe to miss opportunities—so I pushed her and made sacrifices to ensure she'd have the have the best I could manage to give. In addition to dealing with an absentee parent, Tiombe was going through the typical trials and tribulations of adolescence; a father's presence makes such as difference during this difficult stage in a young person's life.

I hadn't given up on trying to bond with my biological father. I wanted to make up for the twenty years that he hadn't been in my life. Dad kept to himself a lot, so every month I initiated a trip to his house. We had many enjoyable moments discussing politics and his years of teaching Pan-African Studies at California State University. He avoided discussing truly personal things, like my mom and the years they were together—the things I wanted to know about. What I really wanted were answers to why he had abandoned me. My first attempt to get them was during a visit in 1993 when I asked him, point blank, what happened between him and my mother.

He remained expressionless during his terse response. "You know, you've always been the most inquisitive child in the family, even when you were just a tiny girl. If you want to know, well, I'll tell you. I married your mother, but I didn't really love her. Now, that's that!"

He leaned toward me from his recliner when he spoke those last three words. I could tell by the way he was fidgeting with his hands and by the way he abruptly crossed his arms when he finished speaking that he didn't intend to say more.

I sat for a few seconds, speechless, staring into his eyes. I wanted to probe deeper, but I didn't know my father well enough to predict how he would react and he already seemed perturbed. Dad had a lot built up inside him, a lot he hadn't dealt with, that made talking with him the way I wanted to a problem. Still, how could he not love my mother when they had four children together? There was clearly a lot of anger and pain beneath the surface that he hadn't dealt with, and I was forcing him to open up old wounds.

Part of me wanted to keep trying to peel the onion, one layer at a time. Another part acknowledged that I may never fit all the pieces of my life together, and that if I really wanted to have a relationship with my father I should stick to the safety of discussing politics, the war, and history—not any of the personal matters that made him so uncomfortable. I had to accept the fact that this was as close as my father and I were going to get.

On January 17, 1994, at exactly 4:31 in the morning, there was an incident that drew me closer to my own child—the Los Angeles earthquake. Tiombe and I were among the millions of Angelinos who felt the impact of the 6.7 quake. The bucking and shaking of the earth rousted me from my bed just before the tilt of the ground below would have thrown me out of it. I landed on my feet, convinced I was witnessing the Rapture. I yelled for Tiombe.

"Earthquake! Earthquake! Tiombe, are you okay?"

"Mom, Mom, where are you? I can't see! I can't see!"

"Just feel your way toward my voice. You'll find me," I said. I had never experienced an earthquake before. I moved the only way I could, slowly, to the living room, which divided my daughter's room from mine. I kept stubbing my toes on furniture that had been shaken to the floor.

"I can't get to you, Mom!" Tiombe cried.

I could hear dishes from the cupboards crashing onto the floor. The antique crystal stem glasses I'd inherited from Mom Frances were gone forever. The contents of the refrigerator were emptied onto the linoleum.

I moved at a snail's pace, my body hugging the wall. I couldn't see a thing in the blackness, but I continued to reach for Tiombe, knowing we would eventually find each other.

"There. We did it!" I said to her as we fell into each other's arms in the middle of the living room. I could feel Tiombe's heart pounding against my own chest as she fell limp against me. She had a gash on the front of her leg, from when her upright desk toppled over, blocking the door of her room. It had only missed her head by a few meters. We were both thankful to be alive.

Tiombe and I heard groans and cries from neighbors who had managed to escape onto the sidewalk. They were wrapped in blankets and talking loudly and frantically, predicting when the aftershocks would come. Many of the apartments on Vineland Avenue, the street we lived on, were severely damaged. For the first time in the city's history, there was a total blackout.

We had no power, but I managed to get Tiombe's old battery-operated boom box to work.

"LA has just gone through a major earthquake. It felt longer than it was, folks. They're calling it the Northridge quake, pegged at 6.7 on the Richter scale."

When our electricity was restored, I was able to see the insane results of the quake on television. It was shocking. The city looked like a war zone. People had been trapped and crushed under buildings. The damage was going to cost over thirty billion dollars to repair. Some homes were destroyed beyond repair, forcing hundreds of people to sleep in tents. Apartments had collapsed, trains had derailed. Gas leaks had caused massive infernos. Freeway overpasses had collapsed and some had split wide open. Sadly, some fifty-seven lives had been lost.

The story that I found most unforgettable was that of Clarence Dean, a Los Angeles motorcycle officer. He was driving to work and flew over the edge of a severed ramp when a section of the Antelope Valley Freeway collapsed. He plunged to his death. I couldn't imagine the pain his family must have felt. I thought of the many times I traveled that same freeway.

After the quake, my daughter and I valued our lives together more than ever. I accepted her decision not to be involved in entertainment, although it was hard because I knew how talented she was, and I didn't want to see that talent wasted. We discussed her going to Burbank High School or maybe to the LA County High School for the Arts at California State University. Tiombe opted to be with her friends at Burbank High School.

In the summer of 1994, we moved to a two-bedroom apartment in a quiet neighborhood in Burbank, only six blocks from the high school. Once we settled in, I noticed we were the only blacks in the fifteen-unit complex—the only ones in the neighborhood, in fact. I heard the city was prejudiced, but I hadn't experienced any of that in my new place. The landlords, a husband and wife, were welcoming. The city was different, though.

I observed that white folks would never speak to blacks; they would just look away when they saw us. Tiombe said she experienced incidents of prejudice several times when walking home from school with her friends. Sometimes elderly white women would clutch their purses as they passed black kids on the street. Someone wrote "nigger" on the school wall.

In addition to being disturbed by the racial prejudice, I wasn't happy with the path my daughter was taking. She had joined the choir, but didn't like the music and dropped out. The renewed closeness we experienced after the quake was short-lived; Tiombe was talking back to me excessively and threatened to run away from home.

"Go ahead. Just don't take anything with you. You came into this world naked, so leave this house naked," I told her once.

I was fed up with Tiombe's shenanigans. About two months into the school semester, she got into a fight that I later learned from her counselor was provoked by the other girl. Shortly after that, I went ballistic when I found bidis in her backpack. It was time to intervene.

"I love you, and I've given you a chance to do this your way. It's not working. I can't sit idly by and let you destroy your life," I told my daughter, who sat listening quietly and attentively.

"You're not gonna get caught up in the usual cycle—getting pregnant, getting hooked on drugs, getting sent to juvenile detention—because there's no father at home. So, straighten up, get involved in the choir at school, or get into some kind of sport. Whichever one will keep you off the street. I didn't raise you to run the streets, and I'm not having it. Now, what are you going to do?"

"I don't know. I miss my music, Mom. The choir's good, but it's not my style. I know you've sacrificed a lot for me, and I appreciate it. I just need time to think. Maybe you could get information on that other school."

I wasted no time. Before the end of the semester, Tiombe was auditioning before a panel of judges at the LA County High School for the Arts. She had to sing one classical and one contemporary song. They loved her voice, and she began at the school the winter semester of 1995. It was a no-nonsense place. There was no skipping classes, and all school rules had to be strictly followed. If a student had excessive violations, that student would be sent back to his or her home school.

Another rule that Tiombe had to adjust to was the selection of one major: music, dance, or visual art. Outside auditions in Hollywood were discouraged; they were a distraction to the school's purpose. Initially, it was challenging for the two of us, driving ten miles one way by 8:00 a.m., rehearsing for a performance after school at 4:00 p.m. until 8:00 p.m., then a pick-up and return home. We eventually got acclimated by keeping our eyes on the overall goal.

Tiombe was at last on the right track. Then something unexpected happened that helped me find a certain peace as well. Closure might be the more accurate way to describe it. I answered the phone one day and a woman asked to speak to Gloria Lockhart.

"This is she," I replied.

"Mrs. Lockhart, this is Mrs. Jones from Atlanta."

"Yes," I said with great trepidation. My relationship with Kurt had ended some five years ago. I couldn't imagine what she wanted now.

"I'm calling to let you know that my husband died from cancer. I thought you'd want to know. I'd like to send you a copy of the memorial bulletin."

How in the world does she know about me? I thought. The remorse from all those years came flooding back and landed like a lead balloon in the pit of my stomach. I couldn't breathe or speak.

"I knew about your relationship with my husband all along," Mrs. Jones told me, as if reading my mind.

I was humbled by this woman's noble reaction to my presence in her husband's life. This wasn't how I'd imagined a conversation between us at all. Tears welled in my eyes.

"I'm so sorry, Mrs. Jones. Please accept my condolences. I'd also like to say that I'm sorry for what I did. It was wrong. Your husband was a generous and kind man, and he helped me get over a lot of bad times."

"Yes, he was a kind person."

"I truly hope that you can forgive me, Mrs. Jones, because from my heart, I'm very sorry."

"I forgive you," she said softly. "What's your address?"

I gave it and thanked her for calling, then quietly put down the receiver. When I received the bulletin, I shredded it. Afterward, I somehow felt lighter.

Yet, there was something in my life that I couldn't keep from the forefront of my mind. A day never went by that I didn't think about how I'd been molested. I replayed the incidents in my mind to the point of obsession. I still blamed myself. I blamed everyone except the perpetrator, the person who was to keep me safe. *If I hadn't gotten in the bed. If I hadn't been afraid of the storm that night. If Mom had been there. If my biological mom had kept me. If, if, if* was all that went through my head day and night. It was torture. When I was a child, I showed signs typical of victims of sexual abuse; I was withdrawn, suffered from nightmares and low self-esteem, and I didn't want to be home alone with Dad Harry. But no one recognized these as signs.

When I could no longer suppress them, the memories of being molested surfaced with a vengeance. I began having suicidal thoughts again. It was January of 1997, the beginning of a new year, but instead of feeling hopeful I was thinking about jumping off a bridge or overdosing on aspirin to end my pain.

As a social worker, I knew that thoughts of suicide were an attempt to murder the individual who had caused harm to you; instead, you're so fraught with guilt over these thoughts that you kill yourself. I didn't allow myself to carry out my suicide plan because I had to live for my daughter. I loved her so much, and she was dependent on me for everything.

I also thought about my extended family. I believed in my heart that if I broke my silence, they would embrace me, just as they always had when I'd experienced challenges. I knew it wouldn't be easy, but as with everything in life that was difficult, I needed to look to God for courage and strength.

I began researching cases of molestation, incest, and rape. I read books on the subject of sexual abuse. I tried to seek therapy, but it was too expensive, and the therapists who seemed to be the most culturally sensitive had no experience with incest or molestation. The books helped. They led me to acknowledge my pain. It became clear that the first step forward on my healing journey would be breaking the silence. I needed to be heard and believed, to have my pain validated. I needed to tell my secret.

When my daughter wanted to start dating, I found myself more uncomfortable with the idea than I'd expected. I didn't want guys talking to her, or for her to have guy friends at school. In my mind, men were always up to no good. I could understand why I felt this way, but these feelings were causing me to stifle Tiombe socially. It wasn't fair to her. I wanted to protect my daughter, but I also wanted her to enjoy her life. My pain was my pain, not Tiombe's; in order to protect her from it, I had to share it.

As Tiombe and I sat swinging at the playground across the street from our apartment in North Hollywood, I tried to work up the courage to tell her about the molestation. I stalled and stammered. I fought back tears. All I could manage to get out was that I had something serious to talk to her about.

Finally, she said, "Mom, what happened? Did you murder someone? Whatever it is, I'll still love you."

"I know, honey, it's just so hard. What I have to tell you, I've repressed for over forty years. I haven't told a soul. And because of it, I haven't allowed you to be a real teenager. I'm holding on to you too tightly. What happened was, when I was about nine years old, I...I...I was molested by my adopted father."

It took hours of swinging to get those three words, *I was molested,* out. Once I did, it felt like a mountain had been lifted off my shoulders. Tiombe didn't say a word. She just threw her arms around me, and we embraced each other for several minutes. When I felt strong enough to disengage myself from my daughter's loving arms, we had a good, long talk. Tiombe's acceptance meant the world to me, and the fact that I respected her enough to trust her with my biggest secret meant the world to her.

I knew it was important to tell Mom Frances. Dad Harry had died in 1979, so it was too late to confront him. Mom Frances was the next closest person to the situation. I decided to wait to talk to her in person.

In the interim year, I continued my healing journey. I traveled to Minnesota to see my sister Eva and her family. I told her my story sitting among the 520 stores in the Mall of the Americas, the largest mall in the United States. Eva sat listening, speechless, stunned, but never disbelieving. I thought she might be mad at me for bringing this out into the open, but instead she was angry with Dad Harry. I was so thankful for Eva's support. I held my breath waiting for her to answer when I asked if she or our sister Lydia had ever been molested. When she told me that they hadn't, I felt like I was breathing again for the first time in years.

Just before Mom Frances came to LA from Michigan in 1997, I prepared for our talk by reading *Betrayal of Innocence* by Craig Buck and Dr. Susan Forward. I decided to sit down with her two days after Tiombe's graduation. It was the morning of Sunday, June 22, and we were preparing for church. We never made it.

The first step I had to take was confrontation, the greatest single step to empowerment. Although I couldn't afford professional counseling, my social-work training served me well during this process. I was kind and respectful, but forthright. "Mom, there's something I need to tell you, something that happened to me when I was a child."

"What I'm going to tell you, you had nothing to do with. I just need you to listen. There are four things I need to tell you. This is what happened to me. This is how I felt about it at the time. This is how it affected my life. And this is what I want from you."

I was feeling so proud of my ability to take my journey to the next level. It was as if I was still on the top of Kilimanjaro, climbing past the first summit to that second, more obscure one. *Pole, pole,* I reminded myself.

"Okay, I'm listening," Mom Frances said softly, patiently.

"Remember when your mother and father were in a car accident?" I asked.

"Yes, I remember. I went down South to take care of them for a spell."

"That's right. Well, one night while you were gone, a real bad storm came through. I was so afraid. I ran from my room and jumped into Dad's bed."

I looked into Mom Frances' eyes, but there seemed to be no inkling in them of what I was going to say next.

"Well," she said, so innocently that I knew she never had any idea of what her husband had done.

"Mom, late that night I woke up, and Dad's hand was touching my vagina. And it wasn't just that night. He continued to molest me for a long time."

Mom Frances sat motionless. I noticed that her face turned light pink. I couldn't tell what she was thinking, what was coming. I remembered how she used to slap me so hard when I was a little girl that my nose would bleed. I braced myself.

"How in the world could he do something like that?" she said softly. "How in the world, to a child?" Mom Frances paused. Then she said slowly, "I'm so sorry, Gloria. I should have been there for you. I shouldn't have gone to Tennessee. I shouldn't have left you." Then she started to cry.

"Mom, you're not to blame. You had no idea that would happen. What I wanted you to know is how hurt, angry, and guilt-ridden I am. I've felt this way since I was a little girl. I must get rid of those feelings, rid my soul of them, so I can go on with my life."

"So that's why you were always running, is it?"

"Yep, that's why. Running keeps me sane. It makes me forget for a bit, but I never really do, not for long. I have to eventually deal with it head-on. I must rid myself of these demons now. That's why we're talking about this today."

I went through my four points. When I was finished, I felt pounds lighter, but I could see the weight had shifted to Mom Frances; I could see how heavy her heart was at that moment.

"If that man were alive today, I'd run him outta the house. I'd hit him over the head with a frying pan and knock some sense into him!" Mom wasn't crying anymore. She was angry. I was just so glad it wasn't at me.

Mom hugged me close to her and spoke the words I'd longed to hear. "I'm so sorry. I'm sorry you've had to bury this inside all these years. It wasn't your fault. Don't you dare blame yourself, you hear? You were just a baby. Just a baby."

Mom was a changed woman. She was no longer the strict, unflagging disciplinarian she was when I was growing up. She had evolved into a loving, compassionate mother—the mother I'd always wanted. I felt I had to love her more than I did when I was growing up, that I had to protect her.

"Mom, you might need counseling when you go home. This is a bitter pill to swallow. Don't be afraid to get help," I told her.

"My best friend is a nurse. I'd feel comfortable telling her. Don't you worry about me. I'm just glad you shared this with me. Thank you."

"I wasn't sure if you would believe me."

"Why wouldn't I? You were my child then, you're my child now. I do hope one thing."

"What's that, Mom?"

"I hope you can find it in your heart to forgive. For your own sake."

"I'm working on that—it's a process that happens over time."

When we embraced again, I felt a strong bond between us, a feeling women have toward each other only when their spirits come together.

Mom never sought help when she returned to Lansing. Instead, she threw herself into the church just as she had done all her life. She continued teaching Bible study, attending Sunday service, preaching, singing to lift the hearts of others, and visiting the sick. That was her way of healing. We never talked about the molestation again because, shortly afterward, she began to suffer memory loss, which was later diagnosed as dementia. Her body was holding up just fine, though, at eighty-seven years old.

As for me, I had freed myself of the guilt I'd carried all those years. I felt vindicated, proud that I had broken my silence. The anger and hatred I felt toward my perpetrator was slowly dissipating.

Shortly after, I went through a special ceremony. Alone in a room, I imagined Dad Harry in front of me. I screamed at him. I cried until I didn't have another tear left in the ducts. Then, later that day, I went on a long run, the last of its kind, so to speak. With every stride, I symbolically stomped Dad Harry into the ground. It was my own private purification process, and it enabled me to release the anger, hatred, and guilt that had been keeping me from reaching the heights I was truly meant to. I ran so fast it felt like I was going to take off into the sky. After forty-two years, my journey of healing was over. But my journey wasn't.

CHAPTER SIXTEEN

In the fall of 1997, Tiombe chose to go as far away from LA as she could. She wanted to soar on her own, to choose a flight pattern of her own making. That fall, she was accepted at the New School University in New York, where she would major in jazz and contemporary music. I was the proudest mom in America in June 2002, watching my daughter receive a bachelor's of fine arts degree. I couldn't hold back the tears when I thought about the journey of faith we took together when we moved to LA, not knowing how our lives would end up.

Tiombe was a talented child who listened to the beat of a different drummer. She held on to her musical instincts when everyone was telling her to go in a different direction. Today, she's an accomplished young woman. She's a successful writer, producer, and singer in New York—she has a unique sound that belongs to her alone. She has found joy in producing music videos and writing music for herself and others.

I, too, succeeded in my calling. I've continued to find pleasure in social work, in helping others restore their lives, including working as the director of a city-funded youth violence prevention program based in adolescent medicine at Children's Hospital Los Angeles.

My greatest professional satisfaction was working at an organization called Girls and Gangs, which afforded me the opportunity to go to juvenile halls and probation boot camps and help redirect the lives of troubled girls, girls at risk of not getting their chance to soar. When I was their age,

I experienced pain similar to theirs, only I found a constructive outlet for it. My personal history and work with vulnerable young women led me to develop gender-specific curricula for girls in lock-up for an organization called Peace over Violence.

More than anything, I wanted these young women to know that just because they were hurting and facing a tough time, that didn't mean it was always going to be that way. They had to become an agent of change for their own lives, and then give back by being an agent of change in their community. This is the same advice I gave my own daughter. I wanted these vulnerable girls to know that they weren't alone, even if they didn't have a mother to call their own to make them feel safe and loved. Others, like me, would be there to help them along their path, if they would just let us in.

My goal remains to guide these young women, to share my story so they can see the possibilities life has to offer and then choose a destination worthy of all they are and can be. The social worker in me, the mother in me, will not back down from this mission.

Eventually, I came to act as my biological father's social worker. The only way to get close to the man was when he desperately needed my help, and I gladly gave it. Sometimes he needed a ride to a doctor's appointment at the VA Hospital in LA. Other times, he needed me to advise him about social-service programs for him or my sister—my dear baby sister, Ethel, also needed me in ways I'd hoped she never would. I was grateful I could be there for her, especially in 2002, when she suffered a nervous breakdown. I was able to perform the crisis intervention that saved her life.

My father called and asked me to come to the house immediately. He said Ethel was on pain killers and experiencing symptoms of withdrawal. She hadn't eaten in several days. When I arrived I noticed her weight had dropped from one hundred and twenty to about ninety pounds. She was in a fetal position on the couch; she seemed lethargic, almost lifeless. She readily consented to my help, which I offered as a sister and social worker.

I asked Ethel what was wrong. She confirmed what Dad said—that she had been taking an excessive amount of pain pills to get rid of her chronic headaches. I assessed that she needed immediate help. I contacted my supervisor, Susan Rabinovitz at Children's Hospital to get recommendations for nearby clinics. My father took her to the closest one to receive the medical attention she needed.

"You sure know your business," one of the intake social workers at the clinic later told me. "If you hadn't gotten her help in time, you would have lost her."

I did know my business; I knew there was more to Ethel's breakdown than met the eye, that there was something more than migraines behind her over-medication. When she was discharged from the clinic, my sister was transported to the psychiatric ward at LA County Hospital. I wouldn't know the reason she needed this type of help so badly until 2005, when our father was diagnosed with leukemia.

As our father lay dying, Ethel took me to a peaceful garden in the hospital courtyard, where she expressed her appreciation to me for helping her get through her breakdown; she was finally ready to tell me the secret that had contributed to it. There in the garden, Ethel revealed to me that when she was eight years old, our father had raped her. It was only because I had opened up to her about my molestation that she was able to open up to me. As an adult, she confronted Dad, but she never sought help.

My heart went out to my sister. It didn't matter that we hadn't grown up together. It could just as easily have been me strapped in that bed in the psychiatric ward three years earlier. When I looked at Ethel, I saw myself as a child, suppressing trauma and keeping my problems bottled up inside. But, unlike my sister, there came a time when I sought to better understand how to deal with those problems and use my experience to help others. That's what led me to social work in the first place.

I provided as much counseling as I could to my sister that day, to help her address the pain of our father's heinous act. Ethel was fragile, but she was strong. She had survived so much. We were about to lose Dad, and less than two years before she had experienced the devastating loss of her only child, Ricky, when he committed suicide. Ricky shot himself in the heart and didn't leave a note to explain why. Ethel knew his difficult marriage had taken its toll, but he did have two beautiful, young children to live for—children who, like their grandmother, would forever mourn Ricky's death.

It's unfortunate that it took bonding over these traumatic events to bring my biological sister and me together, but at least we were together. Time has a way of unmasking the truth, and, finally, we were a family again.

In, 2005—after thirty years in social work administration—I had planned to retire. But God had a different plan for me. My life hadn't fully evolved. I was offered a position as executive director of Toberman

Neighborhood Center, a non-profit multi-purpose agency in San Pedro. The goal was to provide services to low-income individuals and families in the Harbor area so that they could move from dependence to self-sufficiency. It was an offer—and a mission—I couldn't turn my back on.

I do feel I was destined to arrive at this place of serving, redirecting, and helping to empower the lives of individuals, children, families, and neighborhoods. My journey to empower myself prepared me well for this work.

Finally, at the end of 2011, after thirty-nine years in social work, I retired from the field. I went on to consult part-time as a senior advisor for Councilman Joe Buscaino, and his staff in the Fifteenth Council District of Los Angeles. This area includes the Harbor and Watts. This gave me the opportunity to serve as a coach to a new generation of professionals rising up through the ranks. It was gratifying to be able to share with them the benefit of my leadership experience working in the community, in politics, and in partnership building. I appreciated being embraced in this manner, and only wish more seasoned professionals were given the opportunity to share the wisdom of their experience.

In terms of my personal life, I remained single; before I retired, I didn't have time to date. I was always taking care of others and not myself. When I stopped working full-time, I promised my family that I would finally focus on my well-being—settle down and one day remarry. But my idea of "retirement" has been a little unconventional. The desire to effect change is still strong within me, and there are so many individuals who need help. I still want to save the world. I've rededicated myself to doing so through writing and public speaking. It is my goal to share my story with as many troubled young women as possible, so that they may find their own inner strength and definition of success.

I am very pleased about the close relationship I've built with my own daughter. Tiombe and I talk throughout each and every week. We spend Christmas together, with our other family members in Los Angeles. Like me, Tiombe is waiting for a good man to come along, but no moss is growing under her feet while she does. I'm so proud of her new role as a young entrepreneur. I'm also proud that she has a healthy relationship with the opposite sex, and didn't allow my divorce from her father to have a negative impact on her as an adult.

I hope my ex-husband, Henry, has found his truth. I haven't communicated with him in about thirty years. I also hope that over the years he's matured in his treatment of women.

My sister Ethel is the only surviving sibling in my biological family—Robert and Bobbie died from colon cancer, only a few months apart. Although circumstance kept me from having nearly enough memories of happy days spent with my biological family, those who are gone are definitely not forgotten. Mother Dear is remembered not only by me, but with affection and respect by the citizens of Eudora to this day. I continue to cherish any time I can get with my family. Ethel calls me a few times a year to let me know she's fine; she resides in a homeless shelter in downtown Los Angeles awaiting transition to apartment living.

For as much as I've achieved—as a mother, sister, daughter, social worker, community organizer, story teller, mountain climber, and proud black woman—I have every intention of continuing my journey, unmasking more and more of my journey, pushing the envelope further. No matter what my future holds, God will be my foundation; I have never known life without the Lord. Anyone can have a relationship with Him that offers the same benefits I've received, regardless of what church they go to, or even if they don't go to church at all. In a synagogue, at work, or at home—God is there to support and sustain us all.

In looking back on my life, there is one thing I regret not having done sooner: *forgiving those who had caused me pain and harm.* I spent a great many years blaming—blaming myself and blaming others. While many of those "others" certainly deserved it, living with so much anger and bitterness didn't punish them. It only hurt me. The answer lay within my core value system. I needed to reach beyond my circumstances, to continue my climb onward and upward. And, in order to do that, I needed to forgive.

Forgiveness is a process, but the sooner you begin, the sooner you release yourself from the anger and grudges that take up the space in your life that should be filled with happiness and light. When you don't forgive, you block anything good coming your way. It takes diligence and patience to try over and over again, to reach that place where you're truly unburdened of your resentments. It takes faith to believe that you can reach that place. That faith is well-placed; over time, you will heal, forgive, and move on with your life.

When you forgive, you set yourself free. When you give yourself permission to let go of anger and embrace laughter, hope, and goodness, you're releasing yourself from the shackles that bind you and are embracing freedom. Forgiveness is empowering; it is about taking back your power.

As I reflect on the facial expressions of the girls the day I shared my life experiences, I recall thinking how my journey has shaped my passion for life. I learned that it's imperative to be open to the unlimited opportunities that life has to offer, instead of focusing on the slights of the past. When I learned how to forgive, my mind was no longer encumbered by all the negative thoughts that had held me in bondage. No longer would I have a heavy heart filled with blame, shame, and regrets. I'm continuously determined to be all I'm created to be because now I'm free.

END

AFTERWORD

I embraced the idea of writing a memoir when I moved to Los Angeles with my daughter in 1991, with the goal of encouraging, nurturing, educating, and restoring hope to those on a journey of healing similar to mine. Before I could begin the book, I had to finish my journey.

Over the years, I kept journals; I wrote notes on napkins and pieces of scrap paper and in the pad I kept next to my bed. But because this is a story about my life, in a way I've been writing it since the day I was born. Family separations, coupled with the debilitating effect the passage of time has on one's memory, left many holes in my history that I needed to fill when I began to officially put words to paper.

Some of the information included in this book I stumbled across over the years by chance, but much of it I actively sought. Sometimes what I learned brought me to tears, such as news of another untimely death. There was good news, too, though. I was so proud to learn that my high school crush, Ronnie Rainge, had gone on to become a prominent physician. Although I haven't seen Ronnie in decades, I feel like our triumph over the low expectations set for black youth in our high school is part of a much larger narrative.

And, of course, I share a narrative with my family that goes back long before I drew my first breath. In researching this book, I uncovered many things I never knew about those who came before me. One of the stories that touched me most was that of my granddaddy Earl Young and the injustice that was passed down to my mother, and then to me, through the injustice done to him. I worked hard to promote equality in our communities, so that my daughter would be exempt from the discrimination

231

faced by previous generations—the type of discrimination faced by her great-grandfather.

In Chapter Two, I write about my granddaddy Earl's work at the Maury Milling Company, or "the mill," as it was known in my family. The mill was something to be proud of. It occupied five city blocks and employed up to thirty people at a time, and it was always buzzing with activity. It was the best and most reliable place for blacks to find work in Mt. Pleasant.

Farmers nationwide shipped in raw grain they harvested directly from the fields—dry corn on the cob, wheat, barley, rye, oats, clover, and hay. These crops were processed at the mill to produce corn meal, flour, and a full range of cattle and poultry feed. Railcars full of these commodities were then shipped throughout the country, including to the United States military.

Granddaddy Earl worked at the mill every day, full-time for most of his life; he almost never took a vacation. Maybe it's because of the loyalty he felt toward the Maury Milling Company that he never discussed how it was stolen out from under him. It was only through the research my uncle L.D. conducted for a book he wrote titled *L.D. Rocketry, Race, and a Colorful Journey* that the story became known to us.

From digging through the *Tennessee State Library and Archives* in Nashville and annual reports filed on the mill, Uncle L.D. confirmed that my granddaddy Earl's father, James Erwin Goodrum, was a stockowner in the mill from 1908 until his death in 1922. Granddaddy Earl was the rightful heir to at least a portion of the mill, but he inherited none of these assets. Granddaddy Earl served as manager of the mill for fifty-three years, until his stroke in 1961; annual reports show increases in capital stock throughout those years. Yet the only income Granddaddy retired with was Social Security. It's clear that when my great-grandfather died, his shares were absorbed by the remaining white shareholders. Nothing got passed down to his son, my granddaddy Earl, and his siblings.

When Granddaddy Earl died, a man by the name of James H. Jones, Jr. spoke what seem to be revealing words at his funeral: "Earl," he said, "I am so sorry. I had nothing to do with it."

James was most likely referring to the fact that Granddaddy Earl wasn't allowed to inherit his father's stock because although he was of "mixed" blood, under the law he was considered black, and that made him ineligible to collect what was rightfully his.

James Jones did inherit his father's shares of the mill when he passed; it's believed that James's father shared the mill's history with James as a way of clearing his conscience, thus leaving his son to carry the burden of guilt that came with knowing my grandfather had been robbed of his legacy. In those days, if a black man took a stand against a white man, the consequences were potentially deadly, so out of concern for his family, my granddaddy Earl stoically accepted the position as the mill's lifetime manager and kept quiet about the injustice.

Keeping quiet about things is a trait I did inherit and something I did too much of for too long. In writing about my family, I'm breaking not only my silence, but theirs. Although some of the details I've provided in this book are intimate, I've written them down here with the belief that not just forgiveness, but the truth, will set all of us free.

ACKNOWLEDGMENTS

There are many to whom I pay tribute for inspiring me on my journey of writing *Unmasking: A Woman's Journey*, which began in 1991, when I made Los Angeles my home.

To the memory of my parents, may they rest in peace—I am deeply grateful for my biological parents, Robert and Thelma Twiggs, and my adopted parents, Harry and Frances Ewing, who did their best to raise me under conditions of segregation, integration, racism, sexism, and social contempt.

To my sisters, Eva Clark, Lydia Ewing, and Ethel Watson, thank you for your love and support, which helped keep my dream of writing alive; and to my brother-in-law, Pastor Steven Clark, your pastoral guidance through the years has been invaluable.

Uncle L.D. and Aunt Maureen Young, I am grateful to you for being the patriarch and matriarch of our family, keeping our history alive, and teaching lessons of persistence and tenacity.

I am thankful to other members of my extended family who stood by me during the entire journey: Linda and William Humphries, Lisa and Archie Newton, Lorie and Daryl Richardson, Jerome Robertson, and Jocelyn Whitaker.

Those who supported my campaign on Indiegogo.com, I am appreciative of your financial contributions along the way: Ronnie Rainge, M.D., Lana Parrilla, Rick Morris, Taz and Susan Latham, Jennifer Moore, Gary Foster, Mark and Lynn Colangelo, Sandy Bradley, Rochelle Gonzalez, Sandra and Hal Clayson, Alexandra Chamberlain, Irma Guzman, Richard Allen, Bill and Joyce Sharman, Earl and Geraldine Butler, Daoud and Dahn Dior Balewa, Jennifer Zivkovic, Robin Reed Kaswick, and Rosetta and Robert Brunk.

To my sista-friends, Joyce Sharman, Pearl Baker, Patty Koester, and Cindy Simmons, I thank you for constantly reminding me that I have a story to tell, and to "hurry up" and finish it because the world needs to hear it and be healed.

Nikki Luna, my administrative assistant—I am appreciative of the valuable help you gave, which was beyond expectations.

Linda Grimes, my dearest friend, I cannot thank you enough for the countless hours of public relations work given to prepare me for my new career as an author.

Alma Angeline (Albertson) D'Aleo, I appreciate the time you gave as an early reader of the manuscript; your editing helped to shape the final book.

Karen Ceaser, my friend and business strategist, thanks for keeping the momentum of this journey going. You pushed and prodded me to the finish line of publishing.

Patricia Gill, I owe you big time for your ideas and creation of my new website to ensure that we embrace social media into the book campaign.

Gabriel Maldonado, I am grateful for your youthful energy; and to Earl Butler, my mentor, thanks for always being by my side imparting your wisdom.

Pastors Brad and Carolyn Kuechler, I am thankful to you for providing the spiritual guidance to help me understand God's word and how to apply it to various phases of my journey.

Timothy Mc Osker, Esq., your legal advice was helpful and I could not have finished the task of writing without you; and Constance L. Jackson, I am grateful for your legal experience in publishing.

Terrelle Jerricks, managing editor of *Random Lengths*, thank you for the pre-publicity article; and to Quincy Oliver, author, I owe a special gratitude to you for guiding me through the maze of publishing.

Eddie Mc Kenna and Ricky Magana, fitness trainers at Crossfit Heyday, your grueling work outs helped clear my mind for the completion of this book; and to Michele Jones, fitness instructor at the YMCA of San Pedro, kudos to you for the boxing regiment that got me through writer's block.

Katie Cordes and Jeremy O'Kasick of Thomson Safaris, I appreciate your careful review of my Swahili for accurate translation; and to the women of SHAWL House, thanks for reading my manuscript during the early stages...you helped me find my voice.

My editor/writer, David Woolfe, thank you for trusting my story and instincts; your patience with the many draft manuscripts kept me on track; and to Darla Bruno, editor, I am grateful for your guidance and helpful suggestions to the end of this writing journey.

Finally, this book is dedicated to those who believed in me from childhood until this book became a reality. Thank you for planting a positive seed; I will always be grateful. And to those who said I would never amount to anything, your words only propelled me toward my dreams. Be cautious of the words you plant in a child's life; words can impact your life, either in a positive or negative way.

CRISIS INTERVENTION RESOURCES

These are resources that we have come across that may be helpful to you on your journey. Please understand we are not recommending or endorsing them. It is up to you to determine if they offer something you need and if they are appropriate for you. We have researched the list; however, hotlines change and some of these may not be active. Give them a try.

A

Adult Children of Alcoholics (ACA)
National Council for **Adoption**
(866) 212-3678
www.adoptioncouncil.org

AIDS Info
(800) 448-0440
www.aidsinfo.nih.gov

Al-Anon Family Group Headquarters
(800) 356-9996 or (888) 425-2666
www.al-anon-alateen.org

Alcohol & Drug Treatment Referral
(800) 454-8966
www.recoverynowtv.com

Adult Children of Alcoholics (ACA)
World Service Office
(562) 595-7831
www.adultchildren.org

National Council on **Alcoholism & Drug Dependence**
(NCADD)
(800) 622-2255
www.ncadd.org

B
Bullying
(800) 273-8255
www.stopbullying.gov or
www.stopbullyingnow.com

C

Child Abuse Hotline
(800) 422-4453
www.childhelp.org

Childhelp USA/Hotline
(800) 422-4453
www.childhelpusa.org

Children of the Night
Child Prostitution
(800) 551-1300

Citizenship & Immigration Services
(800) 870-3676 forms
(800) 375-5283 info
www.uscis.gov

U.S. Commission on **Civil Rights**
(800) 552-6843
www.usccr.gov

Covenant House Hotline
(children trafficking/homeless
youth)
(800) 999-9999
www.covenanthouse.org

Cutting Hotline
(800) 366-8288
www.selfinjury.com

D

Drug Alcohol 24-Hr Helpline
(800) 281-4731 or (800) 799-7233
www.recoverynowtv.com

Domestic Violence Helpline
(800) 978-3600 or (800) 799-7233
www.thehotline.org

Domestic Violence Hotline
(800) 621-4673
www.safehorizon.org

National **Domestic Violence** Hotline
(800) 799-7233
www.thehotline.org

Nat'l Institute on **Drug Abuse**
Hotline
(800) 662-4357
www.samhsa.gov

E

Eating Disorders (Ref &Info Center)
www.edreferral.com

National Center on **Elder Abuse**
(800) 677-1116
www.ncea.aoa.gov
www.eldercare.gov

National **Eating Disorders** Helpline
(800) 931-2237
www.nationaleatingdisorders.org

F

Food Addiction
www.eating-disorder-treatment.com

G

Gamblers Anonymous
(888) 424-3577

www.gamblersanonymous.org

**Gay, Lesbian, Bisexual, &
Transgender**
GLBT National Hotline
(888) 843-4564
www.glbtnationalhelpcenter.org

H
Anti-Defamation League
(hate crimes)
www.adl.org

Health & Wellness for Girls
www.iemily.com

Hepatitis (A, B, & C) Help
(888) 443-4372
www.aac.org/hotline

HIV/AIDS & STD Hotline
(800) 235-2331
www.aac.org/hotline

Homework Hotline
(877) 275-7673
www.askrose.org

National **Women's Health** Info
Center
(800) 994-9662
www.womenshealth.gov

I
Incest Hotline
(800) 656-4673
www.rainn.org

J
Office of **Juvenile Justice &
Delinquency Prevention**
www.ojjdp.gov

K
KidsPeace (mental health services)
(800) 257-3223
www.kidspeace.org

L
Learning Disabilities
C.H.A.D.D. Children & Adults with
Atten-Deficit/Hyperactivity Disorder
(800) 233-4050
www.chadd.org

Nat'l Ctr for **Learning Disabilities**
(888) 575-7373
www.ncld.org

M
Find the Children (**missing children**)
(888) 477-6721
www.findthechildren.com

Mental Health America
(800) 273-TALK
www.nmha.org

Missing & Exploited Children
Hotline
(800) 843-5678
www.missingkids.com

Missing/Abducted Children
(under 17)

AMBER Alerts
www.amberalert.gov

Mothers Against Drunk Driving
MADD
(877) 623-3435
www.madd.org

National **Mental Health** Association
(800) 969-6642
www.nmha.org

N
N.A.A.C.P. **(Civil Rights)**
(410) 521-4939
www.naacp.org

O
Office for **Civil Rights**
U.S. Department of Education
(800) 872-5327 (800) 421-3481
www.ed.gov/ocr

P
Panic Disorder Hotline
(888) 826-9438
www.findthelight.net

Poison Control System
(800) 222-1222
www.aapcc.org

R
National **Runaway** Hotline
(800) 786-2929
www.1800runaway.org

Rape Hotline (RAINN)
(800) 656-4673
www.rainn.org

Rape, Sexual Assault & Incest
Hotline
(866) 689-4357
www.safehorizon.org

S
National **Sexual Assault** Hotline
(800) 656-4673HOPE
www.rainn.org

Self-Injury Hotline
(800) 366-8288 (DON'T CUT)
www.selfinjury.com

Sexual Abuse—Stop It Now!
(888) 773-8368 (prevention)
www.stopitnow.org

Social Security Benefits Info
(800) 772-1213
www.socialsecurity.gov

STD Hotline (Sexually Transmitted
Disease)
(800) 227-8922
www.ashastd.org

**Substance Abuse and Mental
Health**
Treatment Referral Routing Services
(800)662-4357
www.samhsa.gov

Substance Abuse Treatment Facility
Locator
(800) 662-4357
www.findtreatment.samhsa.gov

Suicide Prevention Center and
Veterans Crisis Line
(800) 273-8255
www.suicideprevention.org

Suicide Prevention Hotline
(800) 273-8255
 www.suicidepreventionlifeline.org

T
Teen Crisis Line (homeless shelter)
(800) 914-2272
www.casayouthshelter.org

National Teen Dating Abuse
Helpline
(866) 331-9474
www.loveisrespect.org

Teen Hotline
(800) 852-8336
www.teenlineonline.org

V
Ctr for Preven of School Violence
(800) 299-6504
www.cpsv.org

National Center for Victims of Crime
(800) 394-2255
www.ncvc.org

Nat'l Org/Victim Assistance
(800) 879-6682
www.trynova.org

Office for Victims of Crime
(800) 851-3420
www.ovc.gov

REFERENCES

Books

Buck, Craig, and Forward, Susan, *Betrayal of Innocence: Incest and Its Devastation*, New York: Penguin Books, 1988.

Potter, Joan and Constance Claytor, *African Americans Who Were First*, New York: Cobblehill Books, 1997 (reference made in Chapter Nine about Pamela Fanning Carter).

Young, Lee D., *L.D. Rocketry, Race, and a Colorful Journey*, New York: Vantage Press, 2010.

Photographs and other Published Materials

Photos and other published materials in this memoir are from the author's archives. Every reasonable effort has been made to identify copyright holders; however, if there is an oversight, correction will be made in the subsequent printing of this book.

Photo 1: Maternal grandparents, Violet and Earl Young, Mt. Pleasant, TN.

Photo 2: Biological mother, Thelma Young Twiggs, Eudora, AK, 1950s.

Photo 3: Biological father, Robert De Leon Twiggs, II, Eudora, AK, 1950s.

Photo 4: Adoptive parents, Rev. Harry and Frances Ewing, Lansing, MI, early 1950s.

Photo 5: Biological mom and second husband, Harry Hoffenkamp, Lansing, MI, 1958.

Photo 6: Eva Marie Ewing, my adopted sister and me, Lansing, MI, 1959.

Photo 7: Me and Santa, photo courtesy of Knapp's Department Store, Lansing, MI, around 1954.

Photo 8: The beginning of my track career, Sexton High School, Lansing, MI, 1963.

Photo 9: "Lansing Girl To Try-Out For Olympics," photo courtesy of *Lansing State Journal*, August 16, 1963.

#10 Article: "Girls Enter Flint Meet," article courtesy of *Lansing State Journal*, July 1964.

#11 Article: "Talent From Sexton," article courtesy of *Lansing State Journal*, 1964.

Photo 12: "Cheers By Ear," photo courtesy of *Lansing State Journal*, March 5, 1965.

#13 Article: "Popularity Poll," article courtesy of *The Zodiac*, J.W. Sexton High School, May 25, 1965.

Photo 14: "Espana Tierra de Amor Sexton 1965," senior prom photo courtesy of J.W. Sexton High School, 1965.

#15 Article:"Huron Girls Compete In Track," article courtesy of *The Eastern Echo*, Eastern Michigan University, May 24, 1968.

Photo 16: "Students, police clash in four day protest," photo and article courtesy of *The Eastern Echo*, Eastern Michigan University, May 8, 1970.

Photo 17: My family attended my graduation from Eastern Michigan University, 1970.

Photo 18: My love for children and the community began in 1974.

Photo 19: My visitation with Chief Nana Boafo Asiedu, II of Ghana, West Africa, 1975.

Photo 20: My climb to the summit of Mt. Kilimanjaro, Tanzania, East Africa, 1976.

Photo 21: I received a citation for climbing Mt. Kilimanjaro, Tanzania, East Africa, 1976.

Photo 22: Mom Thelma and Mom Frances escorted me during my wedding, 1977.

Photo 23: A special moment with my daughter at Disney World, 1981.

Photo 24: My daughter interviewed the legendary Rosa Parks, photo courtesy of Gloria Ewing Lockhart, 1987, Atlanta, GA.

Photo 25: My one-woman show at Ebenezer Baptist Church, Atlanta, GA 1988.

Photo 26: Ku Klux Klan march in Jonesboro, GA; photo courtesy of Gloria Ewing Lockhart, 1988.

Photo 27: My daughter sang at a rally for the Honorable Nelson Mandela, Atlanta, GA; photo courtesy of Gloria Ewing Lockhart, 1990.

Photo 28: I finished the LA Marathon, photo courtesy of MARATHONFOTO, 1997.

Photo 29: Ordinance restricting alcohol and tobacco advertising on billboards 1,000 feet from schools and public venues where children and families congregate, Santa Monica Elementary School, East Hollywood, CA; photo courtesy of Gloria Ewing Lockhart, 1998.

Photo 30: I organized the first "Peace March" in Hollywood, 2000.

Photo 31: I was appointed by Los Angeles Mayor Antonio Villaraigosa to the Harbor Area Commission, 2006.

Photo 32: "Woman of the Year" presented by former California Assemblymember Betty Karnette and former Speaker of the California State Assembly Karen Bass, Sacramento, CA; photo courtesy of Russel Collins Stiger, 2008.

Photo 33: A proud moment with my daughter at her film debut of *Inside A Change*, NY, 2009.

Made in the USA
Lexington, KY
18 December 2012